WITHOUT FEAR OR FAVOR

ODYSSEY OF A CITY MANAGER

LeRoy F. Harlow

D1124586

Brigham Young University Press

Views expressed in this book are not necessarily those of Brigham Young University or The Church of Jesus Christ of Latter-day Saints.

Library of Congress Cataloging in Publication Data

Harlow, Le Roy F
    Without fear or favor.

    Includes index.
    1. City managers—United States—Biography.
2. Harlow, Le Roy F.   I.   Title.
JS344.C5H28   352'.0084'0924 [B]   76-40172
ISBN 0-8425-1461-9

Brigham Young University Press, Provo, Utah 84602
© 1977 by Brigham Young University Press. All rights reserved
Printed in the United States of America
77 2.5M 18108

To Agda
and Our Seven

Contents

Foreword

Here is a fresh approach to the difficult task of explaining city hall from the inside. Some of the problems described here are of basic importance.

This account, drawn from episodes in various widely differing communities, takes us through a broad sample of the challenges that face city administrators: developing efficiency, combatting graft, balancing development against the preservation of shade trees, coping with garbage handling and snow removal, dealing with businesses that locate just beyond the city limits, and vivid examples of the difficulties in hiring and firing key officials.

I knew the author in one of his most difficult periods described in the book, at Fargo, North Dakota. In fact I was with him through much of the Fargo experience. One week after I went to work as City Manager Harlow's principal assistant, a businessman telephoned to inform me he was one of a group organizing to drive Harlow out of town. He suggested I quietly leave town before I was run out. As inducement, he said his group would secure for me a higher-paying position in Minneapolis. This would reflect an advancement opportunity too good to ignore, and would look good on my record. A few weeks later, the police chief called me to his office to say he was securing legal counsel on how to separate me from my job. Both of these initial incidents were in response to major assignments given me by Harlow—to help establish a city merit system and centralized purchasing.

From this experience, I would suggest that, if anything, the author has understated the volatile setting within which he and many other local officials have struggled. It can be a rugged and vicious environment, not recommended for the fainthearted.

Since those tumultuous days in Fargo, I have had the opportunity to serve in federal policy level positions under five presidents of the United States, both in agencies and in the Executive Office of the President. These types of assignment expose one to tremendous pressures from political and special interest groups. The harsh lessons of Fargo described in this book made an indelible impression on me that provided far more than invaluable guidelines for serving the public efficiently. From the author's example, I learned about personal courage in the public service, the importance of open government, the excitement of fighting assaults upon integrity in government, and the necessity of being fully prepared to risk one's own job in the course of these battles. If those who became enmeshed in Watergate could first have had the benefit of learning about government from a person such as LeRoy Harlow, I believe there would have been no Watergate.

Dwight A. Ink
Director
Sponsored Research and Continuing Education
The American University
Washington, D.C.

Introduction

Overtaking a neighbor walking toward his office one Saturday morning, I offered him a ride. He had scarcely settled into the seat beside me when he said, "Tell me, what do you think about local government?"

Laughing, I replied, "Why don't you ask me to tell you what I think about life; it would be about as simple."

"Well," he said, "years ago a high school teacher of mine told our class we ought to have better local government. I've thought a lot about that. I've wondered if it's because of people like me that government, even in our own community, isn't better than it is."

He continued. "You see, I love this country. It has been awfully good to me, and I'd like to show my appreciation some way. I think I'm a pretty good citizen. I always vote, and I obey the law. But I don't feel that's enough. I'd like to do more, but I don't know where to start to do anything else."

This launched us on a two-hour discussion about the problem any good citizen might have who wants to "do something" to help improve government in this country, at any level—federal, state, or local—but doesn't know where to begin or what to do after he begins.

As I drove away, his words kept turning over in my mind— not only his words but the earnestness of his desire to make a contribution as a good citizen and his obvious frustration at not knowing where to start. I wondered how many other citizens felt the same way—maybe dozens or even hundreds of them in every community.

These thoughts answered a related problem for me. From the

time of my first city-manager job until today, including many consulting assignments with local governments and several years of teaching graduate students local government administration, seldom has a conversation come up about my work with local government that someone has not said, "You ought to put that in a book, so people can understand the problems of getting better local government."

Over the years I accumulated a file of materials that might some day be used to help others understand a little better what goes on behind the forbidding counters, frosted windows, and big doors of city halls, district offices, and county courthouses. I hoped the information might also let citizens know what life is like for some local officials who have chosen to be servants to the people in their communities. I've incorporated many of those materials in this book.

There are 78,000 local governments in the United States. They employ over eight million people (compared with fewer than three million federal civilian employees), and they spend about $120 billion a year of the people's money. Of course, no one person's experience can encompass all the varied situations that might confront citizens and officials in these tens of thousands of counties, cities, towns, villages, boroughs, school systems, and special districts—dealing with everything from collecting and disposing of sewage to abating mosquitoes. Nor are the decisions and actions of any one administrator, when faced with the real world of local government, likely to receive universal approval.

But the five cities of which I was manager constitute a rather comprehensive cross section of communities: a war-boom logging and lumbering town, called by nearby FBI agents "the toughest town in Oregon"; a solid city with diversified industry in the upper Midwest; the largest city in one state; a metropolitan suburb; and a world-famous Southern ocean beach resort city. Moreover, the decisions I made while serving those cities were based on reasons that, at the time, seemed to me to be in the best interest of most of the people.

The detailed studies I have made of other local governments from Connecticut, New York, New Jersey, and Virginia—to Georgia, Texas, Utah, Idaho, Washington, and California may round out the picture of local government. Hopefully, what follows can be of interest and use to anyone—private citizen, public official, or student—who now is, or may become, involved in the level of government that most affects the lives of all of us, and where an individual or a small group can have the greatest influence.

Sweet Home, Oregon

Boomtown problems
Unbusiness-like public business
Some by-products of illegal gambling

Prelude to a City Manager's Career

Mayor Stewart Weiss and I stood side by side in the center of the graveled street. He seemed preoccupied, looking up at the weather-beaten red barn with the rickety wooden porch hanging on its front. In a gesture of resignation he shrugged his broad shoulders and turned to me.

"Roy," he said, "this is our city hall. The whole town is in about the same condition. Whatever you think needs doing to make a city out of this place, go ahead and do it. No matter what you do, you can't make it any worse than it is."

We talked a few minutes about what I might do to turn the old building into a functioning center of city business. Then he changed the subject.

"I guess I ought to warn you," he said. "You'll probably have trouble with old John Russell. He owns the weekly paper. John isn't happy with our choice of city manager. He wanted the council to appoint a local man. In fact, he wanted us to appoint a friend of his who has done some surveying for the city. John's old and he's stubborn, but you'll have to try to get along with him."

This was my introduction to Sweet Home, Oregon. It was my first city-manager job, and I was Sweet Home's first manager. But I'm getting ahead of my story, which really began eight years before.

I was a sophomore engineering student at Iowa State College in Ames, Iowa, trying to decide whether to become an aeronautical engineer or an industrial personnel manager. During the college's annual Religious Emphasis Week, a group of YMCA and YWCA student officers were meeting informally with the principal speaker of the week. Having heard that he had chosen the ministry over a promising Hollywood acting career, I asked him why he had made that decision.

He paused, forming his reply. "When I neared college graduation, I realized I had to decide what I wanted to make of my life. With that need in mind, I looked for *the place where the fight was the thickest and the lines the thinnest*. I concluded that place was the ministry. That's why I'm here."

His words startled me. I had never thought of a career in those terms; certainly I was not applying this measure to the career choices I was then considering. That started my search for a field of work to fit his formula.

Sometime and somewhere in the next few months I heard of something called "city management." The words intrigued me, but none of my immediate acquaintances knew anything about it. My college department head gave me a sketchy notion, then suggested I make an appointment with the man who was the city manager downtown in the city of Ames. I did.

What I learned from the city manager about the purpose of a city and the role of a city manager, including both the satisfying and the unpleasant parts of the job, seemed to be the answer to my quest. From then on, I chose college courses and extra-curricular activities that might prepare me for this new career. The summer between my junior and senior years I worked as an "apprentice" to the city manager of Mason City, Iowa, and the day after graduation I went to work for the city of Ames as an inspector of construction of sidewalks, streets, and sanitary sewers.

At that time, few managers were hiring assistants, and even small cities looking for managers set "previous manager experience" as a prerequisite. Consequently, before the Sweet Home city council hired me in the fall of 1943, I had worked for the federal Public Works Administration and Social Security Board, had taken a year's leave of absence from the board to get a graduate degree in public administration, and had sent out nearly two dozen applications for city-manager positions. I was in my second year with the U.S. Bureau of the Budget in the Executive Office of the President, Washington, D.C., when Mayor Weiss telephoned and offered me the Sweet Home city-manager position.

During the long, hot, wartime drive across the country from Washington, D.C., to Oregon—at my expense and with a salary cut—I pictured how I would attack the problems the mayor had outlined over the telephone. I envisioned organizing the city's government and practicing the management principles I had learned in graduate school at the University of Minnesota. In my mind I designed an accounting system to protect the tax-payers against payroll padding and other possible defalcations. I created imaginary meetings with citizens and city employees to present changes that would make things better for all the people in our community. In my reveries the proposals always met with understanding, harmony, and agreement. In short, I dreamed of the kind of city government I was sure every American wanted for his fellow citizens and himself—one that was efficient, courteous, humane, impartial in service to the citizens, and honest. These were the thoughts that filled my mind as my wife Agda, our one-year-old Steven, and I neared Sweet Home.

Without Fear or Favor

A Town with a City's Problems

In October 1943, Sweet Home, Oregon, was a crowded, busy place. Although it had been incorporated in 1893, at the outbreak of World War II Sweet Home had fewer than 200 inhabitants. But wartime demands for timber, draft-deferred employment in the woods and mills, and shot-and-shell prosperity brought loggers, millworkers, businessmen, and their families pouring into Sweet Home. Most of the estimated 3,300 residents had arrived in the last three to four years, bringing changes deeply resented and actively opposed by the old-timers.

Workmen and their families were crammed into trailers, cabins, and shacks. Rickety frame buildings and a few masonry structures housed half a dozen drug, grocery, and department stores. Fix-it shops and secondhand stores were doing a land-office business selling galvanized tubs, foot-powered grindstones, used sawhorses, reconditioned motors and "as is" refrigerators and washing machines. Every business in town was booming.

Offices for most of Sweet Home's twenty-eight logging operations, as well as seven churches and seven taverns, were strung along five or six blocks of U.S. Highway 20 and Long Street, the town's two paved streets. A plywood plant and half a dozen lumber mills were located in various places, inside and outside the city limits.

Between daybreak and dark, log trucks rumbled through the city on U.S. 20 in both directions. Going west, many carried a single giant log that filled the forty-by-eight-foot trailer to capacity. Returning to the woods after delivering their loads to log ponds and "cold decks" of storage logs, the trucks made a steady stream of growling, roaring truck tractors piggybacking their empty trailers.

No matter what the weather, whole families worked day and night, using green lumber and cedar shakes and shingles to build simple but roomier housing. Long after midnight, power handsaws whined, hammers banged, and men's shouts rang out all over town.

In the background of all this motorized and human commotion was the bedlam from mills and plants—mills screeching, humming, and howling as they grappled the huge logs onto carriages, rushed them back and forth—slicing, rolling, slicing again—then cutting to dimension-size lumber; and the plywood plant peeling sectioned raw logs into long, veneer-thin ribbons

8

City Hall, City of Sweet Home, Oregon, October 1943—before remodeling.
(Courtesy *Western City* Magazine)

to be cut and glued into plywood sheets for building prefabri-
cated buildings and the famous PT boats. The air was rarely free
of the pungent smells of green wood, sawdust, and the smoke
from burning bark and millends.

Not long after my arrival in Sweet Home, William Tugman,
managing editor of the *Eugene (Oregon) Register-Guard* wrote
an editorial about Sweet Home in which he summed up our city
government's situation in these words: "Here is a town which
needs practically everything a city needs, and in a hurry—water
supply, sewers and sanitation, streets, sidewalks, more adequate
police and fire protection." He could have added that big
money, hard work, gas rationing, and boring, rain-filled nights
and weekends made the town a magnet for people who make
their living on liquor, high-stakes gambling, and prostitution.

Getting Acquainted with the Problems

When Mayor Weiss and I finished our brief visit in the street
outside City Hall, he took me inside and introduced me to the
only person in the building, a young woman who was working
temporarily and part-time as the acting city treasurer. He asked
her to contact the department heads and arrange for me to meet
them. When the mayor left, I began two "To Do" lists—one of

9

projects to start immediately and one of things that could wait. I had to put several items at the top of the list because it was obvious we would have to work simultaneously on more than one project if we hoped to make headway against the backlog of things to do.

In the next couple of days I met individually with the key city employees: the full-time police chief, street superintendent, and water superintendent; the part-time city attorney and part-time municipal judge; the volunteer fire chief and volunteer librarian; the contract garbage hauler; and a few others. I drove around town with the streets superintendent to observe first hand his street, bridge and drainage problems. The water superintendent took me through the water plant and showed me where he was extending water lines and installing new services. We climbed up a small mountain to the city's only reservoir. The fire chief showed me what equipment the city owned and what it was borrowing from the U.S. Office of Civil Defense. The garbage contractor and I inspected the open dump a few miles west of town.

Except in the case of the chief of police, my getting acquainted with the department heads, their operations, and their problems, was routine. But when I asked the chief if he had any problems, he said, "Yes, two."

Both problems involved ex-convicts and gambling. "Doc" Lytle had served time in Nebraska and Clare Cotter in Oregon. The chief had first met them in a nearby town where the chief had been a member of the police department and where both Lytle and Cotter had operated until they moved to Sweet Home where the pickings were bigger.

Lytle and Cotter were running card games with high stakes. The chief had noticed several newcomers hanging around Doc's and Clare's places, who seemed to have no visible means of support, and he figured that wasn't a good sign.

I asked the chief what he thought we should do. He said he thought we ought to try to get Doc, at least, to leave town. Doc was the older of the two men, he said, and the bigger troublemaker. The chief thought if we could get rid of Lytle, the police could keep Cotter under control. He felt sure Doc Lytle would have no trouble getting someone to buy the cafe he was operating, which had a good trade of its own apart from being the front for Doc's gambling operation.

I told the chief I would back him, that he was authorized to tell Doc to make arrangements to leave, and to set a definite

10

deadline. Every few days over the next month I asked the chief how Doc was coming on his move. "Oh," he said, "Doc says he's going to move, but I don't see any sign of it."

That was the situation two months later, the night Floyd Blankenship killed Doc's bouncer on Main Street—an occurrence I'll describe a little later.

Dealing with Priorities

After meeting the department heads and getting a general picture of the town layout and the city government's facilities and operations, I started down my priority list. First was City Hall. It faced east. You entered by crossing a wooden porch about eight inches off the ground and above the gravel street. The porch roof, which also served as a balcony for the second floor, sagged precariously under the weight of a rusting washtub, three-fourths filled with dirt feeding a single scraggly vine that ran over the side of the tub and the balcony. Entrance to the building was through a door at the center of the wall facing the street. Much of the outside wall was covered with yellowed legal notices and ordinances that no one had bothered to take down after their expiration dates.

Inside, the ground level was divided in two by a partition running north and south. A rough wood floor had been laid in the front half. This was the city council's chamber. A door in the center of the partition opened into the back half. In part of the back half, remnants of the former horse and cow stalls were still recognizable. The other part was the one-room city library staffed by women volunteers. A stairway led up to the abandoned haymow that sometime in the past had been converted to living quarters.

In the twenty- by thirty-foot council chamber, bright green grass and oat shoots were growing up through the cracks between the baseboard and the wall. Many were already two inches above the baseboards. Old maps, more official notices, election posters, and a calendar covered much of the unpainted plywood walls. To one side of center, a pot-bellied wood-burning stove stood in a sand box made of two-by-fours. Dried tobacco juice stained the sides of the stove. The sand was also tobacco-stained and mixed with Bull Durham sacks, crumpled cigarette butts, and burned matches. The stove pipe went in a straight line up through the ceiling and out the second-story roof. The plain wood council table and six wood-and-wire armchairs were arranged in a far corner. Four or five extra chairs lined the wall behind the stove.

This was City Hall.

With the Mayor's approval, I hired a carpenter to pull off the front porch, nail the front door shut, and build a new porch and door on the north side of the building. We added a nine-by-ten room on the south side of the council chamber for my office, and a lavatory. Thus, my office opened off the council chamber and had a back door. We then covered the front and sides of the building with inexpensive asphalt siding.

Inside the council chamber we installed a counter with shelves. We replaced the pot-bellied stove with electric heaters. Next we brought in a secondhand safe purchased at a local mill. The council table did double duty as a working surface when the council was not meeting. Now we were ready to function.

Then I turned to the city accounts. I needed to know where the city stood financially.

Mr. George Corner, a gentleman in his seventies and a pillar of one of Sweet Home's evangelical churches, had been the city recorder for about six years until the new city charter established the council-manager plan of government about three months before my appointment. Because the new charter provided that the city manager was also the city recorder, the council had appointed Mr. Corner municipal judge.

George had kept careful minutes of council meetings, written in his beautiful script in the large buckram minute book. He also maintained a simple single-entry record of the city's income and expenditures. I found both these books at the city hall. But when I wanted to spot-check the original vendor's invoices and statements against recent expenditure figures, I could not find the bills. I called the Judge at his home, where he held court. He declared the bills must be "someplace over there."

On further searching, I found them upstairs in a large cardboard carton. The box was covered with hay, an old window blind, and cobwebs. Each month's bills were strung together on a stout cord tied in a loop. The strings of bills went back to the beginning of the judge's service as city recorder, and they balanced to the totals I found in his books.

For other city records, I went to everyone in town who I thought might know the whereabouts of any city accounts, ordinances, resolutions, contracts, bond registers, and other records. I called on present and former councilmen, department

City Hall, Sweet Home, Oregon—after remodeling. (Courtesy *Western City* Magazine)

heads, and local accountants. Some of the records I rounded up went back more than thirty years. I brought them all to City Hall. As rapidly as we could, the part-time city treasurer and I reviewed, classified, organized, indexed, and filed them.

Our biggest problem was the water system records. A former water superintendent had been responsible for reading the meters, preparing the water bills, and collecting the accounts, as well as installing the water mains, house services and meters, and running the purification plant. The demand for installations kept him busy, and because he was more the outdoor than the office type, he had left the bookkeeping to his wife. She was still handling the work for the city in their home.

She and her sister ran a beauty shop in her home, and she kept the books for the beauty shop and for her husband's business. She kept the individual water accounts, handwritten, in a pocket-sized school notebook. The cross-outs, changes, and scribbled calculations were virtually unintelligible.

In my first meeting with her, I apparently failed to conceal my dismay at the condition of the accounts. Detecting this, she made it plain that in her opinion the city was lucky the records were even this good, considering how little it paid her for "handling this headache."

After a month of working days, nights, and weekends, the

city treasurer and I concluded the water system was going broke. There was a long-term bonded debt of 4 percent non-callable bonds. Nothing we could do there. The bank was holding $16,000 of unpaid city warrants (checks) that were drawing the legal rate of interest, 6 percent. As best we could determine, delinquent customer accounts totaled over $1,600. The system had been designed to serve fewer than 1,000 people but was now required to serve three times that many—at the same time meeting greatly expanded industrial and fire-protection requirements.

A comparison of our charges with our expenditures showed why the system was going broke. We were financing water main extensions to locations that would not pay back the investment in twenty-five years. Also, the city was charging only $21.00 for a new hookup. For this, the city dug a trench from the main to the property line, furnished and laid the pipe in the trench, tapped the new line into the main, supplied and installed a new meter, connected the pipes and meter, and backfilled the trench. The meter alone cost the city $21.50, and the additional labor and materials averaged $21.00 per hookup.

My initial effort to ease this situation was a letter to the meter company asking if there was any way we could reduce our meter costs. Could we, for example, buy in quantity and buy during the slack season? By return mail they replied they regularly gave cities a 40 percent discount, and from then on would extend that discount to the city of Sweet Home.

The next time the meter company salesman came by for an order, I asked him, "How come Sweet Home never got this discount before?"

"Nobody ever asked for it," he replied.

Next, I took a look at our monthly bank statement. I saw that every month we were paying the bank a substantial interest charge. This seemed strange to me since the bank had the city's money to use.

I called on the bank manager. He explained that the bank and the city had a long-standing agreement that whenever the city issued a warrant and there were insufficient funds in the city's account to cover the warrant, the bank would honor the warrant, then convert the overdraft to a short-term note. When there were sufficient funds in the city's account, the bank would use those funds to pay off the note. Of course, he explained, the city was charged interest on the short-term note, the same as any other borrower. He said the city frequently lacked funds enough to cover their warrants.

This made sense to me. But the next month an interest charge again appeared on the statement. By this time, I had been signing the checks and noting our income and bank deposits. I knew the deposits were large enough to cover the warrants we had issued.

Again I visited the bank. The manager explained, "We pay off the warrants on a first-in-first-out basis. It's true you issued some warrants in amounts less than the amount of money you had on deposit. But previously the city had issued a warrant for several thousand dollars. Until there is enough money in your account to pay off that warrant, we don't pay off any."

"Then do we pay interest on those smaller warrants that are backed up behind the large one?" I asked.

"Of course," he replied.

I had another question for him. We were paying 6 percent interest on those warrants, although interest rates generally were down, and almost any city could borrow money for 4 percent or less. When I asked him about this, I learned that under state law, unless the city council took formal action setting the interest rate at a different figure, the bank was allowed to charge the legal rate, which was 6 percent. Since the city had taken no such action, the bank was charging what the law allowed.

The city's accounts were divided into five funds. In accordance with the basic idea of fund accounting, each fund was as separate and distinct from the other as though each were a completely separate business. A surplus in one fund could not be used to pay a warrant issued against another fund. For instance, we might have several thousand dollars lying idle in one fund, such as the general fund used to pay for police, fire and general services, but we could not pay water department costs with that money. We had to continue to borrow from the bank and pay interest on overdrafts in the water service fund.

As soon as I could work out the details with the bank, get council approval, and clear the legal hurdles, we took four actions aimed at putting the water system on a more business-like basis:

1. After discussing our situation with a state auditor who was helping us set up a double-entry accounting system, I followed a tip he gave me. Instead of issuing a single warrant to pay a large bill for meters, pipes, and other materials, I broke the payments into pieces. For instance, if the vendor's bill was

for $650, I issued seven warrants—six for $100 each and one for $50. The first time I did this, the vendor promptly called to ask what was going on in Sweet Home. I explained, and thereafter sent a brief note of explanation along with our payments. Although this was an inconvenience to the vendors, they accepted my explanation and assurance that we would discontinue the practice as soon as possible.

2. I negotiated a lower interest rate on the warrants. The bank agreed to drop the rate to 4 percent on condition that the water service fund warrants were made general obligations of the city with the full faith and credit of the city pledged to their payment. This meant the bank could count on a tax levy, if necessary, as well as revenue from the water system, to get its money.

3. We consolidated all our operating accounts into a single fund. This required careful study of the state budget law and city charter provisions. Although we kept the bond fund separate to protect the bond-holders, we put the general fund, water service fund, water deposit fund, state street tax fund, and road fund together. Thereafter, warrants were payable from whatever monies might be available, regardless of the source. Of course, we maintained individual accounts to be certain we remained within the budget and spent earmarked funds only for the purposes intended.

These three steps enabled us to eliminate most of the interest payments, a saving that amounted to about one-fourth of my annual salary.

We were able to collect only about $1,000 of the delinquent water bills. The council wrote off the other $600, which included a large back bill owed by the former water superintendent. His wife refused to pay, saying the city had not paid her enough for keeping the water accounts.

4. The council passed an ordinance with the following provisions:

    a. Requiring a deposit from all water customers to guarantee payment of water bills;

    b. Authorizing shutoff of water service if bills were not paid in fifteen days and after two courtesy postal card reminders and a twenty-four-hour shutoff notice delivered to the premises;

    c. Requiring water users to share the cost of water extensions where income from the extension would not recover the city's investment within five years;

　　d. Increasing the water charge to users located outside the city.

At the water plant we installed an automatic pump control to eliminate water loss and to reduce pumping costs. The city's reservoir was located high on a hill above the town. It was filled by pumps lifting water from the river. The pumps were controlled by switches in the plant at the river. Unless a man climbed the steep hill half a mile away to visually check the water level in the reservoir, he would never know the reservoir was full unless he saw water pouring over the side. Because this could be seen only in daylight on a clear day, often the pumps ran many hours, pumping water to the top of the hill, overflowing the reservoir, and letting the water run back down the hillside. The new pump control had a float at the reservoir connected to a switch at the pump house. When the water level reached the top of the reservoir, the float switched off the pump, saving thousands of gallons of expensive, chemically treated water and the electricity to run the pumps.

Meeting the Opposition

A day or so before we completed the one-room City Hall addition that was to serve as my office, the carpenter and I were discussing last-minute details when a heavyset man approached us. He was wearing trousers, a plain gray sweater, and an old slouch hat too small for his large head. Without introducing himself, he delivered a string of comments about the "changes" we were making.

"I don't see why we have to spend all this money in fixing up a fancy office when the city needs so many other things so much worse," he said.

He then listed several other things the council was "doing wrong," most of which I knew nothing about. After each item he added with confidence, "The people don't want that."

He left as suddenly as he had arrived, without another word.

"Who was that?" I asked the carpenter.

"Oh, that's old John Russell," he said. "He's the editor of the paper—the *New Era*." I remembered Mayor Weiss's warning.

In my desire to get things rolling before calling on the town's leading citizens, I had neglected this principal opinion maker. Apparently I had offended him. Shortly thereafter, I made it a point to call on Mr. Russell at his combined newspaper office and print shop. The meeting was somewhat stiff. Mr. Russell was busy and self-important. His wife, working at his side, was friendlier, seeming to want to compensate for her husband's general gruffness and occasional near rudeness. I didn't stay long.

Some days later, however, the Russells invited Agda and me to be their guests on a drive over Santiam Pass. It proved a perfect day for seeing the beauty of that forested mountain country.

I sat in front with John, listening to him recite a detailed history of Sweet Home, including the considerable part he and his paper had played in bringing the city to what he considered its present importance. He was proud of the press's role in American life, proud of its independence. He stated and re-stated, emphatically, that any attempt on the part of federal government to put mailing of newspapers and magazines on a break-even basis was a dire threat to the nation's future and an unprincipled attempt to destroy freedom of the press.

We arrived home just ahead of the night, blissfully weary. It had been a memorable drive and an opportunity for me to get a little better understanding of the community, and of John Russell.

A Killing on Main Street

Agda and I planned to spend Friday evening, December 3, at City Hall. While I worked on water accounts, she would do some reading for her new book-review column, "Your Library," which the Russells had invited her to write for the *New Era*.

She was already in the car. I had just closed the back door and started for the car when I heard the phone ring. I went back in the house.

"Hello," I said, "this is LeRoy Harlow."

"Who just got killed up on Main Street?" a voice asked.

"I don't know. Who is this speaking?"

"This is the reporter for *The Oregonian*. Hadn't you better find out what happened?" The speaker hung up before I could get more information.

Going to the car, I told Agda something serious had hap-pened uptown, that perhaps she wouldn't want to go to the office as planned.

"I'll go with you," she said. "I can sit in the car."

As we crossed Long Street, we could see the street in front of City Hall filled with people. Men with hands cupped over their eyes were peering through windows into my office and the council chamber. Most of the crowd was standing back, looking toward City Hall. Others were gathered in groups, talking.

When I turned into the parking space in front of the jail and just outside my office door, I spotted our police chief, Cy Hardy. He was standing in my office, nervously fumbling for a cigarette. Leaving Agda in the car, I entered the office.

"Is there anything I can do to help?" I asked the chief.

"Oh, hello Mr. Harlow," the chief replied. "You'd better ask Curt. He knows better what's going on."

Looking through my office into the council chamber I could see it was crowded. Half a dozen people were leaning on elbows on the counter; some had come around the counter and were standing or sitting against the wall. State patrolman Curt Chambers, in uniform, was sitting, knees spread, at a low typewriter table. Sitting opposite him was a fleshy, dark woman about twenty-five. Black, greasy hair hung to her shoulders. Slumped forward, hands on knees, she was eyeing Curt as he asked her questions and she alternately mumbled or blurted out answers.

For a few minutes, I watched the state patrolman trying to question the woman and type out her answers.

"Curt, can I be of any help? Or maybe my wife can help. She types, and she's outside in the car," I said.

Curt paused. "Maybe that would help. If she could type as I ask the questions, it would speed up taking this statement."

I went outside and got Agda. Curt gave her his seat, took another chair, and resumed his questioning.

"Tell me, again," Patrolman Chambers said to the woman. "What was the name of the fellow with Blankenship?"

"I already told you; I don't know his name," the woman said. "All I know is I heard some guys call him Whitey."

"Where did you meet this Whitey?"

"Well, like I said, the men had come down out of the woods. Me and Curly was spendin' some time at Pat's place. While we was havin' a rounda drinks, I get talkin' to these two fellas, and they ask if I'd like to go with them up to Doc's place. I figgered I wasn't gonna get Curly outa there till nightfall, so why not. They seemed real nice fellas."

"Who's Curly?" Curt asked.

"My husband. Who d'ya think?"

Curt continued his questioning. The woman seemed in a hurry to get it over. She skipped a lot of details necessary to make her story hang together. Several times Curt interrupted her to ask more details.

"You said you and Blankenship and Whitey were headed for Doc Lytle's place," Curt said. "Did you get there?"

"Sure we did," the woman said, thickly.

"What happened at Doc's place?"

"Well, we went in. We sat down at the counter, at the back."

"Where did you sit, and where did the men sit?"

"Well, Whitey sat next to the wall, then I sat between him and Blankenship. There was another guy next to Blankenship—the place was full."

"How many seats does Doc have in his place?" Curt asked.

The woman thought a moment, counting under her breath. "Six—mebbe eight. You know, you walk in off the street and there's the cash register right at the door. Then there's an opening for Doc and his wife and the help to go behind the counter. Then the rest is counter. You walk past the stools to get back where we was. There's a door there, too. The toilets and things is behind the door. That's the way you get to the card room, too, through that door."

"Tell me, then what happened after you sat down," Curt said.

"Well, nuthin' happened. Blankenship told Doc's wife we'd all have a beer, and she brought them and we just sat and talked till the trouble started."

"What trouble was that?" Curt asked.

"Well, I guess that's what we're here for, because of the trouble. It was awful."

"How did the trouble start?" Curt asked.

"I don't know how it started. All I know—when we got up to go, Blankenship went back to the toilet."

"Then what happened?" Curt asked.

"Next thing I know, here comes Blankenship, backing past the stools and out through the door. A big guy with a broken nose and cauliflower ears was followin' him, sayin' somethin' to him."

"What did the big guy say to Blankenship?" Curt asked.

"I couldn't hear. All I heard was Blankenship say somethin' like, 'OK, Brownie, I know you can whip me, and I don't want any trouble.' "

"Then what happened?"

The fat woman looked over Curt's shoulder at a front window.

"Curly ain't gonna like this," she said, a little coyly.

"Isn't going to like what?" Curt asked.

"Me tellin' you all this. He's lookin' at me through that window. He ain't gonna like it one bit."

"Well, you're a witness. We have to get all the information we can from everybody who saw what happened," Curt said.

"Yup, I guess you're right. I'm in it this far, I may as well tell you the rest. But there'll be hell to pay once Curly gets me home."

"What happened after Blankenship and the big fellow were outside?" Curt resumed.

"Well, they went down the sidewalk a little."

"Did you follow them?"

"Kinda. We wasn't very close though."

"Then what happened?"

"I dunno. All I know for sure is I seen Blankenship on his back and the big guy sittin' on him, holdin' him down."

"Yes?" Curt urged.

"Next thing, the big guy was sayin' to Doc, 'Shall I kill the son-of-a-bitch?' "

The woman paused, and looked mockingly at Agda. "Bet you can't spell that—hm?"

Suddenly Curt said to Agda, "Mrs. Harlow, you know what to ask her. Would you mind getting the rest of her statement? I'm going to have to go after the killer."

Agda agreed. Curt left, and Agda resumed the questioning.

"You said you heard the big fellow say something to Mr. Lytle," Agda said. "Then what?"

"Well, in a minute the big guy got up off of Blankenship. The big guy's neck was bleedin'. He said something to Doc, and him and Doc walked back to Doc's place."

"What did Blankenship do?" Agda asked.

"Got up and ran across the street."

"And what did Whitey do?"

"Ran after him."

"And what did you do?"

"Went lookin' for Curly."

"How did you happen to get over here?" Agda asked.

"Well, I went back to Pat's place, lookin' for Curly, but he wasn't there. Then I went to the Tourist. Over there, they was talkin' about somebody killin' Doc Lytle's bouncer. The next thing I know, the Chief come in 'n asked if anybody knew anything about the killin' on Main Street, and I said I did, so here I am."

Agda had the woman read the typed statement. It took her several minutes.

"Do you want to add anything, or change anything?" Agda asked.

"No, guess not. That's just the way it was, as best I remember," the woman said.

"Will you sign the statement down at the bottom then, please?"

The woman took the pen. "Curly sure ain't gonna like this," she said, as she laboriously wrote her name.

In the meantime, the sheriff and the acting district attorney arrived and came into my office. Outside, the crowd had grown, and several people were crowded up to the windows. Out in the main office, Doc Lytle's wife was saying over and over, to nobody in particular, "Brownie Buskirk was the best friend anybody ever had. Yes, sir, he was a fine man. And now he's dead."

Attorney Ed Sox explained that the district attorney was in Portland and he, Sox, was acting in his stead. I invited him to sit at my desk, and offered Agda's help if he needed it. We were setting up the typewriter and a place for Agda to sit next to the attorney when the back door to my office opened. A tall, raw-boned man, handsome and ruddy, was standing there. Patrolman Curt Chambers was behind him. Curt had a bundle of clothing under his arm.

"Go on in," Curt directed the man, and followed him in.

Curt seated the tall, good-looking logger at the desk, opposite the attorney, and took a chair near the corner, between the man and the window. Curt arranged the clothing on the floor in the corner. First he set down the hobnailed boots, and next to them he leaned a pair of heavy canvas logger's "tin" pants. He laid a blue work shirt over the pants and boots. From where I stood in the doorway, I could see that the boots and pants were spattered with red spots, and on the shirt I saw a large, dark red splotch.

"Ed," Curt Chambers said to the acting D.A., "I think you'll want to take a statement from this man."

"All right," the D.A. said. "Mrs. Harlow, if you'll be willing to type the statement as we go along. Sheriff, why don't you find yourself a chair so you'll be comfortable. Chief, you may as well just stay there at the door, in case anybody wants to come in. Curt, would you mind pulling the blinds on these windows? Now, Curt, do you have anything to say in a preliminary way?"

"Well, I might say this," Curt began. "I got a statement from a woman who said she and a fellow called Whitey were with Blankenship here, when this all happened. This Whitey was already on his way here when I started out to look for Blankenship. He told me where Blankenship lived, up in Foster. When I got to the house up there, the Blankenship children told me their mother and daddy were over at the school house. I met Blankenship as he was leaving the school. I took him into custody and we went back and picked up his clothes, and here he is."

"Well, Mr. Blankenship," the attorney began, "we have a pretty serious situation here. A man was killed tonight, and several people seem to think you had something to do with it. Do you have anything to say about it?"

"Yes, sir, I guess maybe I do," the tall man said. He was dressed in a clean blue work shirt, open at the neck, blue jeans, and work shoes. His hair was dark and wavy. As he sat slumped forward, hands clasping and unclasping, dark eyes looking up occasionally from the floor, Floyd Blankenship looked like a man who had worked outdoors most of his life and could handle an ax or saw with ease.

"Mrs. Harlow here will type your statement just as you give it," the attorney said. "Take your time. It is important that you give us all the details you can remember. So, why don't you start out by giving us your name, address, and age, telling us where you're from and where you work, and then tell just what happened?"

Blankenship began, "My name is Floyd Blankenship. I live with my wife and three children at Foster. I came here from up in Washington. I work for Swamp Mountain Logging Company."

"You're how old, Mr. Blankenship?" the attorney asked.

"Thirty-five."

"All right. Go on, please."

"About what happened tonight, I guess maybe it all started about six weeks ago. We had all come down from the woods because of the humidity. You know, when the humidity drops below a certain point, the operators have to shut down.

"We came out of the woods before noon. I figured I'd have something to eat and maybe a couple of drinks before I went home. I stopped at Doc's place for a cup of coffee.

"We batted the breeze a little—Doc and his wife and me—and then I started to leave. When I went to pay for my coffee, the girl at the cash register said, 'That'll be twenty cents for two cups.'

"I said, 'Pardon me, ma'am, but I only had one cup,' and I handed her a dime.

"She said, 'It's twenty cents. That fellow sitting next to you and just left, said he was a friend of yours and you'd paid for his coffee.'

"Well, it wasn't the dime so much, but I never saw the other fellow before, and I didn't know why I should pay for his coffee.

"Anyway, while I'm standing there—and I wasn't arguing, I was just trying to make the girl understand why I didn't think I should pay for the extra cup of coffee—up walks this big fellow and says to me, 'Don't make any trouble for the lady. Pay her what you owe.'

"I started to explain to this fellow why I wasn't paying, when Doc comes over. He says to the big fellow, 'It's all right, Brownie, forget it.'

"From this, I figured this must be Brownie Buskirk, the fighter. The boys been talking up in the woods about Doc's new bouncer. They say he's pretty good with his dukes—has fought Leo Lomski and some of the better fighters. They say Doc brought him here to quiet down some of the boys who've been complaining that the house is getting too much, and getting it too fast, in the card games.

"Anyway, I'm trying to explain, when Buskirk says, 'I tell you, pay the lady and don't make any trouble!'

"Well, I figure it's only a dime. No use making a big fuss over a dime. So I paid her the twenty cents and walked out.

"I never saw Buskirk again until today. I happened to be back in the washroom, and he came in. I said, 'Hi, Buskirk.' He said, 'Blankenship, one of these days I'm going to beat hell out of you, and I've a good mind to do it right now.'

"I said, 'Brownie, I know you're a good fighter. I know you can lick me.' He said, 'You're damn right I can, and I'm going to do it right now,' and he started after me. I backed out the door and through Doc's place and down the sidewalk. He got closer, then I guess he hit me. Anyway, he had me down and was on top of me.

"He had me by the throat with one hand and was holding me down. He hit me a few times. Then I heard him say, 'Doc, shall

I kill the son-of-a-bitch?' I thought he was going to do it. I got scared. I just had to get out of there before he did it. I got one hand loose and got my knife out, and I jabbed him every place I could."

Blankenship stopped. He looked in the faces of all in the room. No one said anything. He looked back at the attorney.

"I don't know how many times I cut him," he said, "maybe two or three, or three or four. Anyway, in a minute he let go of me. He started to climb off. I heard him say something to Doc like 'Can I die in your place? He's cut my jugular vein.'

"When I heard this, I figured I'd better get out of there fast as I could. I ran most of the way home. The kids said their mother was over to school at a meeting. I changed clothes and went over to school to tell her what happened and that I was leaving the country till things cooled off. That's when Officer Chambers, here, picked me up.

"I guess that's all there is to tell. I'm sure sorry. I sure didn't mean to kill him, but I was sure scared he was going to kill me."

The attorney asked a few more questions, then handed the typed statement to Blankenship to read. He read it and handed it back with the remark, "That's the way it was."

The attorney asked Blankenship to sign the statement at the bottom. He did. Then the sheriff took him away.

Next morning the chief dropped into my office.

"Well, Chief, what do you say?" I asked.

"There's not much to say," he replied. "Last night was pretty rough, but at least one good thing came out of it. Doc Lytle's gone."

"Gone?" I said.

"Yep. Gone. Cleaned out. Guess he figured it was going to be too hot for him around here. You know, there were a lot of people pretty sore about what happened last night, and most of them blamed it on Doc."

They put Blankenship in the county jail at Albany. Brownie Buskirk's body was shipped to Tacoma, Washington. Ten days later, Mayor Stewart Weiss and Blankenship's employer went his bail, and he was released to await trial.

Later I saw an official picture of Buskirk's body lying naked on a slab. Blankenship had cut him twice as many times as he had thought. He made six big gashes in Buskirk's chest and belly, he cut a ring around Brownie's left arm that nearly severed the arm at the bicep, he literally cut Buskirk's throat from ear to ear, and he left the broken knife blade in Brownie's head right at the hair line.

The district attorney first charged Blankenship with murder. The charge was later reduced to manslaughter. When the case came on the docket for the grand jury the following March, Blankenship pleaded self-defense. The grand jury found no true bill for indictment, and Blankenship was exonerated.

This closed the case for Floyd Blankenship. With Doc Lytle gone, it also eased one of my first unpleasant situations as a city manager, but it did not by any means solve our law enforcement problem in Sweet Home.

What's in a Name?

Sweet Home needed street names and building numbers and needed them in a hurry. The town was full of newcomers, unfamiliar with old landmarks and their local names. Houses as well as commercial and industrial structures were going up all over. The all-volunteer fire department could not keep up with the locations of new people, new houses, and buildings. And only a few streets in town were called regularly by a name. The main thoroughfare was called Santiam, because it was Highway 20, which formerly had been the Santiam Highway. For some long-forgotten reason, the old-timers called the only other paved street Long Street. But even Santiam Highway and Long Street had only an occasional street name sign; others had no designation.

The need was serious, too. In the middle of a stormy night, people in a burning house or with a choking baby could tell the fire department or the doctor only that their house was "the two-story one up around the corner from that big yellow house, next to the grove of Douglas fir." In fact, a child had recently burned to death in a tragedy that might have been avoided. The fire department was called to a location "by the mill, north of the tracks." While the department was searching for the house at a location north of a track and near a mill, the home was burning to the ground at another location fitting the same description.

But choosing street names that would satisfy the old citizens, then arranging names and numbers in a consistent way was not easy.

In mountain country, streets don't run in straight, parallel lines that form a north-to-south and east-to-west grid. They follow around hillsides and through ravines. About all they have in common is that they can be described roughly as going "up" or "down." It appeared from the city map that the best we could do was arbitrarily put in one group the streets that ran generally east-to-west and put in another group those that meandered in a general north-to-south direction. I accordingly marked them out on the map. I distinguished the two groups by designating the east-to-west routes as *streets*, with a letter-name assigned, and the north-to-south routes as *avenues*, with a number assigned. The numbering of the avenues and the naming of the streets started at a corresponding city limit.

By pure good luck, the number of lettered streets was such that by counting off the streets from south to north, the letter *L* came in the right position for Long Street. Of course, alphabetically *M* followed *L*, and since the Santiam Highway was also the city's main street, it was logical to name it *M* or Main Street.

Next, I started work on a building-numbering system. I hoped to be able to assign the numbers from 100 through 199 to buildings on the lettered streets lying between 1st Avenue and 2nd Avenue, to assign numbers from 200 through 299 to buildings situated between 2nd and 3rd Avenue, and so on.

This called for dividing the street side of each block into fifty equal-length sections. Since blocks were different lengths, this produced different-length numbering sections. In addition, a single building might have three entrances: a basement, a street level, and a second floor.

I tried to accommodate these differences. Where a section was only a few feet long but had more than one entrance, I assigned the whole number to the street-level entrance and the whole number plus ½ to the lower or upper entrance. Where the length of the section spanned two or more buildings, I reduced the section length required for a number. To minimize differences in the numbering of buildings that lay between the same cross streets but faced on different streets, I made adjustments according to where buildings were already in place or where it looked as though future buildings might be placed.

I presented the proposed street-naming and building-numbering plans to the fire department. They approved. I went over the plans with the city council. The council gave tentative approval, with the understanding that I would talk with some long-time residents about the street names.

Here I had some difficulties. The old-timers were not pleased with the street-name plan. They maintained that if we were going to name streets, we ought to name them after the first settlers. Fortunately, there were fewer old settler families to be so honored than there were streets to be named, and all the settlers had names that began with different letters. That problem was solved.

But when I suggested that wherever a lettered street corresponded to the first letter of the family name of an old settler, the street be given that name, one of the old-timers immediately objected.

"That won't do. Their names ought to be given to the streets they lived on." The others agreed with him.

I remonstrated that this would invalidate the whole aim of providing a simplified, alphabetical street-lettering system. But I had no supporters. However, this problem resolved itself. When we went down the list of early settlers' names, the group couldn't agree where they had lived.

The principal opposition to the building-numbering plan came from a few business and professional men whose places were assigned half-numbers. A case in point: While I was talking to our state legislator (formerly mayor) on a street corner, a local attorney approached us. He was obviously upset. Without so much as a "Good morning," he said, "Harlow, you're trying to ruin my business!"

I asked what he meant. "In giving me that half number on my office," he said. "What will people think? They'll think I'm a little two-bit lawyer, running my office from an alley!"

I explained the numbering system to him, how we assigned numbers according to location on the street, and what we were doing where there were separate upstairs or downstairs premises. It didn't satisfy him. We were at an impasse.

The legislator turned to me. "Is the next whole number assigned to anyone?" he asked, quietly.

It happened that that particular business block was short enough that we had more numbers than places of business. I said, "It happens that in this case there is no place of business where the next number is assigned."

"Why not give him the next whole number for his office?" he asked with a smile. "You may never need it, but if you do, you can make the change then."

I agreed, more in deference to the legislator's longer experience than because I thought we should make an exception to the basic plan. It was a good solution.

As a last effort to get community understanding and agreement on the new system, I drew a two-part map of Sweet Home showing all the new street names. ("Cut along line A-A' and B-B' and join together for a complete map.") I sent the map, with a covering memorandum explaining the street-naming and house-numbering system, to every water customer and asked them to let us know of any errors they found.

In the same memorandum, I made my first attempt to get citizens involved in planning their own city. I wrote:

"One other item—your city government has to depend on you to let them know what kind of a place you want your hometown, Sweet Home, to be. Will you take just a few minutes to jot down and return to the city hall a list of (1) the five most important projects you believe the city should undertake during the *next* year and (2) the five projects you think the city should have completed by *five* years from now? Thanks for your help."

I received fewer responses than I had hoped.

We faced our final name-and-numbering hurdle after the council officially adopted the street-name and building-numbering plan: where to put the street-name posts? We wanted to tie them to exact street intersections. By doing so, we could use them both as official markers for the intersections and as guidelines for grading and surfacing streets, cutting ditches, and installing water, and, eventually, sewer lines.

With an official survey map in hand, and starting from a known benchmark, the streets superintendent and I staked out property lines at the intersection nearest the city hall. Our measurements carried us well onto the front lawn of a corner house. We measured again; same result. We moved over to the next block and measured. The same situation existed there.

We were convinced. Through years of use, several roadways had moved gradually to one side or the other of their official boundaries. As a result, the public was actually traveling on private property on one side of these streets, while on the other side much of the front lawns the homeowners had put in were planted in the city street. The people who learned they had more front yard than they thought were happy with our discovery; those who saw they might lose some of their lawn when sewers, sidewalks, and parking strips went in, were unhappy.

During the time we were trying to locate street boundaries, we had occasion to try to get an easement across some private property. The proposed location would straddle the line between two adjoining lots.

We staked out the location of the property line. The two

owners challenged the staked line. They agreed the line was several feet from where our survey showed it. We asked to see their deeds.

When we read the deeds to the two neighbors, they had a good laugh. The metes and bounds descriptions for both properties started from a common point of beginning, then ran north on "a line parallel to a row of apple trees." The apple trees had been dead and gone a long time. The neighbors agreed on a compromise line somewhere between what the survey showed and where for years they had assumed the line was, then recorded amended deeds.

It took time to cut, creosote, and paint sign posts and stencil and attach street-name signs. Most of the work was done by a painter doing time in jail on a drunk charge. Eventually, every intersection in town had a street sign. The city bought house numbers, which individuals put up. Soon thereafter, satisfied citizens were commenting on how much easier it was to get around town. We learned also that at least one potential tragedy was averted because the driver of an emergency vehicle was able to go directly to where he was needed.

An Uneasy Relationship

I did not often see *New Era* editor and publisher John Russell. Although I invited him to send someone to cover council meetings, or to come himself, he preferred to call me the day after the meeting to get a rundown of what went on. I got in the habit of writing a summary of the meetings for his use.

On our first New Year's day in Sweet Home, John telephoned to wish Agda and me a happy New Year. He also said he wanted me to know he would "support 100 percent anything the city did that was reasonable." He didn't define what he meant by "reasonable," and I didn't press him for an explanation.

I had hoped that after getting off to a poor start in my relations with the editor, perhaps our trip into the mountains and my efforts to cooperate from city hall would have healed any ill feeling he might have. Therefore, I was disappointed to learn from Gene Ellis that the hard feelings still smoldered.

Gene, an enthusiastic though realistic community booster, was resident agent for one of the largest timber companies in the state. He had seen the Tugman editorial in the *Eugene Register-Guard*. (Editor Tugman was a member of an American

Legion national committee on postwar development and had just returned from a nationwide survey of what cities were doing to get ready for the return of their servicemen from World War II. Mr. Tugman had written favorably of Sweet Home's progress, as compared with other communities he had visited.) Gene took the editorial to John Russell, commenting that this certainly was a feather in Sweet Home's hat, and probably John would want to rerun the editorial. Russell's response was, "What do they think we old-timers have been doing, long before these newcomers ever got here?" But he did rerun the editorial.

Some time later, I took some printing work to the *New Era*. John got on his favorite subject of federal government efforts to raise postage rates on printed materials. He said he had just received a personal letter from the editor of "a big men's medical magazine," asking him to support the magazine's fight against an unfair postage increase. With obvious pride he handed the letter to me.

John Russell's name and address and the salutation had been individually typed. The body of the letter was duplicated, with a different type face from the name and address. The "men's medical magazine" was *Esquire*.

Speak Softly and Carry a Wet Paintbrush

World War II was at its height. War bond sales were extensively promoted nationally, statewide, and locally. At a bond rally organization meeting, someone suggested auctioning the services of local people to those who bought the most bonds. High bidders would get four hours of a "slave's" time. For example, the local bank manager would chop a week's supply of wood for the family that won his services; the mayor would clean out a horse stable; and I, as the city manager, would scrub floors. Along with this little chore, I volunteered my wife and me to make and paint a large thermometer, to be erected on the corner of a main intersection, to show from week to week how the bond sales were doing compared with the quota assigned to Sweet Home.

I had spent all day Saturday in the vacant lot next to the jail, building the wooden thermometer. It was about 7:30 in the evening; Agda and I were only half through painting the thermometer when a car drove up. Three policemen got out and began to wrestle two drunks out of the car. With a little prodding and steering, one of the drunks was able to walk into the jail under his own power. The other had to be virtually carried.

This was Saturday night and not an unusual occurrence, so Agda and I gave the incident no further attention. We continued our painting, hoping to get finished before dark.

Some fifteen minutes after the police jailed the two drunks, we saw three figures—a man and two women—coming up the street toward City Hall. The man was in the lead, walking rapidly and with determination. The women were doing their best to keep up.

They walked up to us, stopping about five feet away. The man said to me, "Are you the city manager?"

I said, "Yes, what can I do for you?"

He said, "I'm Archie Heseman. You've got two of my men in your jail, and I want 'em turned loose."

I had heard about Archie Heseman. He was a living legend in Sweet Home, a modern "bull of the woods," known for his toughness. The word was that some of the men worshipped him, while others "hated his guts." He was the fellow who, with the mayor, had put up bail for Floyd Blankenship after Blankenship killed Buskirk.

Among the stories told me about his toughness was the one about the time one of his men was crushed to death between two logs as he attempted to steer a log onto a truck. It was 2:30 in the afternoon. Half a dozen men saw the accident.

Ordinarily such an accident so unnerved the men they'd quit for the rest of the day. But instead of shutting down, Heseman had signalled the steam "donkey" to lift the log off the man, then ordered a couple of men to drag the dead man to the nearest tree and lean him against it while the crew finished the shift. As I heard the story, Heseman had said, "We're goin' to get these logs out, and no man leaves till the whistle blows at 4:30."

I now said to Mr. Heseman, "Why did the police pick up your men, do you know?"

"I guess the boys had a drink or two, and were havin' a little fun when those damn nosey cops threw 'em in the lousy clink. These are the men's wives. They want to take 'em home, so let's get 'em outa there."

"Mr. Heseman," I said, "I appreciate your interest in your men. I know these women appreciate your desire to help them. But if the police picked up these men, I'm sure they had good reason for doing so, and we won't be turning them loose until the officers think the men are ready to handle themselves."

"You mean to say you ain't gonna turn my men loose like I told you?" he bellowed, thrusting his face a foot from mine.

"That's right, Mr. Heseman," I said. "We'll probably give them a chance to sober up, and we'll send them home in the morning. In the meantime, they won't cause themselves or anyone else any trouble."

"Why, you _____ " he shouted. "I'll turn this place upside down. I want my men outa there."

Paint can in one hand and wet brush in the other, I didn't say a word. The spit was running over his lower lip. His eyes glared.

Half a minute went by. Heseman just stood there. The women, too, were glaring at me. Suddenly, he whirled around. "Come on," he said, and the three of them started back where they came from. Agda and I silently returned to our painting. I heard nothing more from Archie Heseman.

To Tax or Not to Tax

Under Oregon state law, unless a greater increase is authorized by the voters, a city may not increase its budget in any one year more than 6 percent above its budget for the preceding year. Ordinarily, this limitation places no hardship on a city, but for boom towns like Sweet Home, growing at a very rapid rate and squeezed between shortages on the one hand and inflation on the other, the 6 percent budget increase fell short of the needed budget. It is, however, no easier in boom towns to get people to vote higher taxes than it is in other towns.

In an effort to hold down property taxes yet increase revenue, the city council had passed a new occupation tax ordinance. The ordinance required every individual or organization engaged in an occupation within the city limits, or coming into Sweet Home to do business though headquartered elsewhere, to buy an annual license. The ordinance listed a page or more of occupations and a variable fee schedule. For example, a drugstore might be charged $20 for a license, a grocer $15, a stationery store $15, a bakery $10, a soda fountain $5, and a mill $200.

The city council had estimated the number of occupations in Sweet Home, then set a fee schedule designed to produce $4,000 in revenue. When I came to Sweet Home, the council had not yet started to enforce the ordinance. That was to be part of my job as city manager. It proved to be a major source of trouble for me.

The ordinance contained no definitions of the dozens of kinds of occupations found in even a small town. It gave no directives as to what to do if one business place included two or more occupations. It made no distinctions in fees between large and small businesses of the same kind. These decisions were left to the city manager to make "administratively."

We no sooner sent notices to all businesses, advising them of their obligations under the ordinance than we were flooded with objections and questions. For instance, was a small drugstore with a stationery counter and a soda fountain to pay a license for one occupation, or two, or three? If the drugstore owner had to pay for three occupations, his license fee might be three times that of a man who was in the soda fountain business only, even though the soda fountain business was twice as big as the drugstore. On the other hand, if we decided that the drugstore should take out only a drugstore license, the man who ran a stationery store only would be incensed over the stationery license he had to buy because he knew that the drugstore sold more stationery than he did.

I tried to get agreement among the businessmen on an acceptable maximum that any one store would pay, no matter how many occupations the store included. This idea pleased the larger store owners; but the smaller operators accused me of favoring the larger places.

I advanced the idea of varying the license fee according to the dollar volume of business done by a single place of business, regardless of the kinds or numbers of occupations involved. I suggested an honor system, because if we had to audit every business in town it would cost more to administer the ordinance than the tax would produce. This idea got nowhere. Businessmen pointed out that even though a store had a larger gross sales figure than a competitor, the store with the larger sales might be losing money while its competitor was making money.

This led to the idea that we might base the license fees on a business's net income. I felt out a few businessmen thought to be "friendly" to the council members. They strongly objected. No businessman was going to let anyone at city hall know what his net income was, not even if he was permitted to report his own figure under an honor system and had only to check where his net income fell within a range—for example, between $1,000 and $9,999; $10,000 and $19,999; $20,000 and $29,999; and so forth.

My problem in trying to work out a satisfactory arrangement with the local businessmen was no worse than the police chief's problem in dealing with the milk, bakery, auto parts, gasoline, and beverages trucks that made deliveries in town. It was his job to spot these trucks when they came into town, and to notify the drivers that their employers were liable for an occupation tax. This brought objections from the companies. Some of them had their lawyers call us and threaten to sue the city on the constitutionality of the occupation-tax ordinance.

The local merchants were equally hard on the chief. On the one hand, there were the purely local firms, such as a local dairy or mill, who demanded that the chief "catch" every truck from out of town that was selling goods and products in competition with them. On the other hand, stores and other businesses that depended on out-of-town suppliers charged the chief with "hounding" the out-of-town deliverymen to the point that the outside suppliers were threatening to quit making deliveries, saying there wasn't enough business in Sweet Home to warrant paying the license fee.

Underlying all these problems was the growing feeling that this was the city manager's tax. The council had announced that the tax was to raise $4,000 of additional revenue. This was almost exactly the amount of my salary.

Although the voters had approved the new council-manager charter by a good margin, and most of the businessmen favored a business approach to the management of city government, it was not long before the occupation tax was equated to my salary. The more attention I gave to implementing the council's occupation tax ordinance, the more it appeared that I was going around town collecting my own salary. Some local leaders began to wonder out loud whether the city needed an expensive city manager, a "frill" they had previously got along all right without.

Fortunately, the council repealed the ordinance. But the repeal did not take place before the attention of many local businessmen had shifted. They were now taking their eyes off of what the city needed in the way of improved management and the opportunities for both immediate and long-range savings. Their new focus was on the initial investment, and some of them didn't like what they saw.

Gamblers Galore

When I went to work for the city of Sweet Home, the police department consisted of the chief, two patrolmen, and a couple of part-time officers to help on weekends.

Cy Hardy, Chief of Police, was thirty years my senior. I liked him the instant I met him. He didn't wear a uniform, but he looked neat and businesslike in shirt and tie, well-tailored and pressed trousers, shined shoes, a dark blue whipcord Eisenhower jacket, and a wide-brimmed hat pulled low over the perpetually squinting eyes of an outdoorsman. He wore his badge pinned to his shirt, under his jacket. Unless you were told, you wouldn't know he was the chief of police.

In our get-acquainted visit, he described his years of police service for the city of Lebanon, fifteen miles down the valley. He said in Lebanon he was elected to office by the people. This would be his first experience working under a city manager, but he thought it would be good to have someone to talk to who knew something of the kinds of problems the police have.

The two regular patrolmen were former loggers. One wore a conductor's cap without the railroad insignia—the only thing suggesting that he occupied an official position. The other patrolman might have just stepped out of an old-time western movie. He regularly wore a brown workshirt and loggers' "tin" pants. Over the shirt he wore an army officer's "Sam Brown" belt—with an extra strap. The two straps crisscrossed his chest and helped hold up the two pistols he wore. His badge was a metal star, nearly four inches in diameter, with POLICE engraved in the center. His hat was a wide-brimmed, semiwestern style.

The chief had a tough job. Our problem with the gamblers, not lessened perceptibly by Buskirk's death and Lytle's exit, was a constant worry. Enforcing the occupation tax was unpleasant and had strained the chief's relationships with the businessmen. Further, he was the target of some of John Russell's unfriendly editorials and the outspoken criticism of Tom Burgett, an exlogger who wanted a wide-open town and sent a stream of letters to the editor that John printed in his *New Era*.

When Doc Lytle left town the morning after Floyd Blankenship killed Brownie Buskirk, the Moore brothers joined Clare Cotter at the center of our continuing gambling problem. Although there was another well-known card room in town, we got no complaints about it. The difference seemed to be that whereas the Moores and Cotter were young, ambitious men, bent on making a pile of money as fast as they could, the other operator was about sixty years old, patient, slow moving, and interested only in having things quiet and peaceful. He considered his place more a private club than a fast-moving, big-time gambling operation.

Almost daily the Moore brothers' and Cotter's actions became more brazen. The younger Moore, a good-looking, clean-cut redhead of medium build, dropped in at my office to make what he called "a neighborly social call." He asked me where I had gone to college and what kind of courses I took. I told him I had taken engineering and then graduate work in public administration to prepare for a career in city management. He said he had his bachelor's degree and two years of law school, but he was doing a lot better in business with his brother than any of his classmates who had gone into engineering or other fields.

We talked about earning our way through college.

"Roy," he said, "I earned every cent of my way through college playing cards. I did all right, too—not only paid my board, room, tuition, and clothes, but had enough left over to buy into Jim's place here."

Clare Cotter made a "social" call too. He sat opposite me, tipped his chair back against the wall, put his feet against the edge of my desk, shoved his hat to the back of his head, and began to talk.

"I thought we ought to get acquainted," he said, "since we'll probably be working together on various things, from time to time."

I asked him how business was.

"Oh, fine, fine," he said.

Then he said, "Roy, I came over to tell you I want to cooperate. If there's anything I can do to help this community—anything—I want to do it. You just say the word."

"Clare," I said, "that's nice of you. You have a fine cafe over there. They tell me you put out about the best food in town. Of course, we know you're also gambling. You know you are, and you know that we know you are. So if you really want to cooperate, you'll stick to the cafe business and cut out the gambling, before somebody gets hurt."

"Roy," Clare replied, "I told you I want to cooperate, and I do. I'll do anything you say. Anything, that is, except that." He put on his hat and left.

Chief Hardy brought me a couple reports of log haulers' wives coming in to plead that something be done about the gambling places. Their husbands had played cards all night and by morning had lost the families' entire life savings in the form of their tractor-trailer worth about $18,000. A third wife came to me with the same kind of story and a plea that the city do something.

Another time the chief brought in a gas station owner-operator to tell me the following story: "Business was kind of slow, and Jim Moore and I were standing over in the station, just talking. All of a sudden, Jim looks up and says to me, 'Hey, there's a guy that's got it on him, and I'm going to get it. See you after awhile.'

"I watched him catch up with the fellow, and they went into Jim's place together. They weren't gone half an hour, when Jim was back. He had a big grin on his face. He said, 'I told you I'd get it.'

"I asked him what he meant. He said, 'What do you think I mean? That guy thinks he's pretty sharp with the cards and dice. I just relieved him of his car, that's what I mean!' "

Still another situation: The chief reported to me that Clare Cotter was carrying a gun. That was particularly serious because under Oregon law any person who was once convicted of a felony, if later convicted of possessing a concealable firearm—even if he had previously served out his time—must be sentenced to the penitentiary. The court had no alternative.

"How do you know he's carrying a gun?" I asked the chief.

"I just learned it from Gus, the barber," he said. "Gus was shaving a fellow about half an hour ago. Clare walked into the shop and up to this fellow. He stood there a minute, then took a gun out of his pocket. He said to the fellow, 'Give me the $600 you owe me, or I'll kill you.' The fellow jumped out of the chair, pleading with Clare: 'Don't shoot, Clare; I'll pay you. I don't have it on me, but I'll pay you right away.' According to Gus, Cotter shifted the gun to his other hand, put it in his pocket, and said to the fellow, 'Well, see that you do, fast,' and walked out. Gus says he never saw a man as scared as his customer was."

A New Chief of Police

For several months the chief had been coming into the City Hall about 4:30 p.m. and staying there until his quitting time, between 5:30 and 6:00. Since he was the only officer on duty during the day, he may have thought he could be most easily reached there if he were needed. But this was the peak period for motor vehicle and pedestrian traffic on Main Street. "Crummies"—little buses that carried loggers to and from the woods—were discharging their passengers; other loggers and mill workers were in town or driving through; school was out; and housewives were doing their last-minute shopping. Pedestrians crossed the highway wherever they wished, dodging between cars and log trucks.

From time to time, I made oblique remarks about the problem and hinted that we needed some traffic control uptown. But my hints had no effect. Finally, one day when I returned to the City Hall at about 5:15 p.m. from uptown, where I had again seen snarled traffic, I said to him, "Chief, I think we agree that our worst time for traffic is from 4:30 to 5:30 in the afternoon. Why do you always make it a practice to be here in the City Hall during this period?" He didn't reply; he just walked out.

A few days later he came to the office to tell me he thought he'd be resigning—that his wife's health wasn't so good, and they thought they'd better move back to Lebanon. He said he thought I had better start thinking of someone else for the job. He agreed to stay on until we named his successor, and I began the task of finding a replacement to fill this critically important position.

I gave momentary thought to the two patrolmen and our part-time help. The two ex-loggers were working for the city largely because they were no longer able to handle the hard, dangerous work in the woods. Our principal relief man was young, vigorous, able and popular, but he was a high-rigger, the highest-paying job in the woods. I was sure he would not consider leaving that kind of pay for what we could offer.

None of these men had had any formalized police training, except the little they got at an occasional FBI seminar in which they heard a talk on some phase of police work.

It looked as if I would have to get someone from out of town.

The next time Curt Chambers, the state police patrolman who served our area, stopped at the office, I asked him if he would be interested in the job. It paid more than he was getting with the state, and I knew he was tired of the traveling his state police job required. He expressed some interest and asked for time to think it over.

The next day I was visiting with Councilman George Gessler, whose theatre backed on the same alley as the City Hall. George was a man of medium height, wiry, well dressed and articulate, but he never smiled. His smooth, leather-tan face was like a papier maché mask. He spoke out of one corner of his mouth.

I mentioned that Chief Hardy was resigning and we would need a new chief. Did he know anyone who might fill the bill?

"Yes," he said, "I know a couple of men over on the coast. Either one would make a good chief for us. I know them, and I know how they operate."

I wrote down their names and addresses. Then I said I had approached Curt Chambers about the job. Immediately Gessler's attitude changed. He eyed me sharply, his mouth twisted into a half snarl.

"I'd advise you to stay away from those guys on the state police," he said. "They're all crooks. You can't trust 'em. I wouldn't want any of them around here."

This outburst surprised me. As far as I knew, the city's relations with the state police were excellent. Certainly they had responded promptly to every call we'd made, and they did a good job of helping our officers. They never tried to take over or to take credit for the several good jobs they had done in our town. Moreover, Officer Chambers was personally popular with our men and with people in the community generally.

I tried to be casual about the councilman's remarks, replying that maybe it was true that occasionally a state police officer didn't measure up to high standards but that I'd found Curt and the couple of other officers I'd had dealings with very able, accommodating, and helpful.

"Well," George said, "you had better take my advice and stay away from those guys. We can get better men, the kind we want around here."

I left, both puzzled and concerned: puzzled at the animosity Gessler felt toward all state police officers, including the man I had already invited to take the position of chief of police; concerned that under the new city charter appointments were clearly my responsibility, yet here was a key appointment on which at least one councilman intended to exercise his influence.

Some time later, Curt Chambers stopped by to say thanks, but he guessed he would stay with the state police.

I continued my search for a chief. I sent specifications for the position to the League of Oregon Cities and asked them to circulate word of the vacancy, and I ran newspaper ads in Portland and other cities. I kept in the back of my mind the names Councilman Gessler had suggested, but intuitively I resolved to reach for them only as a last resort.

Although police officers were a draft-deferred class, the wartime manpower shortage made it difficult to get officers. Furthermore, I found that the reputation of our community didn't help matters. When I telephoned the agent in charge of the Portland FBI office to tell him we were looking for a chief, he said, "I don't know of anyone offhand. But even if I did, I don't know how much luck you'd have getting him to come to Sweet Home. We get more calls about Sweet Home than any other place in the state."

The police chief of one of the larger departments in the state wrote directly to the League of Cities in response to the League's notice about our vacancy. The League's executive secretary sent me a copy of the letter. The chief wrote that he had one man who had shown some interest, then added, "But since he talked with a businessman who had recently been over there, he seems to have lost all interest entirely. The picture this man had painted was not very bright, making it look as though they might need one of the old frontier two-gun sheriffs."

Still another man who qualified for the position, when asked if he were interested, responded, "Not me! You think I want to get killed?"

I had continued my search through the spring and into the summer, when one afternoon two brawny individuals appeared at my office. They introduced themselves as Herman "Bud" Richards and Roy Southerland, deputy sheriffs from Clark County, Vancouver, Washington. Richards was spokesman for the two. He resembled a teddy bear with cauliflowered ears and weighed about 225 pounds. Southerland was older and considerably bigger. Richards said they understood we were looking for a new police chief and that he would be interested in the job if we had positions for both him and his companion. He suggested that he be appointed chief and that Southerland, although older and more experienced, be named captain.

I asked about their backgrounds. Both gave a history of several years in law enforcement work in sheriffs' offices and local police departments. They said they'd like to get out of the big Vancouver-Portland area and back into police work in a small town.

I was favorably impressed with Richards except for one thing. Although he spoke enthusiastically about the job, I had the impression Southerland had put him up to making application and that Southerland was really calling the shots. Maybe I got this feeling from Southerland's saying at the outset that he had a military retirement and didn't really need a job. He owned property in southern Oregon and California, and he was offering his services only to help us out. He knew, he said, how tough it was to get policemen in the small towns, and he just wanted to give us a hand if we could use him. He made special mention that if after awhile either he or the city found it wasn't working out, he would say so or I could let him know, and we would part company with no hard feelings.

I jotted down their personal histories and several references and told them I would get back in touch with them. They said, "Fine, we're in no hurry."

Because of the urgency of finding a replacement for our resigning chief, I gave this top priority. The morning after Richards's and Southerland's visit, I called their references, all of them in the Vancouver-Portland area. In addition, I asked the references to give me names of other people who knew both men. I also called the secondary references. Every reference spoke well of both men, citing their good character and good work habits.

Having completed this initial inquiry, and having Richards's and Southerland's permission to talk to the Clark County sheriff (their current employer), I drove to Vancouver. I visited at the sheriff's office and made some other inquiries about both Richards and Southerland. Again, all the reports were favorable.

On my return to Sweet Home, I called Richards and told him we would be glad to have him and Southerland join us. Richards would be chief, and we would create the position of captain and appoint Southerland to that post. (One of our patrolmen had given me notice that he also was resigning when the chief left.) Richards expressed his appreciation and gave me a date on which they would report for duty.

One of the things I had asked Richards and Southerland during our first interview was whether they had uniforms. I thought perhaps one reason for Sweet Home's lax law enforcement was the unprofessional appearance of our officers. They said they had their own uniforms and assumed they would be expected to be in uniform while on duty.

The day Richards and Southerland went to work in uniform

they created considerable comment in town. John Russell wondered, editorially, whether Sweet Home was "ready" for this kind of change. It was soon evident that there were others in Sweet Home who were quite sure the city should not have trained, experienced, uniformed police officers.

One of the first things the new chief did was design a simple, inexpensive, and practical addition to the front of the jail. His idea was to get police activity out of City Hall where Chief Hardy had operated from a desk in the corner of the council chamber. The new office would provide a more businesslike place to deal with the public and a place to keep the department's records and hold their training sessions. We got council approval, and within a few weeks the Sweet Home police department was operating out of a small but adequate facility, with an organized arrest, booking, and records procedure.

The People Speak: Gambling Must Go

We had an adequate antigambling ordinance that had been on the books for years, and the new city charter listed "to enforce all city ordinances" as the first duty of the city manager. But these ordinances are standard equipment in any city. They do not guarantee the people will elect members to the governing body who want that duty performed. In fact, I was surprised more than once by the solid, nongambling citizens who thought that instead of being rough on the gamblers the city should get in on the gambling money.

They reasoned this way: "There's lots of money in town and no place to spend it. The men are willing to gamble it away. Why not take advantage of this? Let the city get a good share of its revenue by licensing the gamblers; then we can get the street improvements, fire protection, parks, and other things the community needs. It will relieve the rest of us from the increasing tax burden."

When a punchboard operator, accompanied by the mayor of another small place across the mountains, came into town and visited a number of our citizens, he added weight to this reasoning. He offered us 10 percent of the gross. The mayor estimated what we could count on and added that the income had sure helped his town.

The combination of nongamblers who could see benefit from the gambling, and other citizens who simply wanted a wide-open town had produced city council majorities who wanted no more than token law enforcement.

But now the council began getting pressure of another kind. Parents of growing children, both churchgoers and nonchurchgoers, and wives whose husbands had lost their whole logging rig in one night at a card table were making themselves heard. They were forcing the council to take a second look at the advantages of an open town. In two instances, I was told, the councilmen's own employees had been victims of "Brownie" Buskirk's manhandling methods and the Moore brothers' fast plays.

Whether as a gesture or as evidence of a sincere change of direction, early in August the city council passed a motion ordering the city manager to strictly enforce all city ordinances, and to let the public know of the council's policy. The council had initiated this action. The brief discussion preceding the vote on the motion indicated that the aim was to stop the open gambling. All seven council members were present and voted "aye" on the motion. It looked as though the council meant business.

In accordance with the council's instructions to inform the public of the council's new directive, I set up a meeting for August 31 in City Hall. Chief Richards personally delivered an invitation to the owners of all taverns and cardrooms in the city and to other key people.

Half an hour before the scheduled meeting time, Chief Richards, Captain Southerland, the city attorney, and I were there, representing the city. We chatted with those who came early. The atmosphere was relaxed and friendly. By meeting time, everyone invited was there: the owners of the seven taverns and cardrooms; the presidents of the Chamber of Commerce, the Rotary Club, the Ministerial Association, the American Federation of Labor (AFL), and the Congress of Industrial Organizations (CIO); the district inspector for the Oregon Liquor Control Commission; the superintendent of schools; and publisher John Russell of the *New Era*.

I thanked them for coming, introduced the police officers and the city attorney, and handed each a copy of a signed statement that I then read. In the opening paragraph I explained we had asked all of them to meet with us so they would "hear the same statement in order that there may be no future misunderstanding or disagreement."

I went on to say, "The basis for successful and progressive community life any place on this earth is law enforcement—

voluntarily self-imposed or imposed from above. America is nothing more than a collection of communities like our own. What we do here is part of what America is doing. We strive for the ideal in which the enforcement of law is self-imposed; we intend that where it is not self-imposed we shall enforce the law to the extent of the authority vested in us by the representatives of all of us—the city council and the state legislature."

After outlining the basic structure of our city government and noting that "the line of authority from the people down to the policeman on the beat is clear, unbroken, and understandable," I invited them to take up with the chief of police questions about the actions of individual officers, to take up with me questions regarding the conduct of the chief, to go to the municipal judge for interpretation of city ordinances or information on interpretation of state law, and to exercise their right to appear at any city council meeting for adoption or repeal of city ordinances.

I concluded my statement with this: "On August 8, 1944, the city council in a regular meeting attended by the whole membership, passed the following motion: 'That the city manager be instructed to enforce all city ordinances.'

"These are our instructions. Until such time as the instructions may be altered, or the ordinances are repealed by council action, it is my duty and the duty of the people working with me—and it is our intention—to enforce the law to the best of our ability.

"We, because we are employees of the city, are no different than the remainder of the community. We have our homes here; we are raising our families here. We shall continue, God willing, to do our best to make this city attractive to decent, patriotic, and sincere citizens who are striving to strengthen our nation by building cities in which we, our families, and our friends can raise our children in decency and in health.

"We solicit your cooperation not alone because we are working for you but because we too are part of the community."

When I finished the statement, I asked, "Are there any comments any of you wish to make, or any questions you wish to ask to clarify what I've just read, or for any other reason?"

There were none. I thanked the group again for coming. Without a word, they arose and quietly filed out, much like men leaving a funeral. Outside the building there was some subdued talk. I heard Pat Moore say, "I don't know why he called me over to this meeting."

Bumpy Road Ahead

The telephone in the new police department office was connected to City Hall so that when there was no one in the police department the girl in City Hall could take the calls. This was helpful, except that she could take only the caller's name, number, and message; she had no way of reaching the officers—a situation that might mean a long delay before an officer responded to the call.

When I discussed this problem with the chief, we hit on the idea of installing a red light atop the utility pole on Main Street that could be seen from the greatest distance and the most directions in town. When a call came for the police, we could switch on the light from City Hall. The officers would check the light frequently; if it was on, they would call or stop at City Hall for the message.

The system wasn't perfect, nor was it as effective as two-way radio would have been. But it was the best we could do, and it was a marked improvement.

Nevertheless, at the first council meeting after the light was installed, the minutes of the previous meeting had no sooner been read and approved than Councilman Gessler demanded to know who had authorized the installation of the red light on Main Street, and why.

I described our problem and said the new chief and I thought this was an inexpensive and practical way to solve it partially.

Gessler snorted, "Well, if you ask me, this is one hell of a way to spend the taxpayers' money. Besides, who needs these policemen anyway?"

I had no answer. The chief, sitting at the side of the room, flushed a little but kept quiet. No member of the council responded. The mayor called for the first item on the typed agenda.

Enforcing State and City Policy

Clare Cotter had attended the meeting at which I had read the statement about the council's policy on law enforcement. Apparently he considered this a challenge. It was not long until Chief Richards came to me with a report that the night officer was having trouble with Cotter over the requirement that there be an unobstructed view from the street into the bar area of any place that held a liquor license, during the time it was serving customers. This was not just a city requirement; it was a well-known State Liquor Control Commission policy and was vigorously enforced.

Cotter's cafe had about a twenty-foot frontage on the street; the entrance door was in the center. The entire front was glass.

After our meeting on law enforcement, Cotter started pulling the blinds on his door and windows at about eleven at night, while he still had customers in the place. The night officer had reminded him of the state policy requiring an unobstructed view, but Cotter had ignored his reminder.

Then the chief took up the matter with Cotter. Clare said he couldn't operate at night with the blinds up. The chief said, "Clare, you know the policy. It's clear. And you know the reason for it. While we want to be reasonable, we have no choice but to require you to comply."

Following my suggestion that if a citizen was not satisfied with the conduct of the chief of police, he should come to me, Clare did just that. He was sore. He said, "Those new cops you've got are trying to harass me right out of business."

"Clare," I said, "the chief told me you and he were having some problem about leaving your blinds up, but I don't think he or anyone else connected with the city is trying to harass you. Anyway, tell me your story and let's see if there's anything we can do about it."

His problem, he said, was this: Almost every night the log train pulled into town a few minutes before his closing time, which was 11:00 p.m. The train crew came to his place for dinner because it was the middle of their work day. Usually they took about forty-five minutes to eat and relax.

This was awkward for him. He wanted their business, but he also wanted to get his place closed on time. He had tried locking the door to keep out other people, but seeing the train crew, the other customers thought his place was open for business and tried to get in. When they found the door locked, they rattled the door and motioned they wanted in. His waitresses felt they had to let the other people in; consequently he couldn't get the placed closed for an hour or more after the time he wanted to close. So he had taken to pulling the blinds. This way, he figured, nobody could see into the place and they would quit bothering him.

I checked the rules. It was plain. If intoxicating beverages were sold, there had to be easy view from the street.

I said, "What about not selling drinks after eleven? Apparently if you're serving only food, you're okay. In that case you wouldn't be taking in more customers; you'd just be finishing serving those already in your place. Then you could close and lock the door, pull the blinds, and there'd be no problem either of violating the law or turning away customers."

"That wouldn't do," Clare said. "Those men have put in half a day's work, and they're tired. They want some refreshments."

"Well, Clare," I said, "if you're going to continue to serve drinks, then obviously the rule about unobstructed view applies, and there's no way to avoid it. Here's another thought, though. Does the blind on your door say 'Closed' when you have it pulled down?"

"No, it doesn't. Why?"

"Because it seems to me that all you'd have to do is have the word **CLOSED** printed in large letters on the outside of the door blind. You could do that by hand. When the blind is rolled up, the sign won't show. But when you close and lock the door, pull down the blind. It will say 'CLOSED.' Any reasonable person, seeing that sign on the door, will leave you alone. This way, your other customers will know you're closed; yet the window blinds will still be up, there'll be unobstructed view from the street, and you can continue serving drinks to the customers in the place. I'm sure this will meet the legal requirements, and it will satisfy the police officers."

"Aw, Roy, that won't work. Those other people seeing the train crew are going to keep trying to get in. They'll bother the hell out of us."

"Clare," I said. "I'm afraid you can't avoid being bothered. You can't have your cake and eat it too. If you want to continue to serve drinks at that time of night, there will have to be unobstructed view into the place. I'm trying to suggest ways in which you can solve your problem, yet not be in violation. I don't know anything else to suggest."

"You can tell those cops to lay off of me, that's what you can do. They're riding me all the time."

"They are?" I asked. "What else have they been bothering you about?"

"Lots of things."

"Well, what?"

"Oh, just everything."

"Clare, you say they're riding you. If they are, let's have it. What are they after you about, other than this matter of keeping your blinds up when you're serving drinks?"

He didn't answer. He got up, put on his hat, glared at me a moment, and left.

First Impressions Can Fool Us

About the time that Clare Cotter came in to complain of harassment, word came from two or three quarters that a pair of professional operators had moved into town and were getting themselves accepted by some of the "best people." It was a man and his good-looking, well-dressed wife. They were friends of Fred and Emma Barnes and were staying at the Barnes' motel. I supposed she was the woman I had seen uptown with Mrs. Barnes a couple of times lately. I had noticed her especially because she was wearing a fur coat and high-heeled, patent leather shoes. This was a bit out of the ordinary in Sweet Home, especially on a weekday.

Word was that the woman was an excellent bridge player and had gotten in solid with most of the bridge crowd. The husband apparently spent most of his time in the various card rooms around town.

At about ten one night I was working on city books when I saw the police car and three other cars drive up in front of police headquarters. Two policemen escorted a man into the office. They were followed by Clare Cotter, Mr. and Mrs. Barnes, and some other people I didn't know.

I waited a few minutes, then walked over to the police office to see what was going on. Mrs. Barnes and the woman I had seen uptown with her were standing in front of the counter. I greeted Mrs. Barnes, and she introduced me to her friend.

"Madge, may I present Mr. Harlow, our city manager? Mr. Harlow, this is Madge Emerson. She's a newcomer to Sweet Home."

Mrs. Emerson turned to me. She was striking—large brown eyes, well-kept, wavy, dark brown hair, and she was dressed more for meeting someone in a leading Portland hotel than for the Sweet Home police department. She acknowledged the introduction in a low but clear and pleasant voice.

I asked her how long she planned to be in Sweet Home. She smiled, and her smile made her even more beautiful. With a look of undivided attention and warm friendliness, she said that would depend on a number of things.

At this moment, the chief came into the office from the cell room. He turned to Mrs. Emerson. "Mrs. Emerson, how long have you folks been in Sweet Home?"

"About two weeks."

"You're staying with Mr. and Mrs. Barnes?"

"Yes, they're old friends of ours."

"Where are you from?"

"California."

"Where in California?"

"Near Stockton. But, Chief," she interrupted the questioning in her pleasant, low voice, "why are you holding my husband?"

"Oh, we just wanted to ask him some questions. I don't think he'll be here for more than fifteen minutes."

"I hope not," Mrs. Emerson said. "The Barneses and my husband and I are to meet some friends at their home up on the Holley Road at about eleven."

"Oh, I think we'll be through in plenty of time," the chief said.

"Tell me again, Mrs. Emerson," the chief probed. "You say you're from near Stockton, California."

"That's right."

"Was your husband in business there?"

"That's right."

"How long did you live in, or near, Stockton?"

"Seven years."

The chief was behind the counter during this questioning. Mrs. Emerson had her arms on the counter facing him. She was giving him her flattering, undivided attention, answering his questions pleasantly, in a low, quiet voice and with a hint of a smile on her face.

The Chief said, "The fact is, Mrs. Emerson, your husband has just been released after spending seven years in Folsom Prison."

For a moment there was silence, then Madge Emerson screamed at the chief. "You rat, you haven't got anything on my husband. Let him out of this place!"

The chief stepped back from the counter as she swung at him with her purse. She stamped her feet, pounded the counter, and continued screaming and letting forth a string of profanity and vulgarities. Gone was the low voice, the quiet smile, the soft brown eyes. Madge Emerson, if that was her name, was a raging female.

Several times the chief tried to interrupt her. Mrs. Barnes tried to get her by the arm and take her outside. The tirade must have lasted five minutes.

When the chief could get Mrs. Barnes's attention, he said, "We have the report from the FBI on your friend Emerson, but we're turning him loose. We don't have anything on him. We just wanted to talk to him and to your husband and Clare Cotter. They'll be out in a minute."

Mostly by force, Mrs. Barnes finally got Madge Emerson through the door, Madge still shouting profanities at the city and at all of us, and still screaming, "You won't get away with this."

In a moment the night officer escorted Barnes, Emerson, and Cotter through the office and out to their cars. They passed the chief and me without a glance of recognition or a comment. When they were gone, the chief said, "That's the couple who have captured the hearts of half the most prominent people in town. Some of these people had better watch out, or they'll be losing their pocketbooks as well as their hearts."

Ahah!

The city council had just disposed of the last item on the agenda when the mayor asked his usual closing question: "Anything else for the good of the order?"

"Yes, I've got something for the good of the order." It was Councilman Gessler. "I'd like to know where these cops came from that we've got out hounding our citizens." George's face was white, his lips quivering.

"Why, George, what's the matter?" the mayor asked.

"I just want to know where these cops came from."

The mayor turned to me.

I said, "George, you know where they came from. When we hired them, I reported to the council that they came from the Clark County sheriff's department."

"Well," Gessler said, "that Captain Southerland used to be a jailer over in Eugene, and he's no good. We ought to investigate him, and Richards, too."

"George," I said, "if there's anything wrong with these men, I want to know it. I checked them carefully with the Clark County sheriff's office. But if you think there's something more we ought to know about them, I'll be glad to go up to Vancouver and over to Eugene with you, and we'll get to the bottom of the story." Councilman Gessler was noncommittal.

The meeting adjourned, and I began gathering my papers before returning to my office. As the councilmen headed for the door, Gessler turned to the mayor.

"Stew," he said, "there are just two men running this town."

"Who's that, George?" the mayor asked good-naturedly, seemingly confident that Gessler would include him.

"The chief of police and the city manager," Gessler snapped.

Next morning I stopped at George's apartment to ask when he could get away to go with me to Vancouver and Eugene. He didn't know when he could get away. In the next two weeks I telephoned or stopped to see him four or five times about the trip to investigate Southerland and Richards. Each time he had an excuse why he couldn't get away.

The following meeting of the council was stiff and formal. Gone was the bantering and small talk that usually preceded the business session. The councilmen stuck close to the agenda items.

They were about through the evening's business when suddenly there was a great commotion on the front porch. The door flew open, and three struggling men squeezed through the opening. Chief Richards and Captain Southerland were "escorting" a man between them. They were holding him so that his toes barely touched the floor. The man was struggling to get loose, cursing and kicking at the officers.

The three wrestled their way past the council table, through my office, and out to the jail. When they closed the back door, no one at the council table spoke for a moment. The man between Richards and Southerland was Clare Cotter.

Gessler broke the silence. "These policemen we've got are ruining this town. I'm for getting rid of the whole lot of them."

"Now just a minute, George," the mayor said. "Did you and the city manager check up on these new men like you talked about doing at last council meeting? If you've got something to report, let's have it."

"No, we didn't. And I don't think we need to investigate them. Everybody knows they're wrecking our town."

"Well, let's get something straight," the mayor said. "You and I may not like the policemen we have, but under the council-manager charter the police department is the city manager's responsibility, not ours. If we don't like the policemen, we can tell the manager so, but we can't fire them. Only the manager can do that."

He paused, then added, "Of course, if we don't like what the manager does, we can fire him."

At this Gessler slammed his fist on the table. "Okay, then, I move we fire the city manager right now!"

For half an hour the argument raged. Nobody would second Councilman Gessler's motion, but neither would anybody stop talking. While three talked at once at the tops of their voices, the other three were shouting, "Mr. Mayor, I want the floor. Mr. Mayor!" Finally, the mayor got a motion to adjourn, and the turmoil moved outside.

I sat in my office, staring blankly at the dark window. I tried to reconstruct all that had happened during the last few weeks and to make some sense out of it. The police were doing their job, and I was doing mine. We were doing just what the council said they wanted done. What distressed me particularly was that clearly Councilman Gessler was not alone in thinking the police were ruining the town. And although nobody seconded his motion to fire me, neither had anybody offered an objection to the proposal.

As I sat trying to figure it out, the chief came in. He apologized for bringing Cotter through the council chamber. He said that in the excitement they had forgotten they were now booking people in the new office instead of at City Hall as they had before.

"Here's something that might interest you," he said, handing me a piece of paper. "It was in Cotter's wallet."

It was a simple receipt form. It read: "Received from . . . . Clare Cotter . . . . Five Hundred and No/100 . . . . Dollars . . . . On Account."

The receipt was signed "Geo. W. Gessler."

I handed it back to the chief for safekeeping in the personal property file. Now I could imagine two or three possible financial arrangements between Councilman Gessler and gambler Clare Cotter that might account for the councilman's objection to our enforcement of the law.

Terminating a Disgruntled Employee

I wanted to back up our new officers, but the statement by Councilman Gessler about Southerland's being in Eugene troubled me. Captain Southerland had not mentioned Eugene in our first meeting when he had listed for me his extensive law enforcement experience. This was my first misgiving about appointing Southerland. Soon I had others.

He stopped Agda and me one evening as we were driving to a movie. "Mr. City Manager," he said, "I don't know how long I'm going to be able to take this hick-town judge you've got here."

This was the first hint I had of any difficulties between the police department and the court. I asked Southerland what was the matter.

"Look," he said, "we're trying to straighten this town out. We're working our heads off, too, and every time we make a good pinch, it gets cancelled out by that Bible-reading judge. He may be a good Sunday School teacher, but he's no judge. He thinks if he gives these drunks a sermon, they'll go home and be good boys and never do anything wrong again. He ought to throw the book at them. That's the only language they understand."

I told Southerland I knew it was tough to work hard on a case and after you get the fellow before the judge, the judge turns him loose. "But that's the American system—the separation of the executive function from the judicial function. Our job is to take the laws of the city council and the state and enforce them as best we can. After we have made an arrest, we're through. We have done our duty; the rest is up to the court." I closed by saying, "Captain, I'll talk to the judge and see what we can do to get him to look at it from your point of view a little more."

"It won't do any good," Southerland replied.

I did talk to Judge Corner. I found it was true that the judge's method of dealing with almost all the men who came before him was to give them another chance—to try to rehabilitate them. Even the promises of the three- and four-timers, he thought, should be accepted if they said they were sorry and would do better. Probably many of these people knew the judge was soft and took advantage of him. Others may have intended to straighten out, but their liquor and other problems had become more than they had will power to overcome. When the judge accepted their promises of turning over a new leaf, the police despaired of making any progress.

Unable to get Councilman Gessler to go with me either to Eugene or Vancouver, I decided to go to Eugene myself and see if there was anything to what he had said about Southerland. I made an appointment with the sheriff of Lane County and drove over to see him.

The sheriff said, yes, he knew Roy Southerland. Southerland had worked as a jailer in his department.

Would he mind telling me why Southerland had left?

Ordinarily, he didn't discuss such matters, the sheriff said, but under the circumstances—since Southerland was working in law enforcement for us, and I was the local government official responsible for his work—he would give me the information.

What the sheriff told me was bizarre almost beyond belief.

Two incidents led to Southerland's dismissal from Lane County. He had served without mishap for some time when the sheriff happened onto an act of such poor judgment and questionable legality it raised grave doubts in his mind about Southerland. Southerland had permitted a prisoner to leave jail and take Southerland's car on an errand of some distance, in return for promise of payment by the prisoner on his release. The sheriff probably never would have learned of this act of indiscretion on Southerland's part if the prisoner had not had a wreck and when picked up told how he happened to be out of jail and using the jailer's car. Southerland admitted to the sheriff all the facts, but on his plea to be given another chance the sheriff let him stay on, with only a reprimand.

The other incident was related to the notorious "Murder in Lower 13." At about 4:00 a.m. on January 23, 1943, as a southbound Southern Pacific passenger train pulled out of a siding at Tangent, Oregon (a small town in the same county as Sweet Home), Martha Brinson James, a twenty-one-year-old wife of a Navy ensign, was murdered in a lower pullman berth. Before she had died, the woman's moaning awakened other passengers. They called the conductor. One passenger, a soldier, claimed he had seen a man run down the car aisle and disappear.

The conductor wired ahead to the station in Eugene to have law enforcement officers meet the train. Southerland was on duty when the message reached the sheriff's office, and he accompanied the sheriff's other men to the train.

Officers searched the train in an effort to round up suspects. Based on what the trainmen and passengers said about whom they had seen the young woman with during the day and the build and size of the man seen running down the aisle, the scant evidence pointed to both a serviceman who had been seen with the woman and to one of the Negro dining car cooks or porters. Evidently, the trainmen were strongly inclined to suspect the latter.

Without the knowledge or permission of the sheriff, Southerland stayed on the train when it pulled out of Eugene and proceeded to make his own investigation. He caused such a commotion among the passengers that the trainmen notified the sheriff, who wired Southerland to get off the train at the next stop. Southerland refused to do so. He continued to interrogate passengers and trainmen. The sheriff had to request the sheriff at Klamath Falls to take Southerland off the train, which the Klamath sheriff did.

These two acts on Southerland's part were too much for the Lane County sheriff. When Southerland got back to Eugene, the sheriff dismissed him.

On my return to Sweet Home, I called Southerland into the office. I asked him to tell me his version of the "Murder in Lower 13" incident. He said it had been obvious to him that the trainmen were trying to pin the murder on the Negro, when it was clear to him the serviceman had murdered the woman. He was determined that justice be done. Moreover, he was still of the opinion that he could have solved the crime if he had been permitted to continue his investigation. (In April 1943, Robert Lee Folkes, a twenty-two-year-old Negro second cook on the train was found guilty of the woman's murder. He was executed in January 1945.)

That night I put together a mental balance sheet. On one side I put our need for police service of the kind Captain Southerland seemed capable of providing and the difficulty I figured we would have in finding a suitable replacement. On the other side I noted his growing domination of Chief Richards (almost always Southerland was along when the chief came to my office, and usually took the conversation away from the chief and spoke for both of them); Captain Southerland's increasing impatience with the judge, the city council, and the "hick" citizens; and, finally, the revelation of what had happened in Eugene. I decided to accept the offer he had made when he was employed, that if it didn't work out, all I had to do was say so and he would go south and take care of his orange groves.

When I told the chief my decision, he seemed to be relieved. I asked him to send Captain Southerland in to see me when he came on duty.

The captain and I passed the time of day for a few minutes; then I asked, "Captain Southerland, do you remember when you and Chief Richards came here, you told me you had other business interests, that you didn't need the job, and that if at any time I felt the arrangement wasn't working out satisfactorily, all I needed to do was tell you?"

He said, "Yes."

I said, "I know how displeased you have been with the judge. I've talked to the judge, and I don't think we're going to get him to change. Furthermore, we aren't going to change the people in this community. We're going to have to work with them the way they are and give them the best service we can. In view of your dissatisfaction with the job, I'm going to suggest that you look around for another job, and that when you find one to your liking you make a change. There's no hurry. Take a month to do so if you need it. And if you need any time off to go for interviews, we'll arrange to get a substitute for you."

Southerland was sitting opposite me, his large frame draped over the far edge of my desk. He didn't say anything, just looked at me. Then, deliberately, he took off his police cap and laid it on the desk. Then he slowly removed his police badge and laid it beside the cap. Finally, he took off his Sam Brown belt with holster and bullet belt and laid them on the desk.

All the time he kept his eyes on me. When he had all his gear laid out neatly in front of him, he said to me in a low voice, "Do you mean I'm fired?"

I said, "No. I'm asking for your resignation. I'm following the steps you suggested when you came here, namely, that if it didn't work out, I let you know. It hasn't worked out. I'm suggesting you arrange to leave at your convenience, any time within the next month."

Southerland pushed back his chair and rose to his feet. He leaned forward, his hands on the desk, and looked down at me. "Step outside, you little _____," he said slowly, "and I'll beat the hell out of you."

I waited for his next move. He just stood there glaring down at me.

"Roy," I said, "I'm sorry you feel this way. Your conduct right now makes me think I probably should have made this move sooner. I'm holding to my offer. You can have a month to make the change. Either accept that, or you're through now."

He picked up his gear, turned, and walked out the door without a word. I saw him go to police headquarters and come out a minute later with the chief. He had on his civilian hat and jacket. He got into his car. I haven't seen him since.

I made no statement about his leaving, but the *New Era* carried this news item:

"Roy B. Southerland, who has been captain on the Sweet Home police force for several months, has resigned his position. On account of Mrs. Southerland's health the Southerlands will change climates by moving to Riverside, California."

Role of the City Manager in Elections

Stewart Weiss was the first mayor under Sweet Home's council-manager charter. In fact, he was almost wholly responsible for adoption of the plan. He had the League of Oregon Cities draft the charter, he wrote and paid for the ads that helped gain public support for the change in government, and he arranged to get the issue on the ballot. The number of total votes on the plan was small, but the percentage favoring the new charter provided a comfortable margin.

The mayor was a strong leader with a record of long activity in the Republican Party. He had organized and headed the Young Republicans in the Portland area. He was licensed to practice law before the Oregon state courts and the U.S. Supreme Court, and he once served as assistant attorney general for Oregon.

With foresight, he anticipated America's involvement in World War II and the corresponding demand for forest products. To be in a position to benefit from what he saw coming, he bought an interest in a lumber mill and was soon the sole owner. This put him among the economically affluent in Sweet Home.

Stew was a large man, forceful and persuasive in voice and manner—a superb salesman. He could sell an audience on either side of an issue and delighted in doing so. For instance, I once watched him persuade a group that they should take a certain position on extension of bus service. (I don't remember now whether he was for or against extension.) A few days later at an official hearing, I heard him argue for the other side on the same issue—and prevail.

When I asked him how he could do this, he said, "Roy, there's no secret to it. I've learned that once I convince myself, I can convince others. Therefore, when I take a case, the first thing I do is convince myself my client's position is right. The rest is easy."

On the city council, the mayor was clearly the strongest of the seven men. Because of his legal training and experience, his success in getting the new government approved by the voters, and his dominant personality, he got his way on every important issue. He was the best informed on the city charter; therefore his presence on the council was important to the continuance and success of the council-manager plan in Sweet Home. Consequently, I was concerned when I heard about a stunt he had pulled that looked to me as if he was asking for his own defeat at the next election.

According to the story, the incident took place at a party given by the owner of one of Oregon's large logging and mill operations. The mayor was feeling his drinks a little and got into an argument about how candidates are elected to local public office. He maintained that with the proper organization and direction, you could elect anyone. Someone challenged him. It ended in the mayor's putting up $1,500 that said he, a lifelong Republican, could get elected as county sheriff an aging, somewhat broken-down political hack that the Democrats had nominated, over a young, popular Republican chief of police from Lebanon.

After I heard the same story two or three times, I asked the mayor if I were hearing right. I was, he said, but there was nothing to be concerned about. His man would win hands down. I surmised he was already convincing himself of the rightness of his action.

When word got around town that Mayor Weiss had wagered $1,500 he could elect the Democratic candidate for sheriff, one of the groups that heard the story and reacted was the Sweet Home Ministerial Association. The Association directed their president to call on me.

The Association president outlined the kind of government the ministers believed I was trying to provide and wondered if members of the city council were supporting this effort. With a majority of the council seats to be filled in the coming election, the ministers planned to pass out handbills at all churches the Sunday before the election and to circulate them to all their members. They intended to urge their members to vote for the candidates I recommended. With candidate filings now complete, whom should they vote for, the Association president wanted to know.

His inquiry put me in an awkward position. The theory of the council-manager plan is that an elected council, whether elected on a partisan or nonpartisan basis, chooses a professional manager to carry out their policies. The city manager refrains from partisan political activity.

At the same time, I was aware that the ministers were more astute and more determined to be an action group for continuation of the kind of government we stood for than any other group in town. They had sensed correctly the situation, namely that some of the council candidates—both incumbents and first-timers—were for getting a new city manager—if not for holding an election to change back to the mayor-council form, with an elected mayor serving as the city's chief executive.

The Association president wanted to know if the story about Weiss's $1,500 bet was true. Since I had heard the story from several sources and the mayor had confirmed it to me, I felt free to say I understood it was true.

Suddenly it occurred to me that this was the clue to solving my dilemma of being politically impartial while at the same time helping those who favored the kind of government we were attempting to provide. I reasoned this way: The affairs of government are the people's business. Under the American system, whenever any citizen or group of citizens makes inquiry about any phase of government, it is the obligation of the governmental officials to fully and accurately answer their inquiries. Although this general rule would not apply to matters of national or community security or when the good reputation of an individual might be involved, in all other situations I felt (and I feel now) that governmental affairs should be an open book to citizens who wish to know. This is so even if the information thus obtained may be used for the citizen's personal gain or advantage or to the disadvantage of those in office, including myself.

To have it otherwise is to make a mockery of our basic concept that the people are sovereign. Unless the people know the facts, how can they act intelligently on the important issues, whether in a small town, a state, or a nation?

So I replied to the Ministerial Association's president in this way.

"You have asked me whom to vote for in the forthcoming election. As city manager, my job is to carry out as best I can the policies of whomever the people choose as their elected representatives. This is the basic concept of the council-manager plan of local government. A manager would not be free to provide impartial administration for the benefit of all the citizens if he either were aligned with or supported any particular individual or citizens' group. And whether I would be personally helped by their support or harmed by their opposition, it is my duty to remain completely apart from involvement and direct or indirect participation or influence in the selection of members of the city council.

"At the same time, as I see it, it is equally a city manager's duty to do all he can to keep the public informed about city affairs. This is why the minutes and all other city records are open to the public, why we put out an annual report, and why managers make radio and other reports to the people.

"In view of these fundamentals of how the council-manager plan is supposed to work, I can't tell you whom I think you or your congregation should vote for. It would be improper for me to urge your support of any particular candidate for the city council. On the other hand, there may be and probably are some things about city affairs that you do not know, but you should know about because they have an important bearing on how well and how impartially the city government is operating. I think it is proper for me to inform you or any other inquiring citizen of these matters. It may then be that with these facts in hand, you and your people will be in a better position to make your own decisions as to whom to support."

The Ministerial Association president was enthusiastic about this approach. He said they had been aware of the underlying principles of the council-manager plan, and some of their number had hesitated to send him to me on this matter. However, others had said if they didn't know where to throw their support, their forces would be divided and confused and as a result of failure to act in unison might contribute to loss of the kind of government they thought the community should have. Where else could they turn, these members of the Association had asked, if not to the city manager who is in the middle of this situation and is best able to tell them what to do to continue the kind of government they now have?

I then recounted the incidents surrounding the Buskirk killing, our troubles with Clare Cotter, and Councilman George Gessler's move to have me fired. I also told him who had filed for council and the nature of my contacts with several of the candidates. As city recorder as well as city manager, I was the chief election official; I had the nominating petitions and could have shown them to him, which might have revealed who was supporting the various candidates. However, he did not ask to see the petitions, and I did not urge him to review them.

We spent two hours or more, covering the above items and others. As we talked, he wrote an occasional note. At the conclusion of our conference, he said he appreciated my refusal to name names. He thought the information I had provided would meet his group's needs in arriving at a decision.

Pride vs. Principle

More than once, Chief Richards was ready to quit the oner-
ous and thankless job of bringing law and order to "the
toughest town in Oregon." In fact, he resigned twice. I was the
cause of his first resignation; I never knew the cause of the
other. Fortunately, he reconsidered both times.

He attended the first city council meeting following his appointment and was at the next several meetings. He came without invitation from me or members of the council. He stationed
himself at the meetings, not in the capacity of a sergeant at
arms or another officer whose services might be required in case
of some disturbance, but as a department head who wanted to
be in on decisions that might affect him or his department.

His presence was awkward for several reasons. First, there
were times when members of the council—not just Councilman
Gessler—had questions about the conduct of the department.
Although under the council-manager plan all directives of the
council to departments are through the city manager, this concept was academic when the head of a department being discussed was sitting at the meeting. Second, other department
heads did not attend council meetings unless they were invited.
They didn't care to spend the time and were satisfied to get
their instructions from the manager. Third, although the chief
was a most personable individual, his presence irritated some
citizens and councilmen.

After several meetings, I talked to him about the problem. As
diplomatically as I could, I told him it would not be necessary
for him to attend the meetings. I may have caught him on a bad
day. Whatever the reason, he took great offense.

He gave me several reasons why he should be there. Basically,
they all added up to his view that as the head of a major city
department he was entitled to sit in on any city council delib-
erations.

"Look," he said, "if they don't want me at their meetings,
and you don't want me there, you can have the damn job. I'm
through. I resign, right now."

I tried to present the other side but was only repeating what I
had already said. It was unacceptable to him. "If that's the way
it is, I resign."

Faced with this all-or-nothing attitude, I said, "I'm sorry,
Bud, but that's the way it is."

"All right," he said, "I'm turning in my badge."

That was a bad night for me. The chief had done an excellent job. Our working relationship couldn't have been better. I knew I would have great difficulty finding a replacement. But as I saw it, there was a principle involved. I was the city manager, and the chief was accountable only to me, not to the council. I was the one solely responsible for administering the policies laid down by the city council. If he didn't see it my way, he would have to go.

When I got home, I told my wife about the chief's actions and how stubborn he had been. Agda listened patiently, without comment. I repeated the story, each time with the emphasis on the principle involved and how unreasonable the chief was. I was still talking about my problem when we went to bed.

A little after midnight, Agda said to me, "Do you think it is possible the chief may be right? Have you looked at it from his point of view?"

"Of course, I have," I said. "That's what I've been explaining to you ever since I came home."

"LeRoy, you may be right," she said, "and you will have to make the decision. But it seems to me that this is not an important enough issue for you to lose the chief's services. You admit he has done an excellent job in every way, and this is the only point on which you two have had a difference. I'm just wondering if you aren't making a mountain out of a molehill."

This disturbed me. Ordinarily Agda and I saw eye-to-eye on things connected with my work, and she accepted my judgment. But here she was saying the chief might have more of a point than I did.

I got up, went out to the kitchen, and sat at the table trying to get my thinking in perspective. Gradually, the chief's reasoning took on greater significance than mine. Then it dawned on me that what I was really doing was mixing principle and pride. Before long, I decided I would go to the chief—the ex-chief—in the morning and ask him to reconsider.

I did. I apologized for being less considerate of his view than mine. We agreed on an arrangement whereby he would see the council agendas before the meetings. If there was anything on the agenda that he thought affected his department directly, he was free to attend the meeting. With this understanding, he went back to work and resumed doing his usual good job.

The chief's second resignation was on election day.

Even in small towns, election day is exciting for the candidates and their supporters. But for the election officials responsible for the hundreds of details involved, it is a trying and tiring time. Where there are no mechanical ways of counting ballots, clerks stationed at polling places may work around the clock; those who must also set up the election facilities may work a longer stretch.

This was my situation. As city recorder, I was the chief election official. Several days before the election I carefully read the election laws to learn the procedural details and to get the city attorney's help in interpreting some obscure and conflicting sections. Then I had to arrange for polling places and election boards. Petitions had to be checked for completeness and validity. Ballots had to be printed and proofed for correct spellings and to see that names were rotated so that no one candidate's name was always in the favored first position.

On election day I had to get books and supplies to the polls well before the opening at 7:00 a.m.; and since elections most often occur in cold November, I had to make advance arrangements for the comfort of the election boards: heat, chairs and tables enough, coat racks, toilet facilities, and usually a place to brew coffee through the long day. And of course the voting booths had to be ready and in working order.

Election day is certainly no time for extra problems and crises. Yet, right in the middle of the busy election day, the police chief insisted on seeing me. When I could find a minute, we met in my office.

"I'm resigning," he announced. "Today. Right now."

To say the least, this was an unexpected and unwelcome announcement. As far as I knew, the chief was getting along fine. (Our fuss over his attending council meetings had been settled months before.) I asked the cause of the trouble.

"This town doesn't want law enforcement, and you can't trust the councilmen," he said angrily.

There wasn't time to get all the details. It was something about abiding by the election laws and selling liquor. I managed to get him calmed down enough to agree to remain in office one more day. By the next day, with the composition of the new council known, he was willing to reconsider his previous day's action. Another day or two of cooling off, and his proposed resignation was forgotten. To this day I don't know the specifics that precipitated that crisis, but with the police problems we still had I was glad he changed his mind.

As for the election results, when election day drew near, the Ministerial Association mounted an active campaign among their members, urging the election of some candidates and the defeat of others. They did not take a position on Mayor Weiss's candidacy; but since he was such an important and powerful figure in city government, their failure to endorse him was tantamount to recommending his defeat. They openly urged the defeat of Councilman George Gessler. In the race of thirteen candidates for the seven council seats, Councilman Gessler ran eighth and Mayor Weiss ninth. Thus, both lost.

More Views on Gambling

The council that took office after the defeat of Mayor Weiss and Councilman Gessler included the older man who ran the card room we had never had any complaints about. The new mayor was Ivan Hoy, a grocer and hardware store owner. He was a quiet, serious man who favored law enforcement and disagreed with those who insisted the town would be ruined if it were not allowed to run wide open.

The new council made no move to either rescind or reinforce the previous council's directive to strictly enforce all ordinances, and it was not long before Mayor Hoy had to demonstrate whether he would stand by his convictions. First, the cook at one of the cafe cardrooms, who was one of Mr. Hoy's best customers before he became mayor, stopped buying from him. When Mayor Hoy went over to get an order, as he had been doing since the place opened, the cook pretended not to know him. The mayor told me afterwards, "I guess these gamblers mean business. I never thought they'd use my business against me, just because we don't agree about whether the town should be wide open."

At a meeting to discuss the need for a sanitary sewer system and what it would cost, the state legislator said, "If the money spent bothering gamblers, buying uniforms for the police, and a new police car had gone to the right place, we'd have a sewer system by now." Mayor Hoy's reply was, "I didn't know the gamblers had been elected to run the town. If they have, I'll resign and they can have it."

On another occasion, word came to me that Mrs. Fred Barnes (the friend of the out-of-town card players, the Emersons) was telling around town she had "proof" the night officer had asked for protection money, saying he had to split it with the mayor and the city manager. When I called on Mrs. Barnes at her motel office to get the details and see the "proof" she said that actually she didn't "know" about the matter; she had only "heard" about it.

When I reported this to Mayor Hoy, he commented, "If there were any payoffs, we wouldn't be having all the fuss we're having from the gamblers."

Together, the mayor and I ran down another rumor, this one credited to Floyd Eaton, one of the larger logging operators and a neighbor of the mayor. Eaton was quoted around town as saying that all the loggers would leave town if gambling were shut down. Mayor Hoy told me he couldn't believe Eaton had made such a statement, and the story troubled him.

My reply was that I thought the best way to get the truth of a matter was to go to the source. "Let's meet with Eaton, tell him the rumor that's circulating, and ask him what he does think."

So we made an appointment and called on him at his home. He was cordial. The conversation moved quickly to the recent election and the changes in the council. Then Mayor Hoy forthrightly asked Mr. Eaton if the statement credited to him was correct.

Eaton laughed. "Hell, no," he said. "I never made such a statement, and it's the farthest thing from my mind. I know loggers, and I know they're no different from anybody else."

But he didn't stop there. He went on. "Most of them want to be with their families when they get home at night. They're tired. Falling and bucking trees, even when they're lucky enough to be using one of the new power saws that are coming into the woods, is hard work. These men couldn't go out on the town every night, even if they wanted to, and most of them don't want to.

"Oh, we've got a few roughnecks, men who've come from someplace in the East or the South. They've seen some movie version of a logger as a rough, tough customer and they try to act the part. You'll find most of these guys never logged before they got out here, and the only reason they're doing it now is because of the big money. They aren't the real loggers. They're the Johnny-come-latelies, and they make most of the trouble, not only in town but in the woods, too. You can be sure that when this war is over and things get back to normal, they'll drift off someplace else. They won't be the ones staying here to make this a good, solid community where a man can make a living and raise a family in decency.

"No, sir. I don't think you'd lose a single substantial logger if you closed out the gambling completely, and I'm for doing it. The fact of the matter is that with gambling wide open, some of the men frequent these places just because they're here. And I know a few of them have lost their shirts, and they wish to hell they'd stayed home like they should have, instead of getting mixed up with these cutthroats who'd just as soon ruin a man as look at him."

Mayor Hoy had his answer.

Rooting out Rumors

The girl who filled the combination job of city treasurer, general office clerk, and my secretary had graduated from Sweet Home High School the previous spring. She was the valedictorian of her class. When I checked her qualifications with the superintendent of schools, whom she had given as a reference, he told me she was one of the most mature and able students they had ever had. He thought she would do an excellent job for us.

After graduation, she worked a few months in a local business establishment, then answered my ad for a secretary and general office girl. She was extremely bright and hardworking; so I was surprised when one of the councilmen suggested perhaps I ought to let her go. He said she had worked for him and that he didn't think she was reliable, that she was a gossip, and I'd probably find myself wishing I hadn't had her in the office.

This concerned me, not only because a councilman was trying to interfere with an appointment—contrary to the charter—but because there were enough situations requiring confidential handling that I didn't dare take a chance on someone who couldn't resist the temptation to talk outside the office about what she saw or heard at city hall and in the police department.

However, when I had hired Jean, I knew she was inexperienced and also that she knew little of what goes on in a city hall. So, after she had had a week or two to get accustomed to the work, I had a conference with her about the confidential nature of some of the things that came to our attention.

I made it clear that I wasn't talking about accounting records, official actions of the council, or our correspondence. That was public information. I was talking about information that involved the personal reputations of individuals. I pointed out that we might get reports about citizens from disgruntled neighbors, personal enemies, or even pranksters—reports that might be largely or completely false, but that if repeated might do irreparable damage to an innocent person's reputation.

I particularly cautioned her about the danger of being trapped into saying something she shouldn't. I told her that one device people sometimes used to get facts was to deliberately misstate a situation in the presence of a person known to have the facts, like herself. Inadvertently, she might try to set the record straight. In so doing, she would be playing right into the hands of the people trying to get her to give them information they wanted. I asked her to make it an unbroken rule to not know anything about these kinds of matters when she was away from the office.

She took this counsel seriously and, as far as I knew, had never revealed anything about city affairs that might do harm to someone else. Therefore, I was puzzled when the councilman came to me a couple more times to suggest strongly that I ought to let her go, warning that I would wish I had.

He was so persistent I decided to ask Jean what, if any basis, there was for his actions.

She said, "I think I know his reason, but I don't think it is reason enough for me to lose my job. But I'd rather not go into the details."

Knowing that she now knew how persistent the councilman was, and having brought the matter to her, I decided to do nothing more for a while. However, the next day I had a call from Jean's mother, asking if she and her husband could meet with me, that Jean had told them about our conversation and was very upset by the whole thing. I agreed and said I would come to their home that evening.

After a short visit, I asked if there was something they wanted to discuss about Jean and the job. Jean's mother said, "Mr. Harlow, Jean just loves her job. She has told us both of your warning about the confidential nature of some things that happen at city hall, so that we will understand why she won't talk even at home about some of the things we hear about. While the decision is up to you, of course, we as her parents would hate to see her lose her job because of what this one councilman has to say.

"You see," she continued, "Jean worked for that councilman at his store for a time. Did you know that?"

I said the councilman had told me that, though he hadn't gone into any details about her duties.

"He had two or three young girls working for him. We don't know how the other girls got along with him, but after Jean had been there a few weeks, one night she reported this incident to us. She said she had to go down into the basement for something a customer wanted. Her boss, the councilman, was down there. He come over to her, seemingly to help her get something off the shelf. Instead, he put his arms around her and tried to kiss her. Jean resisted him, broke away, and went upstairs to try to take care of the customer. Needless to say, she was upset, and when she got home that night she was a nervous wreck.

"We talked it over. She wanted to know what she should do. We advised her not to quit the job, but if he tried that again to say she was not interested in that kind of thing—that she would do her work as best she could, but if that wasn't enough, she would have to quit.

"He didn't trouble her for about a week, until they happened again to be in the basement together. This time he tried to talk her into letting him kiss her by asking 'What's a little kiss, anyway?' Well, you know he's married, has a wife and children, and is a highly respected businessman. Jean just isn't interested in having an affair with a married man, and she told him so. He didn't force himself on her, but Jean told us that night that she knew he didn't like it, and she was afraid she'd have to get another job. It was about this time that she saw your ad and was able to leave to go to work with you."

I suggested they counsel Jean to quit worrying and just continue her good work. Jean stayed with the city as long as I did, performing admirably on her job and never once creating the kind of problem the councilman had warned me about.

Personal Rapport Is Important

In addition to the early history I learned from Editor Russell, I learned a bit more about the early days in Sweet Home when the council sent me to one of the old-timers, Albert Weddle, to try to get him to deed a piece of open downtown property to the city for a street. They prepared me for my call on Weddle by telling me he was very unpopular with the businessmen. "He's ugly as an old bear, from some stomach trouble," they said. "He'll give you hell, and probably run you off his place."

They explained why the businessmen disliked him: When the highway had been improved through town and had become the main street, Weddle acquired a sliver of land between the highway right-of-way and the property line of lots that several businessmen had bought from him. To own clear title up to the highway, they had to buy pieces of that strip of land, in some instances only inches deep. He made them pay what they considered extortionate prices.

I did call on him. He was gruff. But when I happened to mention that my great-grandfather had homesteaded up in the mountains of western Washington much like his father had in Sweet Home and that sometime I'd like to have him tell me something of the early days in Sweet Home, he became very friendly. He told me of his earliest memories—of coming West in a wagon train, of living in a tent while his father sought a home site, of helping build the log house, and of working in his father's general store after the timber companies began logging around Sweet Home. He even told me about his stomachache that he had never been free of since he had worked in the store as a boy.

"You think you've got troubles, with fights, knifings, and killings," he said. "It's no different now than it's always been. We've always had troubles around here. There have always been troublemakers." Then he told me how his father had extended credit for groceries to a poor man with a raft of kids, including two no-good older sons. They didn't pay; so Albert's father told him that if any of that family came into the store to remind them their bill was past due.

The two older boys did come in. They apologized, said they were working now and would pay up soon, then asked for a couple of items for cash. One of the items they wanted was on a top shelf. When Albert stepped up on the ladder to get it, they jumped him. One pulled a knife and stabbed at his belly, ripping him straight up the front, through clothes and all. He grabbed himself, and when they saw blood, they took off.

Albert thought he was going to die if he didn't get help fast. He figured the fastest way to get a doctor was to get to the hotel and have someone call. He held himself with both arms until he reached the hotel and told the clerk what was wrong. By this time he was so weak he passed out. When he came to, he was lying there with his innards spilled out on the floor. Somebody told him they'd gone for the doctor and for him to lie still.

He thought it must have been an hour before the doctor arrived. He didn't bleed much and wasn't in much pain, so long as he didn't move.

When the doctor did arrive, he got some men to help lift Albert onto a table. They tried to move him, but it just about killed him. His intestines were stuck to the floor where the blood had dried. They couldn't get him loose. Finally, the doctor took a knife and ran it between his intestines and the floor, slicing him loose. They got him on a table, put a mask over his face, and put him to sleep with chloroform or ether.

When he came to, he was sewed up and bandaged. The doctor said he'd taken out a section of intestines for fear of infection. He said Albert was lucky to be alive.

We talked about a few other happenings in early Sweet Home and since. Weddle made it plain that although he had made some money when the war boom started, he was unhappy with the changes taking place.

"Sweet Home isn't like it used to be, and I guess it never will be again, but I'd like to keep it as much like it used to be as I can, for as long as I can."

I asked him about getting property for the street I'd come to talk to him about.

"Well, young man," he said, "I don't know whether I will or I won't. There are some mighty hard feelings between me and some of these newcomers. I don't know if I will or I won't."

A year after I left Sweet Home, Mr. Weddle did let the city have land enough for an alley.

An Odorous Problem

High on the city's priority list was the sewage disposal problem. Sweet Home had a central water system, but the older homes still used outdoor privies. The newer homes had septic tanks, but they worked poorly because of a peculiar soil condition. A few feet below the surface of the ground, a virtually impervious stratum of soil, known locally as "hardpan," covered the town like a rubber sheet. Privies were satisfactory if the pits went deep enough. But the effluent from septic tanks could not penetrate the hardpan to seep away. In rainy weather, of which western Oregon has its share, and even during dry weather in areas where there was not enough top soil to absorb the septic tank effluent, it rose to the surface and ran over the ground. All over town, septic tanks backed up into homes, or effluent surfaced and spread over back yards. The effluent was such good fertilizer the heavy growth of rich green grass was a telltale tracer of the route the spilled-over effluent took.

Despite the war and the stringent control of strategic materials and equipment, our problem was so acute the State Health

Department recommended we apply for a federal emergency grant to help finance a sewage collection and disposal system. The state sanitary engineer's supporting letter read, in part, "Raw or inadequately treated sewage from private residences and from business establishments is discharged into adjacent roadside ditches or drainage ways where it is exposed to insects, rodents, and other vectors of disease. This method of disposal is a direct hazard to the health of children who wade and play in the sewage." The first Federal Works Agency engineer who come to inspect our situation showed me his report. It read, "People are living in their own filth; you would have to see it to believe it."

I spent weeks trying to pull together from inadequate records the information needed in our application for federal funds. Because of the difficulties I encountered trying to get from the FWA field staff "yes" or "no" answers on what would make our application acceptable, I loaded into my car a typewriter, records, maps, reports, and everything else we had on our sewer and finance problems and drove to Seattle. I knew from experience as a junior engineer inspector with the Public Works Administration, a forerunner of the FWA, that an applicant had a better chance of writing an acceptable application if he sat down with the legal, engineering, and finance people in the FWA regional office and stayed there until he had put down answers to what otherwise would be a stream of letters asking for "more detailed information," "clarification," and "additional justification."

After two busy nights and one full day in the FWA regional office, where I received excellent help, the application was ready for our mayor's signature.

In addition to the visible filth reported by the state sanitary engineer and the FWA engineer, the stench from undigested sewage often was nauseating throughout large areas of the city. In fact, the stench was one of the most convincing evidences that we needed a sewerage system. Consequently, I was discouraged at the conclusion of the final inspection of our condition made by a second federal official before our application for financial assistance could be approved.

The FWA man came down from Seattle. He arrived during a dry period, when the frequent septic tank overflow and seepage were not as visible to the eye as usual. However, the stench was as bad as ever.

As we went from point to point throughout the city—to the

war housing project, between a double row of new homes, and through some low areas—I asked him to note the sickening odors. He was noncommital, seeming not to notice them. When the inspection was completed and we were back in the office, I was so concerned about my inability to convince him of our need that I pressed further on the odor problem.

"Mr. _____ ," I said, "it's difficult for me to imagine how we could have toured this whole city, covering some of the worst sewage problem areas, yet you tell me you didn't smell any sewer odors."

"Oh, that," he said. "About three years ago I had surgery on my nose, and since then I haven't been able to smell a thing."

The Handwriting on the Wall

When in early May I submitted my second annual report and budget to the city council and budget committee, the committee objected to the amounts estimated in the budget, eliminated the secretary's position in city hall, and cut the police department back to three men, including part-time help. This last step brought Police Chief Richards's resignation, which was final this time.

Chief Richards agreed to stay until I found a replacement, but for a limited time only. The man next in line was about to be inducted into the service. This left us with the third man and the part-time officers we were using. I asked the chief to recommend one of these men. Although probably 80 percent of Sweet Home's residents had been in town less than three years, I decided the community had had about all the "outsiders" it could take—namely the city manager and the police chief.

The chief selected one of his men and brought him in for an interview. He was alert and diligent, with an easy and friendly personality of the kind I thought would be liked by the people in the community. I outlined what we were trying to do in the way of law enforcement and general modernization of the city government, and how important I considered the police chief position. This seemed to fit his interests exactly.

"How's your personal record?" I asked. "Anything on it that might cause us to hesitate to name you to this position? If there is, you may as well tell us now, because we'll be taking your fingerprints and sending them to the FBI for a report. (I had learned a lesson from the Southerland incident.)

"No," he replied. "I've got a good record, I'm proud to say."

When I finished interviewing the man, I told the chief the man looked all right to me and asked the chief to take his fingerprints and send them to the FBI in Washington with a request for a report. The chief was surprised at this, and hesitant too. He wondered if this might not indicate lack of confidence in the man.

I said, "If the fellow's record is clean, well and good. In fact, if it is, he shouldn't mind our checking him. If not, we'll know about it. I have no reason to doubt that it's as he says, perfectly okay. But I have a feeling that from here on, we ought to make such a check before we hire people, in the police department or anyplace else."

Apparently Chief Richards and the new man talked about Richard's desire to be relieved within a month, because the next day the man came in to say he had some property matters to take care of and would be available in about thirty days.

Some ten days later, the chief stopped at my office one morning after mail time. He looked unusually grim—didn't say a word, just handed me an official-looking letter. It was a form letter from the FBI with a report attached. The report was on our about-to-be chief of police. At first glance, I could see it contained an unusually long list of entries. Closer examination revealed at least half a dozen arrests. The shock came when I saw that our man had fairly recently completed a prison term for grand larceny.

I looked at the chief.

"Roy," the chief said. "I'd never have believed it if I hadn't seen it with my own eyes."

When the man returned from taking care of his personal business, I handed him the report and asked, "Why didn't you tell me you had a record when I asked you? You must have known we would find out sooner or later, especially if we were going to send your fingerprints to the FBI?"

He smiled pleasantly. "Well, there's always a chance of a slipup. You might have forgotten to ask the FBI for a report, or they might not have gotten around to sending it."

"What," I asked in exasperation and perplexity, "do you expect me to do now?"

"Oh," he said, "I suppose I won't get the job."

He was right.

I asked several close friends, including former Mayor Weiss, what meaning they read into the budget committee's action. Some of them commented that probably city managers, like school superintendents and ministers, can overstay their period of usefulness. They noted that the school board had not renewed the school superintendent's contract and that a prominent local minister had just gone to another charge after differences with his congregation. Their counsel helped me decide to accept a standing offer from Public Administration Service, a Chicago-based consulting organization. On June 4 I submitted my resignation to the city council to be effective the middle of July.

On July 2 I received telegrams from our United States senator and congressman that our application for the sewer grant had been approved.

On July 14 Agda and our two sons and I left Sweet Home for Phoenix, Arizona, to join the PAS team on an administrative survey of Phoenix's city government. My part of the assignment was to study and recommend improvements in the organization and activities of Phoenix's public works, transportation, and water departments. By coincidence, the lead article in *Water Works Engineering* magazine, July 25, 1945, titled "Sweet Home, Ore., Treats Itself for Growing Pains," was one I had written describing our efforts to improve the operations and financial management of Sweet Home's water utility.

Albert Lea, Minnesota

Interdependence of the private and public sectors
Applications of organization and management principles
Employer-employee relations
The downtown parking problem
Fundamentals of community planning
Methods of budgetary control

Prescribing for Ailing Governments

I completed my part of the Phoenix survey in one month—the month World War II ended. Seven years later an article by a Phoenix city employee in the November 1952 *Public Works* magazine showed that the public works and utilities reorganization and operations recommendations had been adopted almost verbatim. Twenty years after the administrative survey the full report was still required reading for all new management interns employed by the city of Phoenix.

We went from Phoenix to Medford, Massachusetts, where I was to undertake a comprehensive organizational and administrative survey for that city.

Medford is in Middlesex County on the Mystic River—route of Paul Revere's famous midnight ride "through every Middlesex village and farm." But early American history was not the only thing that excited my interest in Medford. Equally intriguing were the local government finance practices that kept the people of Medford from knowing what was going on in their city government. Some of the more interesting of these practices were these: making large "economy cuts" in the budget when it was under the news spotlight but restoring the cuts soon after public attention shifted to other local news; presenting budgets without revenue estimates to facilitate manipulation of expenditure figures; inflating the assessed value of property, thus enabling the city to increase the *amount* of taxes without increasing the tax *rate*; and delaying publication of the city's year-end reports until they were useless to citizens who might want to do something about them. These practices would discourage any but the most persistent and dedicated individual or citizen group from following through on opportunities for improving the city government or its activities.

My Medford work was interrupted a few weeks while I went to Charleston County, South Carolina, to help on the public works part of the comprehensive study Public Administration Service was making of that county's government.

Over all, the Medford assignment took about six months. Some time later the voters of both the city of Medford and of Charleston County adopted a council-manager form of government, based in part on our survey reports.

Shortly before we completed the Medford administrative survey, I received a letter from Clarence C. Ludwig, executive secretary of the League of Minnesota Municipalities and director of the Bureau of Municipal Research at the University of Minnesota. Ludwig had been my major professor in municipal management at graduate school. Also, he had been the first city manager of Albert Lea, Minnesota, fifteen years earlier. He said Albert Lea was seeking a city manager. Was I interested? If so, he would be glad to introduce me to the city council.

Although, in my opinion, Public Administration Service's consulting work was important, Agda and I had discovered that moving a family from one end of the country to the other on short assignments during the severe postwar housing shortage was almost unbearable. In addition, Albert Lea had an unusual reputation. It had been the pilot community used by a task force from the United States Chamber of Commerce, by the recently formed Committee for Economic Development, and by other prestigious groups to demonstrate how communities could prepare for reemploying returning GIs. The "Albert Lea Plan for Postwar Employment" had received international publicity.

I told Mr. Ludwig I was interested and flew to Minnesota for an interview. We spent the day visiting community leaders, the publisher of the daily paper, former city officials, and some of Mr. Ludwig's longtime friends.

Three points from these conferences particularly impressed me. One was the number of leaders who put a city plan at the head of their priority list of community needs. Another was their dissatisfaction with the city's progress and their determination to "catch up" now that the war was over. Third was their praise of Ludwig's four years as city manager. Several mentioned his requiring the banks to put up collateral to secure the city's deposits.

This is the way that had happened: State law required banks handling city funds to deposit an equal amount of securities at another location as collateral to protect the city in case of bank failure. Ludwig found the banks were not complying with this requirement. He asked them to do so, but they resisted. He said he would withdraw the city's funds if they failed to comply. Reluctantly, they complied—just before they went under.

The city had all its money intact; other depositors suffered severe losses. More than one person declared to me, "If C.C. hadn't done another thing during his four years with us, he more than paid for his salary by that one act!"

Late in the day I met with the city council, was offered the city manager position, and accepted.

Without Fear or Favor

The Need for Policy

The first week on the job I was invited to meet with the board of directors of "Jobs, Inc.," the local nonprofit industrial development corporation, backbone of the famed Albert Lea Plan. I thought it was a courtesy, get-acquainted invitation.

Instead, the directors were conferring with two foundry owners from another city about setting up a foundry in Albert Lea. The meeting had not progressed far when I realized I was there because the group of independent, private businessmen were stalled in their negotiations until they could get some assurances from the city.

They reviewed the developments to date. The foundry was needed; local stove manufacturers and others could promise enough sales to make it profitable; Jobs, Inc. could arrange the capital financing; and a land owner was ready to sell the site they wanted at a satisfactory price. The unanswered questions depended on the city.

First was the need for a street. The site was a pasture at the north edge of town. It was ideal because trucks could reach the foundry without going through town. But there was no street into the site. Before the businessmen could complete their negotiations, they needed assurance that the city would build a street—one that would hold up under heavy loads of foundry sand and castings.

Second, the foundry needed large quantities of water. The only available supply was from the city-owned-and-operated system. Again, private enterprise was stymied until the city would guarantee the amount, quality, and pressure of water needed.

Third was a question of zoning. Although the proposed foundry site was outside the city limits (the foundry management had purposely chosen a site outside the city limits to avoid city taxes), they needed assurance that the city would zone the property across from their site inside the city limits, for either industrial or commercial use. If this were not done, homes soon would go up in the vicinity, and the foundry management would be hounded by the nearby homeowners about smoke, noise, traffic, and appearance.

As they talked, I grew uneasy. I couldn't relax and enjoy the meeting as an observer because it was moving toward some critical decisions I was not prepared to make. I had another reason for being uncomfortable. By looks passing back and forth and an air of unfriendliness and impatience, the visitors and Jobs, Inc. directors revealed their resentment at having to depend on the city in what they considered a purely private business matter.

While they discussed the total situation, seeking alternatives to various problems, my mind raced ahead to what I might soon be asked about. Streets, for instance. What was the city policy about building costly streets to serve a single industry, especially one located outside the city? Would the city use general funds that came from all the taxpayers in town to help serve this one firm? Or would there be some kind of joint venture, with the city and the industry sharing the cost?

And extending the water service. Almost everyone would like to escape city taxes. What if any industry or homeowner could live outside the city, yet get water service and fire protection? Why would anybody locate inside the city where he had to pay for these conveniences?

In brief, to what extent should the property and people within the city subsidize an industry outside the city, even though it did bring jobs and generally help the local economy?

On the zoning problem, I didn't know the present zoning. I did know that if the property in question were already zoned residential, it would take considerable time to get the zoning changed. Certainly the law would require notice and hearing; the zoning or planning board would have to view the property and make recommendations to the city council; and the council would have to make the final decision.

With the current housing shortage, if the property were now zoned residential, chances were the owners were counting on subdividing their land and selling it in residential lots. This might seem a more promising way to get their money out of the land than to wait until a commercial or industrial development came along. In that case, the owners would probably object to rezoning, and the zoning board and city council might agree with the local people and turn down the rezoning, despite the city's strong desire to help the industrial development effort.

My thinking was interrupted by a direct question from Mr. Myers, president of Jobs, Inc.

"Mr. Harlow, will the city put in a heavy-duty street?"

"I'm sorry, Mr. Myers, but I don't know whether we can or not. I don't know what the city policy is. All I can say is that I'll find out just as soon as I can, because I know you men want to go ahead with your plans."

He continued to press for answers. "Will you recommend to the council that the city put in the street?"

"I can't answer that either. If there is no policy on this, we'll need to establish one. Before we can do that, the whole thing will have to be thought through carefully."

In anticipation that the city might not be able to do all they were asking, I took a moment to say to them that city officials don't have the same freedom of action as they have in private business. I made this comparison: When one of their customers pays them for a product or a service, the money is theirs to do with as they and their board of directors decide. But it is different with the city. Every one of our "customers" is also a stockholder in our municipal corporation. Our stockholders are not always willing to let their money be spent for the benefit of only a few, especially if the few the money is to be spent on are outsiders or competitors.

I could see the men were getting restless, so I tried to bring the conversation to a close and get gracefully out of an awkward situation. I said, "Gentlemen, I think it is the city council's desire to work with Jobs, Inc. And personally I think you are on the right track, having private business provide employment instead of waiting for government to do it. But you have asked me some questions I can't answer now. I promise you your questions will get high priority, and I will get you the answers as quickly as I can."

Accordingly, the first thing I did on my return to the office was to go to the city clerk, the assessor and the city engineer to ask what our policies were. Their answers were that we had no clear-cut policies on extending streets and water service outside the city. The city had a program for financing water extensions inside the city, but each case of the kind I was asking about was handled "on its merits." At the first opportunity, I consulted the council about these items. They, too, told me there were no fixed policies.

This concerned me. The war was over, and change and growth were coming at a fast pace. Unless there were established policies for dealing with certain classes of situations, much time would be wasted on individual cases. Moreover, decisions might be inconsistent. In that case, if the city put in a street or water extension for one citizen or firm but not for another, it opened itself to charges of favoritism or worse.

The council left it to me to draft and recommend policies. I immediately began pulling together ideas about financing streets. The basic idea eventually adopted was that abutting property owners would pay for a minimum standard width and quality of street. If the use of the street required a width or thickness beyond the minimum standard, the general community would pay the extra cost through city general funds. Where there were special requirements that would benefit only a few properties, the benefited few would pay the extra costs, the amount to be agreed upon through negotiation.

The water extension problem was different. It seemed fair that the users of water pay according to the amount they used, insofar as that could be ascertained and with certain adjustments for volume. In many cases, individual users were unable to provide the initial capital investment for ditching, pipes, meters, and installation. In those cases, the city would borrow the money, make the investment, then recover its money from regular charges over a period of time. Users outside the city would pay a surcharge.

These city policies were precipitated by that first meeting about a Jobs, Inc. project. As far as I know, the city was never an impediment to Jobs, Inc.'s objectives. Albert Lea's leaders knew the private sector and the local government needed each other. The relationship was mutually beneficial.

Let the Facts Decide

Not only geographically but governmentally, Albert Lea was markedly different from Sweet Home. Due largely to Ludwig, a certified public accountant and later a nationally recognized authority on local government, the city of Albert Lea was one of the more advanced municipalities in the country.

For instance, the city's budgeting, accounting, and reporting systems reflected his influence. Budgets showed revenue sources and objects of expenditure in an orderly fashion, with comparative data for previous years. The accounting system included basic cost accounting so that the city knew the average cost of doing each unit of certain kinds of work as well as its total expenditures. Each year a pocket-sized annual report was published promptly after the books were closed. This handy little booklet included a directory of city officials, pictures and descriptions of major municipal activities during the past year, financial information in understandable form, and salaries of all key city positions.

But Ludwig had been gone from the city for thirteen years.

Along with the rest of the nation, Albert Lea had passed through the Great Depression and World War II. The city had not kept up with physical, social, and economic changes that required updating and modernizing the city's organization, procedures, and programs.

Internally, we needed to reorganize the departmental structure, install work simplification methods, mechanize more of our operations, and improve our personnel administration.

Externally, our most pressing problems were automobile parking, the physical condition of sidewalks and streets in and near the business district, the need for city planning, more recreational facilities, water safety, and elimination of lake pollution. As in Sweet Home, I went to work on several projects at the same time. I was like a cook with four burners going and a casserole and pie in the oven.

First I tackled the departmental organization problem, because unless we were better organized we wouldn't be able to carry out the other projects. The biggest problem was the city manager's span of control. Over the years as new organization units had been added to accommodate the growth of population and demand for services, they had been placed directly under his supervision.

The span of control problem is not new. As far back as Old Testament days, Moses was commanded to organize his nation of an estimated two to three million people into four groups of three tribes each, and his father-in-law counseled him to delegate the judgment of small matters to others.

There is no ideal or final number of subordinates any one person can supervise effectively. The number depends on the supervisor's personal energy and competence, the ability of his subordinates to handle delegated authority, and the complexity of the decisions the supervisor must make. But in my judgment we had too many people reporting to the city manager. Moreover, we were denying some of these people the opportunity to develop their leadership abilities by solving problems themselves.

We put the separate city engineer's office, streets department, and water department in a public works department headed by a public works director/city engineer. Later we created an inspection division, in which we combined all building, plumbing, and electrical inspection work in one position and placed it in the public works department also.

We did essentially the same thing in the finance area. The city had a separate city clerk, city treasurer, city accountant, and city assessor, all reporting to the city manager. We combined the city clerk and city treasurer positions under one person and named a finance director-assessor. Now the clerk-treasurer and city accountant reported to the finance director. Financial matters that did not come under their jurisdiction and those of the assessor were handled by the finance director-assessor as part of his finance director duties.

The net effect was to reduce by five the number of people reporting to the city manager, thus removing him as a possible bottleneck to getting prompt and knowledgeable decisions from capable people in the organization.

Although we spelled out in writing the new organizational arrangements and the jurisdictional areas of the several departments and their divisions, from time to time jurisdictional issues arose that had to be resolved. A case in point was a brief controversy between the parks department and the public works department over the use of a gravel loader.

I first heard of the problem the day the parks superintendent came into my office, clearly upset.

"What are we going to do about the gravel loader out at the pit?" he asked. "Every time we want to load gravel or topsoil to use in the parks, the public works department says they have to have it to haul materials for the streets, or waterworks, or something.

"I thought the loader belonged to the parks department; we bought it out of parks department money," he said. "We ought to have it when we need it, and not have to have our men and trucks stand around waiting for the streets men to get through before we can use it."

This was a typical management problem, involving two management principles—unity of command, and duplication. Did the loader operator have two bosses, the parks superintendent and the public works director? He should have only one. Of course, each department head would like to have the equipment under his control, available whenever he wanted it. But this would mean duplicating equipment, when as a matter of fact, even when serving two departments, the loader was not always busy.

In this interdepartmental rift, I wanted to make a decision on facts and avoid any feeling I was favoring one department over the other. Fortunately, we had cost-accounting data that showed who used the loader, the number of hours each user used it, and the hourly cost of use. The figures showed that the streets division, now part of the public works department, was a far bigger user than the parks department. Other units in the public works department also used it, but less than the parks department.

I asked the public works director/city engineer and the parks superintendent to meet with me about the problem. I laid the figures before them.

"It seems to me that I should not make an arbitrary decision between you two men," I said. "The facts ought to point the way to a decision.

"Obviously, both of you have good reasons for wanting and needing to have a loader available to you whenever you need one. However, the record shows that even our one loader is not used full time. Furthermore, the use has never been so heavy at any one time that we've had to rent an outside unit. Would you agree we are not justified in buying another loader?"

They agreed.

"The records also show that public works uses the loader about five times as much as parks. Does that suggest anything to you?"

"Maybe the streets department should have bought it in the first place, with their money," the parks superintendent said.

"Herb, I want to compliment you for your pride in your department and your interest and protection of it," I responded. "And I can appreciate how you feel about what you call 'parks department money' and 'streets department money.' But I hope we can be a team, all working together—that we're working, first, for the city of Albert Lea, and second, for our individual departments. Actually, of course, all the equipment we're using belongs to the people of Albert Lea—they paid for it—and we ought to use it the way that is best for them."

"Well, if that's the way it's going to be," the parks superintendent said, "maybe we ought to assign the loader to public works and hold them responsible for keeping it in good running order."

"And charge it against my budget?" the public works director asked.

"Charge it against your budget, yes, but on a revolving fund basis so you can recover part of your costs from other users in proportion to their use," I replied.

"This raises another question," I noted. "If public works does 'own' the loader and is responsible for its upkeep, should others who use it—other departments, the county, and so on—provide their own operators? I can see some risk in this. Not being responsible for the unit, they may abuse it. I suppose, though, we could leave instructions for its operation on the machine, or we could arrange to have the public works department check out other operators before they're put on the machine."

The public works director interrupted. "I'd rather assign one of our own men to the loader and keep him on it. Then, if anything goes wrong, I'll know who is responsible. Otherwise, every time we have a breakdown it will be 'somebody else's fault.' We can charge the using departments, or outsiders, just what it costs us for the unit and the man."

"Herb, what do you think of that?" I asked.

"That's all right with me," the parks superintendent said. Turning to the public works director, he added, "Then, it will all be your headache, Bill. Repairs, costs, assignment of a man, priority of use—everything.

"But I see one other problem," he went on. "If Bill's department is going to 'own' the loader, how do I know I can get use of it when I need it?"

I turned to the public works director. "What do you say, Bill?"

"We can work that out," he said. "Herb, do you ordinarily know a day ahead of time whether you're going to need material, and how much?"

"Yes, except in an emergency—a washout, or something like that—we'd know the day before."

"Good," the public works director said. "If you'll try to let me know a day in advance, or longer if you can, we'll schedule our work so we don't need gravel hauled when you have your trucks in the pit. The same with us. Except in an emergency, we can adjust our work schedule to fit yours. I don't know any reason why you can't count on getting materials without delay, any time you give us twenty-four hours notice."

Thanks to the cooperative attitude of the two department heads, we were able to avoid an unnecessary expense or a continuing source of irritation between the two departments.

Work Smarter, Not Harder

America's private industry is world renowned for its know-how and skill. Much credit for this reputation is due industrial engineers who have found ways to do almost everything better, faster, cheaper, and easier. Unfortunately, with few exceptions, local governments have not shared this enviable reputation. That doesn't mean they couldn't, if we could release the experience, the knowledge, and the creativity of hundreds of thousands of people who work for our counties, cities, towns, and other local governments. I tried to do this in Albert Lea, starting with an opportunity less than twenty feet from my office door.

The main office in City Hall was in a large room on the ground floor. My office was partitioned off in one corner of the room, and the entrance to the main room was diagonally across from my office. Just inside the entrance was a long counter, running nearly the width of the large room. Two women, the city clerk and her assistant, took care of the counter from desks facing each other and about six feet behind the counter.

When anyone came to the counter for service, one of the women got up from her desk, walked to the counter, found out what was wanted, and often had to return to her desk to get a form, type something, or otherwise take care of the request.

I suppose two things triggered my thinking about work simplification at this location. First, the middle-aged city clerk had a handicapping congenital hip injury. She had difficulty getting up from a chair, and she walked with a severe limp. Second, although both women were as willing, dedicated, and able as I have seen in any office, they sometimes took undue time finishing an assignment I gave them.

I observed this was not their fault. It resulted from interruptions to take care of the counter when more than one customer came in to be served. If either the clerk or her assistant was serving the counter and the other was doing work at her desk, customers became impatient if the one at her desk did not get up to help them. More often than not, both women were occupied with counter work, when one could have handled it almost as expeditiously.

I found a moment when they were free and invited them into my office, where I voiced my concern about their work load.

"You girls must get up and down from your chairs to service the counter a hundred times a day," I said. "Do you ever get tired?"

"Tired?" They blushed. "The first of the month, when people pay their water bills, we're exhausted!"

"Have you ever thought of ways to make your work easier?"

They looked at each other and at me with embarrassed surprise. They said they didn't know what I meant.

"What I am trying to say is that there is so much work to be done I think we ought to do it by the easiest means possible. I think we ought to be lazy about our jobs, in the sense that we don't do things the hard way if we can be equally or even more effective doing them an easier way. With that thought in mind, can you think of any ways in which you can make your work easier?"

Again they exchanged glances, still embarrassed. They shook their heads. They couldn't think of anything at the moment.

"Suppose we were to reverse the positions of the counter and your desks," I said. "Then, instead of your getting up and going to the counter to meet the public, they would come to your desks."

They looked at each other, puzzled, then smiled. They just didn't know how it would work, they said.

"Let's think about it a few days," I said. "We don't have to make a decision right now. During the next three or four days, talk it over between the two of you. Try to imagine how it would be if we made that change. Of course, we won't change anything until we've all had a chance to mull it over."

Then I added. "While you're thinking about this, please give some thought to something else. If we move the counter back to where your desks are now, why don't we mount a glass partition on top of the counter? This will separate the space up front from that behind the counter. You can see if the desks get so crowded people are having to wait to be served. But if there are not more than two or three people up front, and one of you is working on something behind the counter that you should not interrupt, you can stay at it. The public won't expect you to come out from behind the counter area to wait on them as they would if you were sitting right in front of them."

To explain the idea, I told them something I'd read somewhere. A partition with a door in the middle separated a shop from living quarters in the rear. The proprietor left the door open so that he could see customers from the living quarters and so that air could circulate. But when there was no one in the shop, customers would walk into the living quarters.

The proprietor mentioned his problem to a psychologist friend. The psychologist suggested: Tack half a dozen five-foot strands of cord to the top of the door frame, about two inches apart. Skeptically, the proprietor followed the simple suggestion. To his amazement, it worked. Customers stayed outside the privacy barrier, and the proprietor got the unobstructed view and the ventilation he wanted. I said, "Perhaps we can get the same results with a glass partition built up from the counter."

A few days later, the girls asked if we could get together. They had some ideas which they hoped I wouldn't think were silly. They were excited about switching the counter and their desks. They had thought of two or three other changes that might help. "After moving the counter back, instead of having one end attached to the wall as at present, why not leave a space to go around both ends of the counter? This would save steps. Also, what about placing a supply of frequently requested forms where the public can help themselves, instead of having to wait for us to give them the forms?"

"You've caught on," I said. "Those are good ideas; we'll do that."

We made the changes, which were really very simple. We got no complaints from the public. I estimate we reduced the energy expenditure of the counter help by 20 percent.

Other employees were encouraged by word that suggestions were welcome. In addition to the mechanization of our operations with purchased equipment, some employees designed and built mechanical equipment for city use. The *American City Magazine* ran a filler news item in their August 1946 issue describing these improvements.

A Voice for All City Employees

Soon after my appointment, I learned that some city employees were on the verge of joining a union, a somewhat unusual move for local government employees at that time. They did organize Albert Lea City Employees Local Union 1018, and a few employees joined. A John Jorgenson came in to tell me he was now representing those employees as the business agent for their new union.

Although I had no objection to employees' joining a union, it did seem to me that *all* the city's employees, not just the few who paid dues to an outside organization, were entitled to a voice in matters related to their work that were vitally important to them and their families. Therefore, I discussed with several employees the idea of an employees' advisory council to consider such things as the need for pensions, hospital insurance, written personnel policies, grievance procedures, social activities, and other items, whose members could encourage every employee to make suggestions for improving our ways of serving the taxpayers.

All the employees I talked to thought there was merit in the idea. I sent a ballot to all full-time employees asking them to elect three members to the EAC. The three employees receiving the highest number of votes would serve with the finance director and the city manager as members of the advisory council.

Three able people were elected. They proved to be helpful in surfacing problems outside the regular routine of city business, and at arriving at satisfactory resolutions of these problems. They were instrumental, also, in sponsoring some outstanding social activities that brought the employees and their families together on a friendly, personal basis.

With the help of the advisory council and the union agent, we designed a compensation plan with certain objectives in mind. One was provision for automatic annual pay changes as the cost of living changed. The purpose was to put annual compensation adjustments on a factual basis. (This was some years before industry generally adopted the idea.) Then there was a series of pay steps for each position; therefore, the difference between steps was an equal percentage of the preceding step, not an equal number of dollars. The pattern was five pay steps for each position class, with 5 percent intervals between steps. As a result, the maximum pay for any position class was about 22 percent above the minimum pay for that class.

Since the minimum pay for the positions with more responsibility was higher than the minimum pay for positions with less responsibility, the 22 percent range resulted in several more dollars of increase for the more responsible positions than the less responsible ones. The purpose was to reverse the trend toward the same pay for every position regardless of the level of responsibility.

Also, we had a provision for starting experienced people on a step above the minimum. Although I generally favored a promotion-from-within policy, the purpose here was to enable the city to attract some qualified people to city service from outside (not necessarily outside of Albert Lea, but outside the city service) to get the benefit of their wider, more varied experience.

We drafted an ordinance that incorporated the main elements of a position classification plan and the pay plan, and included a number of other essential provisions. For example, it provided for placing the classification and compensation plans in effect, for keeping the plans up-to-date, and for vacation and sick leave, performance ratings, and extra pay for long service. The city council adopted the ordinance.

The city council did not automatically rubber-stamp every recommendation I made for the development and installation of the personnel program. They were mature men, alert to what was going on outside Albert Lea. They knew what the city needed and made numerous practical suggestions. They were cooperative. In one instance they acceded to the demands of a handful of employees for salary increases that would have destroyed the principles of fairness and equal pay for equal work we were trying to establish. I asked for a special meeting of the council, where I pointed out the effect of their action. Having committed themselves to the employee group, they stood by their word. But to avoid upsetting the balances we were trying to establish, they brought the other classes up to what they had promised the small group. As a result, the pay relationships established by the new program were not disrupted.

Will the Voters Like It?

Three months after I went to work at Albert Lea, I had to begin preparation of the budget for the next fiscal year. Fortunately, the accounting system and records were excellent.

As I reviewed the past revenues from taxes, license fees, and sale of water, and the corresponding expenditures for fire, police, streets, parks, and the water utility, I noted the operating costs of the water utility were rising faster than the income. The figures showed that only a few years earlier the city water system had a sizable surplus, but the surplus was being rapidly depleted. Operating and capital improvements were running ahead of income, and the difference was being made up by dipping into surplus. If these trends continued—and there was no reason for thinking they wouldn't unless we took some action—it would not be long before the water system went broke.

I started inquiring about possible savings. Did we have excess personnel? I found that, for an operation that ran 24 hours a day, every day of the year, and was of vital importance to the health and safety of the community, we had a very small crew.

What about purchase of supplies: were they on a competitive

basis? They were. We were getting as good or better prices as other cities in the state.

Could our power bill be reduced? No. This had been negotiated with the power company, and evidently the company was doing as well by the city as we could reasonably expect.

What about the financing of water main extension and lateral lines? This was already under study as a result of my first week's meeting with the Jobs, Inc. people about our extending water to the proposed foundry. There might be some savings to the city here. The city was carrying users for several years before the investment costs were liquidated. But this was a small part of the total financial picture for the water utility.

Finally, I looked into our bill collecting practices. Were we promptly collecting money due the city, and in full? Yes. The city had a good system, and it was being followed.

Satisfied that we were running a tight operation, I asked the city accountant to make a comparative rate study, with a view to a possible upward adjustment in the rate schedule. This involved getting rate information from other municipal water systems, by classes of customers: industrial, commercial, residential and off-peak.

I think I'll never forget his response when I suggested we might have to recommend an increase in water rates to keep the system solvent.

"The voters won't like that!" he said.

"Probably they won't," I answered, "but this is a business proposition. Water is essential to this community, and it is already cheaper than dirt. (It was, too; you could buy a ton of Albert Lea water delivered to your home for less than you had to pay for a ton of dirt.)

"Our job is to keep this system solvent so we can continue to provide pure water in adequate supply and pressure to the homes and industries. Moreover, we have to maintain an adequate supply and pressure for fire fighting when it is needed.

"If the income from the users is not enough to cover our expenses, and we have reduced our costs to a minimum, we simply will have to try to get the council to raise the rates. Now, how can we do this and be fair in the way we distribute among our various users any increase that might be necessary?"

The accountant undertook the assignment, but with great reluctance. Throughout the entire assignment, he remained adamant that "what the voters like" should be our guide, not the need to operate the city-owned utility on a business basis. I might have expected this from someone who had to get elected to office; but I was astonished to hear it from a person whose job, like mine, was to guard the financial health of the people's business. Eventually, we got the rates where they had to be to keep the system financially solvent.

Parking Meters—the Businessman's Friend

The curb parking along our business streets was jammed, particularly on Saturdays when the farmers came to town. We had no off-street parking in or near the downtown area; consequently cars continuously circled the principal city blocks looking for parking spaces. Further, a survey we quietly conducted (recording license numbers of parked cars, then getting the owners' names from the state auto license bureau) revealed that most of the precious parking space was occupied by owners and employees of the business places. These were the very people from whom we were getting complaints that their customers couldn't find a place to park.

Faced with the problem and armed with these data, we determined to make a three-pronged attack: Try to generate turnover in the use of the limited parking space; make it unprofitable for the merchants and their employees to monopolize what space there was; and raise revenue to finance land acquisition and off-street facilities. All three approaches pointed to the need to install parking meters as the initial step, to be followed by finding more parking space. Both steps challenged our ingenuity and later put a strain on our good city-community relations. In fact, there were times in the next few months when it looked as if the odds were too much against us.

We started with a handicap because only one other city in the state had installed parking meters, and under public pressure that city had taken them out after a short trial period. I checked their experience. It appeared the city had overmetered. I resolved to avoid that pitfall. Instead of filling the nearly 700 possible meter locations, I decided to install fewer than 100 and to put them in the places of greatest need.

I had in mind not only the other city that had had to take out the meters; I knew we would have objections from some local people, because there are always those who resist change. In addition, there would be the farmers and other out-of-town customers to whom Albert Lea was the major shopping center. Their attitude would be that they were already spending their money with Albert Lea merchants, and for the city to require them to pay for the privilege of spending their money in town bordered on outrage. They would threaten to go to some other town to shop "where they appreciate our business." I was afraid the objectors and those they could bring along with them would be numerous and vocal enough to discredit the meter program before it had time to prove its worth.

Despite my determination to go slowly, I still was not comfortable about going ahead. My uneasiness increased the day I got a call from Carl Jacobsen, owner-manager of the principal hotel.

"Harlow," he said, "meters won't work in this town. We know they won't work. About six months ago a committee of us from the chamber made a tour and visited several cities about our size in the Midwest where they have meters, just to find out about them. Nobody likes them. They don't get the results their promoters claim for them. And we are in unanimous agreement; Albert Lea doesn't need parking meters, and they shouldn't be installed. They're not for our town."

I didn't argue with him. I didn't know they had made the tour, so I was interested in what they had learned.

I did say, "Carl, if we do install them it will be for a trial period only. If we find they don't help the parking situation, we'll take them out."

"Well, you'd better not put them in," he said, "because the businessmen in town are against them."

The removal of meters in the other city, the opposition of our own businessmen, the fact that we were sticking our necks out to be one of the first to try meters—all these facts chased through my mind, when suddenly I remembered an idea I had read someplace—I think in Elmer Wheeler's book, *Don't Sell the Steak, Sell the Sizzle!*. The circumstances were entirely different from ours, but the principle seemed to be the same.

As I recalled the story, the owner of a soda fountain was losing money and was about to go out of business. He hired Wheeler to help rescue him. Wheeler's analysis showed that the fountain's biggest seller was milk shakes, and the owner made the most profit on a shake if he could sell it with one or two eggs mixed in. Watching them work, Wheeler observed that the soda clerks were asking the customers, "Would you like an egg in your shake?" This gave the customers a choice between one egg or no egg. He suggested the owner have the clerks hold up two eggs and ask, "Would you like one egg or two in your shake?" According to the story, the fountain owner adopted the idea, his profits from milk shake sales soared, and he stayed in business.

It occurred to me that if our public had a choice between two kinds of meters, it might switch their attention from whether or not they liked meters at all. Encouraged by this idea, I devised a three-part plan for installing the meters. For the first part of the plan, I decided we would install two types of meters, the manual and the automatic. We would alternate them down the street.

The second part of the plan would be a little shock treatment. That is, after the meters had been in use a few days, and most of the people who would ultimately be subject to them knew about them, we would issue parking violation "tickets" every few hours to about every other car parked in the meter area. The tickets would look like the real thing—same size, shape, color, and printed heading. But instead of being a real ticket, it would be a courteous explanation of our problem and a suggestion that the motorist help make a future decision about parking meters in Albert Lea.

The third part of our plan was to choose one of the most popular, easygoing policemen on the force—one who could listen to complaints all day without getting riled up or impatient—to courteously point out the reasons for the meters without seeming to force the idea on people. After a week or so we would have to start enforcing the meter ordinance, with tickets and fines against violators, but until then he was to be very casual, show people how to use the meters, point out the different features, ask them if it seemed easier to find a parking place near where they wanted to park, and then say we would like their help in deciding which of the two types of meters motorists preferred.

We prepared a supply of the tickets and followed through with the plan. We received a mere handful of complaints about the meters. From time to time, I checked with council members and city employees. It was the consensus that the public did not object to meters. The strongest complaint came from a merchant who telephoned me to say he was about to make a $500 sale when suddenly the customer's wife rushed in and said the meter was about to expire. The customer and his wife ran out to put more money in the meter and never came back. I suggested that other merchants had told me they were telling their customers that if the customer got an overparking ticket while

CITY OF ALBERT LEA
"TRAFFIC TICKET"
(Please Read)

Dear Motorist:

University tests prove that driving around a block once (we actually drive 4 blocks, or ⅓ mile) costs more than 5c. And that is the kind of expensive—and exasperating!—driving you've had to do. There just hasn't been enough turn-over of cars using the limited amount of parking space we have.

We're aiming to give you a better chance to get a place to park. Since there's just so much parking space along the curbs, and the stores are open only so many hours, the problem is to pro-rate this space among all of you who wish to use it. Parking meters seem to be one way to do this, so we're going to give them a trial for a few months..

Meters have been installed in over 750 cities in the U. S. In only a dozen cities has their use been abandoned. Where no more meters than necessary have

(over)

been put in, folks heartily approved their use, after a few months, because they found it easier to get a place to park.

Never in history have so many people been shopping in Albert Lea. A survey by an interested airline shows more than 96,000 people in this trade are.

But the worst (or best) is not yet. Highway experts tell us the number of cars on the road will be DOUBLED by 1956. Whew!

If these meters increase turn-over (and they have in other cities) you are going to be money ahead. Working together we can give this thing a fair trial. Let's see how it works out. After a few months, let us know what you think of them.

Yes, history repeats itself. Here we are, back to hitching posts!

Sincerely,

CITY OF ALBERT LEA

P. S.—The "quick pick-up," 10-minute stalls, are still free.

Mock traffic ticket used to solicit motorists' help in solving the parking problem, Albert Lea, Minnesota.

in his store, the merchant would pay the one-dollar fine.

The climax to our parking meter installation effort came the day I had another telephone call from Carl Jacobsen, the gruff, outspoken owner of the Albert Hotel who had previously warned me that meters would not work in Albert Lea.

"Harlow," he said, "this is Jacobsen. I'm leaving for Florida for the winter. But I wanted to call you about those damn parking meters. I don't know what's happened in the last six months, but I was wrong. The people seem to like them, and they're doing the job. I just wanted you to know I was wrong."

I thanked Carl, and hung up with a great feeling of relief.

City Manager, Spare That Tree

Although we intended to purchase off-street parking sites with some of the meter revenue, I hoped we could find better ways to increase the number of parking spaces. Site purchasing has a double disadvantage: sites have to be close to business districts or motorists will not use them; this means the city has to pay the premium prices such high-value land commands; also, every such property the city acquires comes off the tax roll.

In my search for some way to increase parking space at minimum cost without reducing our property tax base, I came on an opportunity to do so at a location within walking distance of one end of the principal business district.

It was a city park, one block in size. Across the street to the west was the high school; to the south the Lutheran Church with the largest church congregation in town; to the north the popular Presbyterian Church; and to the east two or three homes. The park itself was bordered by a double row of stately mature shade trees inside the property line. The four streets surrounding the park were rather narrow.

By widening the streets we could replace much of the parallel parking with diagonal parking, increasing the number of parking spaces by nearly 50 percent. This would benefit the business district, the high school, and the two churches. So I took the initial steps toward the improvement: I got the city attorney's opinion that our removal of some trees and widening the streets would not invalidate the city's deed to the property; I met several times with the two church boards and got their approval; I got an okay from the school officials; and I visited the homeowners surrounding the park, finding no objections.

With these approvals in hand, I asked the council—already completely informed of our planning—for permission to proceed. It was granted. Mistakenly, I thought the rest would be smooth sailing.

First, the engineers staked out the area. This aroused the curiosity of a few passersby, but to no great extent. A few days later our park and street crews began removal of the outside row of park trees. They sent men up the trees to saw off the branches and strip the trees down to bare trunks. Of course, the branches fell to the ground in great disarray and left large wounds on the trunks where the limbs had been removed.

Then the men dug around the bases of the trees to provide room to get down into the holes and chop off the large roots. This freed the trees to be pulled over, sawed in sections, and hauled away.

They had reached this stage, which took two or three days, when I got a telephone call. The man on the other end virtually exploded in my ear. What, he demanded to know, did I think I was doing, ruining the city's finest park? Didn't I know that that park had been deeded to the city for park purposes and that what we were doing meant the city would no longer have a park? I answered that I had checked this with the city attorney and that he had assured me we were in the clear.

But the caller was not satisfied. He demanded to know if I had been in the park that morning and had seen what the city crews were doing. I acknowledged I hadn't been there that morning but said I knew what they were authorized to do and had a pretty good idea how far along they were. He hung up, exasperated beyond words.

Next morning, I made it a point to go through the park on my way to work. This time I ran across another citizen who was boiling mad. He could hardly contain himself.

"What stupid fools we have at City Hall," he said. "I thought this administration was trying to do something for the city, and look at what they've gone and done. Look at those trees! Look at the whole park! They've ruined it!"

I must confess that seeing it through his eyes it looked pretty bad. Already the leaves on the big branches were shriveling and losing color. There were great mounds of dirt like newly dug graves by every large tree. But the worst were the great white chips that lay strewn around from the axemen's work. Every one of them seemed to be a sign of a horrible, irreparable attack on a stately but helpless tree, a grand creation that could not defend itself against the ruthless onslaught of unthinking barbarians. After glaring red-faced at me for a moment, speechless with rage and disappointment, the citizen turned and walked away.

During the next several days I had calls from citizen after citizen. Members of the church congregations demanded to know who had authorized this terrible thing. A couple members of the church boards called to say they never intended to approve any such vandalism and useless wreckage as we were making. Councilmen, too, had many calls though no one of the councilmen criticized me directly about what we were doing or how we were doing it.

Under this avalanche of criticism, I instructed the public works director to do everything possible to expedite the project. Also, I asked him especially to do whatever was necessary to leave no refuse or traces when the men were through, even if it cost additional money to resod the areas where trees were removed. I wanted no evidence of the changes.

He carried out the instructions to a T. His men did an excellent job. Within a week after the job was completed, one would never have known there had been a change. Even the newly laid curbs and pavement had taken on a used appearance.

The public immediately began use of the parking areas. The first Sunday they were open they were filled with cars of people who had heretofore parked several blocks away. I think it is safe to say that even the trees were not missed.

But I had learned an important lesson. Trees in a city, unlike those in the country where they might be a nuisance or might interfere with land cultivation, have a special place in the hearts of many people. To a lesser degree, but with similar emotions, many city residents hate to see grass torn up and raw earth left exposed. Although in recent years the public has become more accustomed to seeing bare dirt, roots, upturned trees and torn-out shrubbery for freeways and housing developments, many are angered when they see the natural look disturbed.

I share this feeling. At the same time I recognize that like surgery on the human body, sometimes we must temporarily injure part of a community to assure its long life and good health. After this experience, I resolved that if it were possible I would never again expose a destroyed and mangled tree to the gaze of the public. Thereafter, I would try to collect the evidence of destruction as we went along and get the agony over as quickly as possible.

Our other efforts to deal with the parking problem were not as strenuous as that one. The city bought and developed an off-street parking site in another location near the main business district. And I negotiated at some length with the state highway department before they finally consented to let us use space under a highway overpass for parking. This was largely a task of getting a long-established bureaucracy to permit what they feared might set an undesirable precedent.

Let the People Choose

Despite Albert Lea's reputation as a progressive and up-and-coming city, the sidewalks all over town and especially in the main business district were broken, unsightly, and in many places dangerous. Except for the main thoroughfares, many of the street surfaces were also broken and pot-holed, and other streets were not surfaced at all.

At first I assumed the streets were a war casualty, a result of the time when men and materials had not been available. But on closer inspection I could see that these problems were more than four or five years old. Then I learned the reason the city had not initiated the necessary improvements: it did not have the authority.

The charter provided that sidewalks, street surfacing, and similar improvements could be initiated only by the abutting property owners. This was an example of a charter provision that was meritorious at the time it was adopted but had outlived its usefulness because of changed conditions. Presumably it was put in the charter to protect property owners from unreasonable financial burdens placed on them by ambitious city officials. Also, presumably, when the charter was adopted in 1928, Albert Lea's population was quite stable. Most of the property was owned by people who lived on it or at least lived in the community.

But by 1946 this had changed. Title to much of the property was with absentee owners or estates managed by trustees, neither of whom had much interest in what happened in Albert Lea, and who did not wish to pay for improvements they would not be using. Moreover, the city had made little effort to contact absentee owners for their approval of needed improvements.

Faced with this legal barrier, we planned a campaign to get a charter amendment which would permit the city to initiate improvements and assess the abutting property. We organized a speakers' bureau. We told the story to as many organizations as we could and to the general public by radio and newspaper publicity. The amendment was put on the ballot and received overwhelming approval.

After passage of the charter amendment, rather than take

upon ourselves the job of deciding where repairs were most needed, we formed an independent citizens' committee and asked them to designate for us where they thought repairs should be made.

This was not a pleasant duty. It involved the risk of alienating friends and property owners. But the committee approached its task good-naturedly. It went up and down the main business district, marking sections of sidewalks that in their judgment should be repaired and the cost billed to the abutting property owner. Few people objected—probably fewer than if the city's personnel had done the selecting.

Beware of Citizens Bearing Gifts

On a couple of occasions in Albert Lea, developers wanted the city to accept little tracts of land to be maintained as parkways in the middle of or in the intersections of streets. They reminded me of my first learning experience about citizens' motives.

I spent the summer between my junior and senior years of college as an apprentice to the city manager of Mason City, Iowa. (Today we would say I was an intern.) I was given a variety of short-term assignments, one of which was to do some drafting in the city engineer's office.

A man came in to see the city engineer. After a moment of casual talk, the man said, "Chet, I've lived in this city a long time. As you know, I've been pretty successful. The town has been good to me. And now I want to do something to pay back part of my debt to the city.

"I've been thinking about this for some time, and I've concluded I ought to give something to the city that all the public can use."

I was eavesdropping, intently. For the nearly three years since I decided city management was where I might make a contribution, I had been picturing what it would be like to work for a city. I envisioned everybody cooperating, helping one another, grateful that they were part of the community, and wanting to share. And here was a citizen doing just what I had imagined they would do.

I heard the city engineer say, "So?" in what seemed to me a negative tone. But Mr. Stevens was elderly, and not well. He wasn't always pleasant to everybody.

"Yes," the citizen continued, "I've been thinking that with

all the property I have scattered around town I ought to give the city some land for a street. The piece I have in mind is located over on the west side. In fact, I have it marked on a plat here."

He unfolded a map he had in his hand, spread it on a drafting table, and pointed to the place he had in mind.

"There ought to be a street right through there," he said. "It's a great inconvenience for the public to have to go clear around that whole section to get back and forth from downtown."

The city engineer didn't say anything, and the citizen continued.

"That's real valuable land. I doubt that the city could buy a strip through there big enough for a street for less than $5,000. But, as I say, I want to do something for this city that's been so good to me. I'm willing to give this land to the city—donate it, no strings attached, an outright gift. All the city would have to do then would be to grade it up a little and put a little light surface treatment on it—tar, oil, or asphalt—and it would have another street and would be helping all those people at that end of town. What do you think?"

I expected the city engineer to respond with the enthusiasm I felt, to grab the opportunity. But he didn't. He asked a few questions to be sure he understood the location. Also, he asked about the lay of the land—was it pretty flat through there, did it ever get flooded, were there any big trees that would have to be removed?

The donor-to-be answered that the land was "flat as a board, no water ever stands there, and there are only a few little scrub trees on it."

The city engineer said, "Carl, we'll think about it."

As the man left, I felt embarrassed. The engineer had rebuffed one of our good citizens. In fact, he had been rude to him, it seemed to me.

When the man was out of earshot, I said to the city engineer, "Mr. Stevens, I don't understand. The man who was just here wanted to give the city a street, free, and it sounded to me as if you practically turned down his offer. Why did you do that?"

He looked at me for a moment, plainly irritated by my question. Then, with a half smile, he said, "Roy, you'll learn." He told me to bring to his desk a certain subdivision plat. "It's in that map case, in the second drawer down," he said. I leafed through some large blueprints and tracings until I found the one he'd asked for and handed it to him.

"Let me show you something. See this big section in here, with no streets cut through?" He pointed to an area that looked to be about four square blocks in size. "Guess who owns all that land."

"I have no idea," I said.

"No, that's right, you wouldn't know. Well, I'll tell you. Every square foot of it belongs to our friend who was just in here."

I still didn't understand.

"So, what does that have to do with it?" I asked. "He's willing to give the city a big piece of it, free. I thought the city would jump at the chance, before he changed his mind."

Chet Stevens grinned.

"He won't change his mind—because he isn't giving the city anything. All that talk about wanting to do something for the city is just hogwash. The site he's talking about would make a good location for homes. As he said, it is fairly level, and it has enough slope to drain well. But without access to it, nobody would want to build a home there. He probably got the whole tract for a song, just for that reason—nobody can sell off building lots until the streets are in.

"If he can get the city to put in the streets, his lots will increase in value five times as much as the cost of the little bit of land he's 'donating'—as he calls it—to the city.

"He made it sound as if he was giving away a really valuable piece of property and that the city's contribution would be minor. The fact is just the opposite. By the time we put a survey crew in there to set a grade so the street will drain when it's built, spend two or three days of bulldozer and grader time to clear and level the ground, haul in several hundred cubic yards of crushed rock for a base, and then put on even the cheapest surfacing, we'll be out two to three thousand dollars. That's the public's money.

"And then our costs are only beginning. From then on, we have to maintain the surface, sweep it occasionally, and plow the snow every winter.

"No, Roy," he concluded, "you've got to watch these 'free' things people are always wanting to give the city. Things aren't always what they seem."

Through the years, the Mason City experience proved to be a prototype of many similar "gift" offers from seemingly public-spirited people. Until we got subdivision regulations, there were other offers of streets. The Albert Lea parkway offers were typical of other offers of little triangles and odd pieces of land, too small for building lots, left over when the subdivider laid out the streets in a pattern that would get the largest number of building lots out of the tract.

Developers would say what lovely little parks these would make, what with grass, flowers and trees. They never mentioned that these little bits of land were too small for any use other than to look at, but that they required the initial installation of water pipe and the planting of grass and flowers, followed by the continuing service of a man and truck several hours a week to water, cultivate and mow. To the citizen, the offers probably seem generous, and the city officials who are not grateful seem rude, unreasonable, or lazy.

Unfortunately, most of us look at things first from our own point of interest. We think it would be nice to have a little green spot out in front of our house or a boulevard running down the middle of the street. And it would be. But a city is a big place. If the city provides and keeps up a little beauty spot in one section of town, every other section is entitled to the same thing—and they will demand it. This is the kind of thing that makes city taxes climb, with so little to show for the increase.

There Is No Limit . . .

Despite a few unhappy situations, Albert Lea enjoyed an open-minded, cooperative approach to community questions that was both rare and remarkably effective. I am sure it was this unusual spirit of community interest and mutual helpfulness that enabled Albert Lea to carry out its plan for postwar employment and for attracting new industry that was the envy of other communities.

How much the Albert Lea spirit contrasted with the all too prevalent atmosphere of uncooperation in some communities was demonstrated the night the state planning director and I were asked to address a citywide meeting in another city the size of Albert Lea.

City officials asked us to talk briefly on the values and general principles of city planning and on what could be accomplished by thinking ahead and avoiding problems. I was to speak from the point of view of a sister community, and the other man from his broader, statewide experience. After our short presentations, we were to respond to questions from the floor.

There were about 200 local citizens at the meeting. Together the director and I had talked from thirty to forty minutes when the chairman opened the meeting to questions. Immediately an individual got to his feet and began lambasting city officials and other citizens about a number of past events—rezoning, property sales, drainage projects. Despite the chairman's efforts to get the meeting on a different track, the whole meeting followed that initial course. The efforts by the state planning director and me to get the group looking to the future fell on deaf ears. Before the meeting adjourned, two and sometimes four people were shouting at the same time, throwing accusations back and forth across the room.

"The only reason you want a zoning plan is so you can get a high price for that useless property of yours," one charged.

"If you'd pay your taxes, we could do something in this town," came from another quarter.

"Who are you to talk? What did you ever do for anybody but yourself? You're still nursing the first nickel your grandfather made in this town seventy-five years ago," another shouted.

I was happy to get out of that meeting.

That night I was the guest of the mayor. We talked into the early morning hours, the mayor detailing the deterioration taking place in his town. Business was moving out instead of in, the city's streets, sidewalks, and sewers were falling apart. There was continuous wrangling—but no action—on what to do about a theatre-auditorium the city had inherited. Several bond issues for new schools and other improvements had been turned down.

Driving back to Albert Lea the next day, I thought of the contrast between the two communities. It seemed to me the community I had just left did not have a single problem it couldn't solve if the attitude were right—if it could have the optimistic "can do" attitude shared by the business leaders, civic leaders, and citizens in Albert Lea.

When I had arrived at Albert Lea, I had never heard of "brainstorming" sessions and didn't until several years later. But looking back, I see that what Albert Lea had was a priceless ability to brainstorm issues in an atmosphere of mutual, unselfish community helpfulness.

For instance, I remember two important public meetings in Albert Lea—one concerning a charter amendment it seemed as though we needed and another about adopting some major city plans.

On both occasions everyone at the meeting seemed to be straining to think what he could contribute to the general direction of the meeting. No one accused anyone else of wrong motives or wrongdoing. On the contrary, everyone tried to add to, improve upon, complement, and strengthen the contributions of the others in the group.

I don't recall the exact verbal exchanges that took place at the many civic meetings I attended in Albert Lea, but I do remember they almost always went something like this: After a brief explanation of the purpose of the meeting by the chairman, whether it was a problem to be solved or a program to be carried through, someone would get to his feet.

"Mr. Chairman, do you think this might move us toward the objectives you have just outlined?" Then the speaker would make a concrete suggestion, offering it as a tentative motion to get the discussion moving.

Someone else would get up. "Elmer," he would say, "that's a great idea! I think it would work. Do you think it would help your idea if we did so-and-so?"

The first person would respond, "Say, that's even better! Mr. Chairman, will you add Bill's suggestion to my motion?"

Time after time in these meetings we came away with ideas and decisions different from those first proposed but markedly better. Those who suggested the improvements seemed to pick them out of the air, inspired by what others had said.

When I called on the Chamber of Commerce secretary one day, I saw a motto on his desk that summarized the Albert Lea spirit. Inspired by the motto, I asked him to get me a copy. During the remainder of my years as a city manager, it hung in a prominent place in my office. The motto read: "There is no limit to the good a man can do if he doesn't care who gets the credit."

Keep Your Vision Before You

I suppose every city manager has many speaking invitations. When the program chairman says, "Choose your own subject," this invitation offers an opportunity to share some personal convictions with the larger community. The invitation to be the graduation speaker for the local school of nursing was such an opportunity. I still have my notes from that talk, and although society's value system has taken several sharp turns since then, I think what I said then is as valid today as it was then. I chose to talk on "Some Elements of a Healthy Democratic Community." Here are extracts from what I said to the graduating nurses, their faculty, parents and friends, and to members of the community.

"We have much in common: we are serving the public, our fellowmen. We are happy in our work when we can contribute to the happiness of others.

"Cities are like individuals. What works for one will not necessarily work for others. Look for these things in your community; if they are not there, do what you can to attain them. (This list is not in the order of importance.)

- First, a community dies at the roots if it does not develop its youth to assume responsibility. See to the health of the children—that they have proper food, shelter, recreation, and medical care; that at least the home environment you provide is wholesome, happy, and challenging; that attention is paid to the moral and spiritual development of the young people; that the schools are given support in the form of encouragement to the teachers, financial aid, and an attempt to look occasionally at education from the faculty's point of view.

- A healthy community has good government, and it has good government because it chooses good people for office. Your right to vote is truly one of your most magnificent heritages. Its very availability and ease has made us forgetful of its importance.

  Do not persecute your elected officials by unwarranted and unfair criticism, causing decent citizens to decline to run for office and leaving only incompetents who have more brass than brains, more crust than character.

  Your vote is important. Use it as intelligently as you can.

- A healthy community plans its future. In other words, it practices preventive medicine rather than relying wholly on remedial measures.

- A healthy community is a beautiful community. It fulfills the desires of men, women, and children to enjoy the beauties of nature and of man-made developments.

"Congratulations to you. You have accepted the challenge to serve humanity; you have already made the sacrifices necessary to equip yourselves to translate your desires into action; yours will be the rewards that come from devotion to duty and service to your fellowmen.

"If I am not mistaken, most of you have aspired to be nurses since you were little girls. Perhaps in no other vocation are there as many active members whose childhood ideals have been held to firmly and brought to fruition in that they are what they made up their minds to be when they were yet young. You once saw a vision; you see it now; keep it before you.

"If I could define democracy in one phrase, it would be as follows: 'That system of government in which men discipline themselves to avoid discipline from another.' This discipline of which I speak causes men to restrain themselves from doing what they know to be wrong and constrains them to do what they know to be right."

Commencement speakers are chosen because they have broader or longer experience than the graduates they are to address. They know from experience that "commencement" is an exact term—the commencement of a real-life journey, during which youths' idealistic plans for the future are often pushed aside by expediency and disillusionment. A speaker may strive on such an occasion to strengthen the graduates' resolve to hold to their ideals. In his effort, he may wave the flag, speak personal convictions, and bare his soul without restraint. I suppose I hoped to crystalize the idealism of these young people, to perhaps rekindle past hopes and dreams of their families and friends, and to transfer some of both to the wider field of mutual community service and cooperation.

Factories Are Good Neighbors—for Other Factories

The day Clarence Ludwig had taken me around Albert Lea to meet various community leaders, they were almost unanimous that city planning was the city's top need. The publisher of the paper pushed hardest of all on this point. Yet by a single headline eight months later his newspaper almost killed the planning program.

But maybe it wasn't the headline; maybe it was the mood the community was in. Communities, like individuals, seem to have their good and bad periods, their ups and downs. There are times when the optimism and enthusiasm in the community make almost anything seem possible. This positive attitude can be followed by a somber atmosphere that communicates itself to the entire citizenry—businessmen, their employees, their families—everyone.

In a community like Albert Lea, where at least the retail businessses depend on farmer trade, these moods change with the weather. If the corn has enough moisture, followed by sun and corn-growing weather, optimism is the prevailing note; but too much rain, cool weather, hail or threats of hail bring on a general depression you sense in talk on the street, over coffee, and at church.

In any case, the city council had authorized me to get a planning program going; I had consulted Walter Blucher, the head of the American Society of Planning Officials, about how to proceed, and we had engaged a professional planner to make a preliminary survey and cost estimate for a full program. Unfortunately, the day following his report to the city council, the paper carried the front-page headline, "Master Plan Cost Is Set at $18,000." If the announced figure had been ten times as much, I doubt that it would have created any more stir and resentment. The town suddenly came apart. For days, it seemed everyone I met jumped on me about "wasting" $18,000 of city money for such foolishness as a city plan.

I can't estimate the amount of damage done to our city planning efforts by that one headline. But I do know the amount of work it took to try to get the community back on its former track. During the next six months I wrote articles, went on radio, and made personal appearances all over town, explaining why we needed planning. Sometimes I had two and three evening meetings a week, including the night of the worst blizzard of the year. I addressed every service club, PTA, neighborhood group, church dinner, business association, and chamber of commerce committee that would listen to me.

My talk had three parts: A brief review of how most American cities started and of how they progressed to their present condition; examples of our own situation, familiar to most Albert Leans; and a description of how we hoped to do the planning for our city, with emphasis on citizen participation in the decision making. Leaving time for questions and discussions, I closed with my true "scrambled eggs" story:

"Cities are like scrambled eggs," I said to my listeners. "We don't have to be very smart to scramble them, but once they are scrambled, the wisest man can't put them back together again." Then I told them of a telephone call I had had about nine o'clock one morning, and what followed.

The woman on the telephone ordered me to get to her house immediately to look at her washing. I could tell by the tone of her voice there was no use asking why I should drop whatever I was doing to go see her morning wash. She was a thoroughly angry taxpayer, and the only way I know to deal with such folks is to show sincere interest in their problems.

I told the audience the general location of her home. All of them knew the area. It was one of our older residential sections. Most of them knew also that right in the middle of the area was an egg-drying plant.

The plant was a long-established part of our local economy. It employed twenty to thirty men who, with their families, depended on the jobs in that plant for their livelihood. Maybe this woman's husband was employed there, too; I didn't know. All I knew was that on this particular morning this citizen-tax-payer-homemaker wanted the city to do something about that egg drying plant, right now.

I told my audiences that when I found the address and parked my car I could see the lady of the house framed in the doorway, hands on hips, poised in a most hostile stance. When I reached the porch she started right out, not even prefacing her remarks with a "Good morning."

"You come with me," she said. "I'm going to show you something this city is going to have to do something about."

I followed her through the house, out the back door, straight to her loaded clothes lines. She stopped in front of one line of freshly laundered sheets, pillow cases, and shirts.

"Look at that!" she said. "That's what I have to put up with every time I wash clothes, and I'm not going to stand for it any more."

I looked but couldn't see anything wrong. When she saw I didn't recognize her problem, she ordered, "Don't tell me you don't see it. Look at those sheets, all streaked with eggs."

She ran a finger across one sheet; then I saw what she was talking about. Her finger collected three or four strands of mucus-like substance strung up and down the sheet.

She flipped the stuff off her finger. "That's what happens every time they run that plant. They let the dried egg dust get out through that cupola on the roof, and it settles on my wash and on all the wash in the whole neighborhood. How can you keep a decent house with a thing like that right in your neighborhood?" she demanded.

I admitted it was pretty bad. I asked a few questions, hoping to convince her that the city was really concerned. Then I said, "This is one of the best examples I've seen of why a city needs planning and zoning."

"I don't know what you're talking about."

"No, I suppose you don't. And you're not the only one. The city charter says we must have a master plan to guide the city's growth and development. The people adopted the charter over fifteen years ago, yet nothing has been done to get an overall plan. Now we're trying to get a plan for the city, and half the people in town are mad at us because of the cost. Actually, the cost is only about one dollar a person and will be spread over several years."

"Well," she said, "I still don't know what you're talking about, and I don't see what that has to do with my problem. Anyone can see you can't keep a decent house with an egg factory practically next door."

"That's exactly what I'm talking about," I said. "Of course you can't keep a decent house next door to a factory—this kind or any other kind. In your case, it's the powder from dried eggs. If it weren't that, it would be bad smells or noise. But even if the plant eliminated those problems, you'd still have a traffic hazard and a general nuisance."

She didn't know it, but I was referring to half a dozen cases that were headaches for us at that very time. One woman was complaining that the workmen loading trucks at a nearby plant used such vile language she had to keep her children in the house. An old man had protested he couldn't sleep on hot nights. His problem was that trucks came in after midnight, and whoever directed them into the loading stalls shouted instructions so loud you could hear him three blocks away. Another current complainer was a newcomer to Albert Lea. She called a couple times a week to complain about the trains switching in front of her place. She kept wanting to know, "When is the city going to move those tracks so we can get some peace and quiet around here?"

At this point I told my listeners that if we had had a plan for the city's growth for the last twenty years we could have avoided most of these problems. We would have had industries in one section of town and residences in another. Where the industries and homes were in the same general area, we would have separated them with green areas—parks, playgrounds, and boulevards—or at least could have put business and commercial zones between the industrial areas and the residential areas.

As for the lady's problem, I told my audience that I had met with the owner-manager of the egg-drying plant, as I had told the lady I would, to see if he could do anything to reduce the problem. He was cordial and cooperative. He didn't have a "public be damned" attitude like some industrialists have.

I had asked if there were any devices he could install, such as moistened baffles to catch the egg dust. He said they had found nothing on the market and that what they had devised themselves was ineffective. He promised to make an extra effort to adjust his operations to the weather, because the problem was worse on muggy days, and to continue looking for some way to solve the problem. Since everyone agreed we needed jobs, and the egg plant manager was doing what he could to alleviate the problem, I knew of nothing more the city could do.

I ended my talks by saying, "Ladies and gentlemen, the problem of this lady and her neighbors is a concrete example of the reason why a city—any city— needs to plan. Only by wise planning, courageously carried out, can we keep to a minimum the frictions that inevitably develop where hundreds, thousands, and even millions of people live close to one another almost every hour of the day and for all the years of their lives.

"Our opportunity to do something in the past is gone. Our city is already scrambled. We have land use problems, traffic and parking problems, and problems of playgrounds and recreational areas. All we can do now is make the few corrections we can and concentrate on preventing more scrambling in the future. That's what we're trying to do in our city planning program."

After almost every one of these talks, one or more persons said to me, "So *that's* what you mean by city planning. Why, I'm for that: I didn't know what it meant."

We adopted a motto for Albert Lea: "The city that plans its future!" It was printed in large letters on a sign a mile or so out of town announcing to the motorist he was approaching Albert Lea. The city council went ahead with the program.

Some four or five years later, when I was directing the work of the Little Hoover Commission for the state of Minnesota, a fellow came up to me during a meeting. He introduced himself and said he had been a reporter for the *Albert Lea Evening Tribune* for a year or so after I was there and that he had heard about the squabble over the city's planning program.

"It would have made quite a difference if the headline had read, 'City Master Plan to Cost *Only* $18,000' wouldn't it?" he observed.

I agreed, "It surely would have."

Firmly Flexible

How much we pay for fire insurance on our homes and business places is influenced by our community's conflagration hazards and the strength of its water system and other fire defenses. As a basis for determining premium rates, the insurance companies' national associations and state insurance rating bureaus classify municipalities according to how well they meet certain standards for water supply systems; fire department organization, manpower, and activities; structural condition of buildings; protective codes, and other criteria. For example, a municipality with no central water supply system or fire department would be in class 10. To be in class 1, a city's water supply, fire department, fire service communications, and fire safety control would have to be topflight.

Cities are classified after an on-site survey by qualified rating bureau personnel. On completion of a survey, the rating bureau files its report with the city officials, detailing where the city is deficient. Since the rating bureau people are experts in ways of preventing and combating fires, their recommendations are useful for more than reducing fire insurance rates; they show a city what it can do to reduce the likelihood of loss of life and property. For these reasons I was interested in the recommendations of the latest underwriters' report on Albert Lea. I hoped we would find ways to cut insurance costs and provide better fire protection.

Albert Lea's fire department had only two full-time, paid men. The rest of the department, including the fire chief, were volunteers. In determining the personnel strength of a fire department as a factor for rating purposes, one full-time man is considered roughly the equivalent of four volunteers. The survey report on Albert Lea showed that the major opportunity for improving our classification was to go to a full-time, paid department. But apart from the dollar savings in insurance premiums was the question whether a full-paid department would increase our fire-fighting effectiveness and whether going to a paid department would alienate an important group in the community, the volunteer firemen.

Only after I had familiarized myself with the operations of all other city departments did I start looking for cost savings and improvement opportunities in the fire department. When I did look, I found expenditures to be in line with fire department costs in other cities. I learned also that the retirement pay for volunteers, though small, was larger than their base active duty pay. This suggested that being a volunteer fireman might be financially attractive and that there might be opposition to reducing the volunteer force.

I called on the fire chief, a local grocer who had been in the department over thirty years and had been chief about ten years. Like all volunteer firemen I know, he was devoted to the fire service. In our first visit he related story after story of the heroism of the volunteers, of the many times they had fought fires in blizzards and at great risk to their own lives. He gave me a detailed description of the night they were racing to a fire and collided with an auto, an accident that left him with a crippled leg for the rest of his life.

When I casually inquired about the possibility of improving our classification, it became immediately obvious that this was a touchy subject. The city couldn't afford the high cost of paid men, he said. Besides, paid men don't have the interest in the fire service that volunteers have. He declared that volunteers could reach fires as fast as paid men, and he bristled each time I suggested we consider other survey recommendations for improving the department.

I discussed the matter informally with the council, some of whom had served as volunteers. To my surprise, they generally felt that the city had outgrown the volunteer system and should move with reasonable speed to a full-time department.

With this kind of backing I sought means of moving toward a paid department while retaining the values that a volunteer department offered. I met with the department more than once to discuss frankly the council's and my thinking and to solicit their cooperation. Though I could not point to any specifics, I sensed some of the men were volunteer firemen as much out of civic duty as enthusiasm to be "smoke-eaters." After all, when a man has been called out of a warm bed or from his business hundreds of times over a twenty-year period—as many of them had—he reaches a point where he is willing to let somebody else have a turn. He may even be willing to pay a little more in taxes to buy this kind of relief.

I didn't push the matter, but from time to time word reached me that the men in the department were giving the subject thorough consideration from every angle. The die was cast when the chief came in to announce he had decided to retire.

Although on the surface this was the opportunity we had

been seeking, implementation would not be simple. We faced the likelihood that the volunteers would expect the new, full-time, paid positions of chief and assistant chief to be filled from their ranks, in the manner they had followed for years, namely through election. In fact, no sooner did the city council authorize the full-paid positions of chief and captain (the second in command) than I began receiving suggestions as to who would be "just the man for the job," and factions began to form in support of certain individuals.

Election of a fire chief might show who was most popular in the department, but it would not necessarily produce the best man for the job. If I judged public sentiment right on the question of fire department reorganization, the council and the people were ready to go all out to obtain the best qualified persons available to a city our size. I resolved, therefore, to widely advertise the positions, to provide a rigorous examination, and to appoint the man who came out on top. This we were able to do, but only after a bizarre fiasco that nearly upset all our plans.

Using the directory of all cities in the United States, I listed every city over 10,000 population in Minnesota, Iowa, Wisconsin, North and South Dakota, and Nebraska. Knowing an impersonal general announcement of our vacancies would be tossed promptly into the wastebasket in many cities because fire chiefs would resent our trying to steal their men, and any interested person would probably feel uneasy negotiating with us confidentially, I decided to go straight to the chiefs themselves in our recruiting effort.

I wrote up a detailed announcement, giving the qualifications we were seeking, the working conditions and the pay, and outlining the examination procedure we would follow. The examination would include a written test, an agility test, and a final appearance before an oral examining board.

The top man in the examination would be appointed fire chief, the second high man captain.

I sent the following letter along with the announcement to the fire chief in each of the cities in those six states:

"Our city is beginning a program of fire department expansion and will need a chief and a captain with initiative, ideas, personality and leadership.

"If you have in your department any men of this calibre whom you would like to see fill positions of the kind we will have, will you post the enclosed notice, please?"

The announcement hardly had time to reach another city before the local firemen began objecting. One of the most vocal was a young member of the department with the appropriate name of Joe Spark. He came in to protest my inviting "outsiders" and "foreigners" to compete for the appointments. He was a war veteran, had served as a fireman with the armed forces in Italy, and belonged to that large group of people who think city jobs should go only to local taxpayers.

I attempted to show him the weakness in trying to man city government by building walls around the supply of talent. I asked him if he knew of any successful business that drew a circle with a three-mile radius from its place of business and refused to go outside that line to get the qualified help it needed.

He argued that this was "different," that the taxpayers were paying for these jobs, and the jobs belonged to those who paid for them.

I tried to counter with two lines of reasoning. First, I said, city government is more technical and more complicated than many businesses. At the same time, in any city there is only one police department, one fire department, one city engineer's office, one water department, and so on from which to draw technically qualified people. There is rarely a pool of trained and experienced people within the boundaries of a city, especially a small city, to man these specialized jobs. If we are going to get competency, I said, and add new blood with new ideas and new enthusiasm, we must not limit ourselves to our own city limits. I added that I heartily agreed we should promote from within the organization or choose local residents whenever we could—and that I certainly hoped he would apply for the positions—but we could not afford to hamstring ourselves by turning our backs on potential employees merely because they lived outside Albert Lea.

Second, I said, I thought the local taxpayers about whom he was concerned—and only two of whom could get the jobs—were entitled to know we were using their tax money to hire the best talent we could get for what we could pay, regardless of where the people came from. And on that score I asked if when he was in the service he found the "outsiders" and "foreigners" from other towns and other states very different from him in their interests and needs and abilities, and whether he felt they were not entitled to the same job opportunities he had in our *United* States.

I got nowhere in our discussion, again proving, I suppose, the old adage: "A man convinced against his will is of the same opinion still."

As he left, I said again I hoped he would take the examination. He wasn't sure he would. "I don't like the way you're handling this," he said.

I had purposely set the examination for nearly two months after the announcement date to be sure to allow plenty of time for word to get around and for candidates to make application and arrange their work schedules so that they could come to Albert Lea to take the examination. Soon after the announcement, inquiries and applications began trickling in. The two full-time drivers, both active members of the employees' union, came in to talk about the new positions. They, too, were displeased that I had opened the examination to "outsiders." I encouraged both of them to file.

The announcement had been out about a month when I sensed increased hostility. The two full-time drivers were less cordial and relaxed than usual. Volunteer members of the fire department whom previously I had found willing to see the two sides of this issue now seemed preoccupied when I met them on the street. The union members in the other city departments, too, were a bit standoffish, less willing to pass the time of day when we met. Even the council meetings were more formal and less cordial than previously.

And although I could see the change occurring: tension, distrust, resentment growing—I did not know the cause. I dared not call the employees together to ask for an explanation, because it was possible I just imagined the hostility. Maybe my reluctance to bring the problem into the open was a product of my strong hope that we would succeed in getting the city off on the right foot in its first venture with a full-time, paid fire department.

The city council meeting on November 13 was more confused than usual. The mayor's previously unbroken rule that council meetings start exactly at 7:00 p.m. had to bow to a Chamber of Commerce dinner, which delayed the meeting until 8:00 p.m. The full agenda was handled with dispatch, and at 10:00 p.m. the mayor banged his gavel, adjourning the meeting.

I had gathered my papers and started for my office when I noticed at the far side of the council chamber one of the councilmen in deep, vigorous conversation with the union business agent and a handful of other people—employees, spectators, and the press representative. As I passed, I overheard someone say, "Why don't you ask Harlow?" I turned to the group, but no one made a move; so I continued toward the door. As I reached the stairs, someone caught up with me and asked, "What goes on about this Ames fellow getting the chief's job?"

I turned to him. "What goes on about what? I'm afraid I don't know what you're talking about."

"You must know something," he replied. "The men in there say you've already promised the chief's job to the fire chief down at Ames."

We returned to where the councilman and the union agent were still talking. By this time, several more had joined the group. As we approached, they all stopped talking and stared questioningly at me. I stood there for an awkward moment. Then the councilman broke the silence.

"Roy," he said, "these men have a newspaper clipping that shows you have already offered the fire chief's job to the Ames fire chief."

"I haven't offered the job to him or anybody else," I said. "Let me see it."

Someone handed me a worn clipping. It was headed "Job Offer to Fire Chief." The first paragraph read: "Fire Chief Sam Long has been offered a job as head of the fire department at Albert Lea, Minn., he said today."

I looked around, flabbergasted. It was obvious that to the men standing there this was no joke. They expected an answer from me.

"All I can say is that it is not true," I said.

But no one was convinced. Somebody put out his hand for the clipping. I gave it to him, then turned and headed for my office.

Fifteen or twenty minutes later the newspaper editor, who had covered the meeting that night, came in. I invited him to sit down.

"What's the story on this fire chief situation?" he asked.

"Tryg," I said, "You've got me. I don't understand it. But if you're wondering whether I did make such an offer, the answer is no."

"You're going to have a hard time convincing anybody of that. The firemen and the business agent have had that clipping for a week. They've shown it to half the people in town. If there's nothing to it, what accounts for the story?"

"I don't know," I said. "I sent our announcement to Ames as

I did to every other city over 10,000 population in six states, but I've never even talked to the fire chief down there. It's too late now, but the first thing in the morning, I'll call the Ames city manager to see if he knows anything about it."

"Okay," he said. "But you'd better give me a statement as soon as you've talked to the people in Ames. This thing is hot."

I assured him I would, and he left.

I turned immediately to the file of fire chief applications for clues to the reason behind the statement of the Ames fire chief. I found that on October 18 I had sent the same announcement to all the cities, including the City of Ames. A week later I had received a letter from the Ames fire chief describing his own background, and writing in part as follows (with language and spelling as shown here):

"I em getting 250.00 here and 5 cents a mile for my Car. so that is not bad and they are talking about another rais whitch I think will be about 25.00 more

"But if you would talk around 300.00 per Mounth for my self and about 250.00 for Captain.

"I think that I could fill the wants for you and put your Department on it feet."

Because the spelling, grammar, and construction of Chief Long's letter was somewhat garbled, I couldn't tell if he was interested in the job for himself. On October 25, I had replied to Chief Long, thanking him for acknowledging our announcement. I said:

"Appreciating, as you do, the importance of having competent and able men in a department, I know that you will bring the announcement of the examination to the attention of the people in your department who might be qualified for that type of work.

"Thank you very much for writing."

In case he was interested, I added this postscript to my letter:

"I'm enclosing an application form which you may wish to complete in case you find that you are interested in the position."

On November 12, the day before the council meeting, I received another letter from Chief Long. Again, I was not certain what the chief was trying to say, but I assumed he was telling me he would not be filing an application. His lengthy letter began:

"I have given this Chief job quite a Conscience in regards to my self and your men.

"I don't know any of your men but it looks like to me that if you had men that been with you as long as some of them have.

"It looks to me that they are entitle to it with all fairness to them. if they have been good enuff to Continue in your service this long it looks like they are the man for you."

He followed this with a mixture of advice and philosophy.

At the time I received this second letter I was amused at the way Chief Long expressed himself but never gave a thought to what may have been his motive. But as I reread the correspondence in light of the Ames newspaper story, it occurred to me he might have been using us to strengthen his position in Ames.

Next morning when I telephoned the Ames city manager, I suggested this to him. He said he had seen the newspaper story and assumed it was legitimate—that I had offered the Albert Lea position to Chief Long. He said he would look into it and call me back.

I then prepared the following short statement for the Albert Lea editor:

"It is extremely regrettable that Mr. Long did not read the announcement that the examination would be held and did not understand that an invitation to take the examination is not an appointment."

The Ames city manager (whose name, incidentally, was John Ames—the man who gave me my first job the day after I graduated from Iowa State, as engineer-inspector on street, sidewalk, curb and gutter, and sewer construction) telephoned me later to say that evidently my hunch was right. He said the chief, who was eligible for retirement, had been putting pressure on the Ames city council for a pay raise, which would give him a higher base for his retirement pay. Perhaps Chief Long thought a statement to the Ames paper about the Albert Lea job would help. City Manager Ames said Chief Long now claimed the whole thing was "a misunderstanding," but that the Ames reporter was sure he had reported the chief's statement correctly and Chief Long had made no attempt to change it.

The next day the editor of the Albert Lea paper called at my office. He asked if he could have all the correspondence between the Ames fire chief and me so that he could give Albert Lea readers all the facts.

I remembered that our firemen and the union business agent had circulated the story from the Ames paper around town in Albert Lea for nearly two weeks without coming to me for my side of it. I knew also we still had ahead of us the problem of selecting a new fire chief, and perhaps naming a nonresident against the wishes of many local people. With these facts in mind, I thought this might be an opportunity to let the public see behind the scenes what we faced in trying to make a needed reorganization of the fire department. I agreed to release all the correspondence, on one condition: that the paper would reprint the correspondence *exactly,* including all the unique spelling, capitalization, punctuation, and grammar. The editor hesitated a moment, then agreed. On November 14, 1946, the Albert Lea *Evening Tribune* ran all the material under a three-column head: "Offer of Chief's Job Denied by Harlow."

The number of inquiries we had had about the fire chief and fire captain positions indicated a potential of several dozen applicants, but by the closing date for filing, the number of applicants was little more than a dozen.

We held the written examination in a high school classroom and the agility tests in the gymnasium. Six men survived the tests by scoring more than 60 on the written examination and meeting designated minimums of strength and agility. The six were three Albert Lea men and three outsiders.

The oral examining board consisted of the fire chiefs of Minneapolis and the neighboring city of Mankato, the engineer for the insurance rating bureau, Clarence Ludwig (executive secretary of the Minnesota League of Municipalities), and one city councilman. I sat with the board and joined in questioning the candidates.

At the conclusion of the oral interviews, the five members of the oral board prepared their individual ratings of each man on qualities of leadership, experience, and general acceptability. I consolidated the individual returns on the written and oral examinations and prepared the final ratings. The top man was a fire captain who was serving as acting assistant chief in the Sioux City department; second was our own Joe Spark, the man who had complained about the way we were handling the selection process; third was a volunteer fire captain from the North St. Paul department.

The following day I telephoned the Sioux City man the results and offered him the position as Fire Chief. He asked for time to give it further consideration. I agreed to wait a week but asked him to make his decision as soon as possible. Until he made his decision I could not move on the appointment of a captain.

The number two man, Joe Spark, had done very well on all

the tests and had the minimum years of experience for the captain position, but he was a few months short of the announced minimum experience requirement for chief. If the Sioux City man accepted appointment as chief, Spark would receive the nod for captain. But if the Sioux City man declined the appointment, I would have to go down the list to the fourth or fifth man on the examination ratings to reach one who met the experience requirement for chief.

The Sioux City man took nearly a week to make his decision. In the meantime, the five other finalists were waiting anxiously for the results. There was great interest throughout the city, especially within the fire department. Finally the Sioux City man called. In view of a pending appointment as permanent assistant chief in the Sioux City department, he had decided not to move and therefore declined our offer.

This left me facing a dilemma. If I appointed a man who met the minimum experience requirements, I would have to name an out-of-town man who ranked well below Joe Spark except for the experience requirement. On the other hand, if I appointed Spark I was subject to criticism for not adhering strictly to the specifications we had set for the position. The decison could be critical to both morale in the fire department and to public confidence in our determination to stick by our declared plans.

I deliberately wrote out the pros and cons of the situation, trying to give proper weight to each point. Then I put the list aside for a couple of days, hoping time would give me a better perspective. When I looked again at my pro and con list, it seemed clear the overriding consideration was the decision best for the community over the years, regardless of immediate approval or disapproval. A few days before Christmas I offered the appointment to Joe Spark. He accepted. I then offered the fire captain's position to the volunteer fire captain from North St. Paul, a young man with great promise, and he accepted. Two days after Christmas we made the public announcement, and Albert Lea entered a new phase of municipal government.

A Fair Rate of Return

The private electric utility serving Albert Lea also held the twenty-year natural gas franchise from the city. This offered a money-saving possibility for the businesses and residents of Albert Lea which appeared to merit exploration.

The gas franchise, which had six years to run, was granted by the city when Mr. Ludwig was city manager. I thought I could see his handiwork in the language of the franchise, because it was carefully drawn with the city's interest in mind. For instance, it did not give the utility an exclusive franchise; it included an agreed fair value of the gas company's property as of the franchise date and required the utility company to file annually with the city the costs of all additions and changes; it gave the city access to all company records of property values, revenues, and expenses; and it reserved to the city the right to purchase the gas system at any time during the franchise period at the agreed valuation as of the date of the franchise, plus the cost of additions and less the retirements and depreciation.

Reviewing the annual audits of the gas company's operations, regularly filed with the city, I noted that the net profit shown for each of the past few years was about equal to one-third of the current value of the system. In other words, the company appeared to be making enough money to pay for its investment every three to four years.

With this information in hand, I invited the local manager of the utility to discuss it with me. I asked him how he felt about a rate reduction or the possible purchase of the system by the city as permitted under the franchise. Of course, he was disturbed by either prospect. He maintained there were other factors besides those shown in the financial statements that justified the rate of return the company was realizing on its gas operation.

A day or two after our meeting, a senior member of one of the county's prestigious law firms called on me. He wasted no time getting to the purpose of his call.

"Harlow," he said, "if you want to kill the council-manager plan in this city, just keep pushing for public ownership."

I laid the audit before him. "I'm not pushing for public ownership," I said, "but I am concerned that the people of this city are paying for the gas system every three years under the present rate schedule. There are a lot of places this money could go to build up the community instead of into the pockets of absentee stockholders."

He made no reply to this but warned me again as he left the office. "Well, mark my word," he said. "The people will throw out the council-manager plan if your proposal goes through."

I had made no recommendation to the city council nor had I made a "proposal" to anyone. But shortly thereafter the utility company announced through the newspaper a gas rate reduction.

Run It Like a Business

During a League of Minnesota Municipalities conference the mayor of one of the northern cities called me aside, saying he wanted to talk to me. "We've got a problem in our city," he said, "that's just about got the council and me down. I wonder if you have any ideas on how we might solve it."

"If you can't solve it, I doubt that I can. But at least I can sympathize with you. Anyway, go ahead—what's the problem?"

He told me they had a superintendent of streets who had worked for the city for years. He said the man was popular with the public, always doing people little favors. Also, he was a real political power. The mayor had no criticism of the man's work. The problem was that no matter how big an appropriation they gave him, he was always out of money two or three months before the end of the year. Every year he promised to stay within his budget, but every year he ran out before the year was over.

The mayor said, "It's as embarrassing as hell, because he makes it look as if we men on the council—ours is supposed to be a businessmen's administration—can't manage the city's finances. We're always having to borrow at the end of the year or take money away from some other department. When we do this, we're in bad with the other department heads. They say, 'Why should we pinch and save to have a little money left over at the end of the year, as you councilmen want, when all we're doing is saving it so the street department can have it?'"

I asked the mayor what they had done so far to deal with the problem. He said one year the council told him that if he ran out of money he would just have to shut down, but that backfired. When the citizens complained because he wasn't cleaning the streets, trimming the trees, cleaning out catch basins, or repairing potholes, the street superintendent told them, "Don't talk to me. Talk to those guys down at the city council. I want to do the work, but they won't give me the money."

The mayor said they sure heard from the public. When they tried to explain that they had given him all the money he asked for and that he had promised to get the work done for that money, the people didn't care what the council's reasons were. They wanted relief from potholes and dust.

					Original Appropriation $36,780		
Department _____					Supplemental "		2,250
Division _____		MONTHLY BUDGET ALLOTMENTS			" "		
Fund _____		19____					

		Jan	Feb		Oct	Nov	Dec
1.	January	2800.00	2800.00		2800.00	2800.00	2800.00
2.	February		2800.00		2800.00	2800.00	2800.00
3.	March				2900.00	2900.00	2900.00
4.	April				2900.00	2900.00	2900.00
5.	May				2900.00	2900.00	2900.00
6.	June				3177.00	3177.00	3177.00
7.	July				3200.00	3200.00	3200.00
8.	August				3200.00	3200.00	3200.00
9.	September				3200.00	3200.00	3200.00
10.	October				2900.00	2900.00	2900.00
11.	November					2800.00	2800.00
12.	December						3103.00
13.	Supplem. Approp.				1250.00	1250.00	1250.00
14.	Supplem. Approp.				1000.00	1000.00	1000.00
15.	Cumul. Allot.	2800.00	5600.00				39030.00
16.	Cumul. Expendit.						38644.42
17.	Unexpended Bal.						385.58
18.	Unpaid Bills					14.17	6.25
19.	Purchase orders on Hand					21.50	0.00
20.	Unencumb. Allot. (Deficits in red)						379.33

*Department and Division Heads. On line 20 above is shown the
unencumbered total of allotments, as of the last month shown, for
your department or division. Overexpenditures or encumbrances in
one month should be offset in succeeding months. Please make every
effort to keep within appropriation and allotment limits.

_____
Manager

Simple budget-allotment form for keeping track of departmental expenditures, to avoid overspending budgeted appropriations.

I asked him if they had considered using a budget allotment system. He said he had never heard the term, so I explained. I said that after they had approved the appropriation for the street department they might want to first set aside a small amount for emergencies or contingencies—maybe 3% to 5%. Then they could divide the remainder into monthly or quarterly amounts.

The mayor asked if I meant dividing the remainder into twelve or four equal amounts. I said, no, because needs vary from month to month. They could have the city accountant go back over expenditures for the last four or five years and see about what percent was spent each month or quarter. Then they could divide the current appropriation into the same percentages, by months or quarters. These would be the budget allotments.

Then they could keep track, month by month. At the end of each month they could compare the street department's actual expenditures for the month with the allotment for that month.

If the department ran over in any month, they could call in the superintendent, find out why, and unless there was a good reason for running over, make him cut back expenditures the next month. In this way they would know before it happened if he was running out of money.

I added that, of course, all this depended on how politically powerful the streets superintendent was. If he ignored the council's monthly or quarterly budget allotment, they might have to decide whether to take the bull by the horns and get themselves a new superintendent or give in to him. I suggested they try the budget allotment system first.

The mayor listened attentively to my long explanation.

When I finished, he said, "You know, it's funny we never thought of this. This is pretty much what we do in our businesses to keep out of trouble. I guess we never thought you could run a city like a business, so we never thought of this. I'm going to talk to the rest of the council about it."

I told him I'd like to know how they made out, but I never heard. I wondered several times afterwards whether they still thought you can't ever run a city like a business.

Let's Have No Second-Class Employees

I worked for the Bureau of Old Age and Survivors Insurance of the U.S. Social Security Board before I went to public administration graduate school. As a result of this experience, when I became a city manager I knew how much employees working for employers "covered" by the Social Security Act paid in Social Security taxes, what it took to be eligible for benefits, and how to calculate benefits for retired people and for survivors in case of a worker's death.

At that time local governments could not join the Social Security program. City employees could not build up the same Social Security benefits and have the same old age and survivorship protection as employees of most private businesses.

This prohibition was hard on both city employees and the cities hiring them. For thousands of general city employees across the country it meant they had no protection; for others who had city pensions (usually the uniformed forces—fire and police), they were locked in with one city, because if they went to work for another city, they lost their pension rights. For the cities as employers, they could not offer potential employees as attractive a compensation package as private industry could.

At Albert Lea I learned we had employees with twenty years and more of city service with no retirement protection. I did some rough calculations of how much life insurance a young man with a family, working for the city, would have to carry to give his family protection equal to what Social Security provided and estimated that his annual insurance premiums would be fifteen to twenty times a private employee's Social Security contributions. This was an astonishing difference.

I put this information to use during the 1947 annual convention of the League of Minnesota Municipalities, when the paid representatives of the uniformed pension systems sponsored a resolution memorializing the Congress of the United States to prohibit the extension of Social Security coverage to municipal employees.

This inconsiderate, selfish move so disturbed me I took the convention floor and argued hard against the resolution, using specific examples from Albert Lea. I pointed out not only that we had employees with twenty years and more of city service and no retirement, but also that if the level of pensions then enjoyed by the uniformed services were extended to other employees of the city who had no retirement protection the city would go broke.

Evidently my arguments were persuasive. The resolution was defeated and returned to a league committee for further study. After the convention, I was appointed with some others to a league retirement committee, to study the whole business of retirement programs for city employees.

Two years later, when I was city manager in Fargo, North Dakota, the American Municipal Association invited me to appear with the personnel director of Kansas City before the Ways and Means Committee of the U.S. House of Representatives in Washington on proposed legislation to make Social Security coverage available to local government employees. This time I had exact figures that verified the cost differences between Social Security and private insurance. Also, I wrote a few members of Congress whom I knew, including Senator Hubert Humphrey, who was mayor of Minneapolis when I was in Albert Lea. Senator Humphrey informed me we faced an uphill battle to overcome the great opposition from the national organizations of the uniformed services. I learned that the directors of state pensions systems were also opposing extension of federal Social Security to local government employees.

This is now history. Eventually, Social Security protection was made available to local governments on a voluntary basis, and I assume that most cities in the country now provide federal Social Security coverage to their employees (except those who have recently withdrawn from the federal system).

Through the Eyes of a Child

Although not every adult citizen held all of us city officials in high esteem, at least our four-year-old Steven gave one of them the benefit of the doubt. The city attorney, our neighbor, related to us this encounter with Steve, and also gave it to the newspaper.

Steven was talking to him in his front yard.

"What kind of work do you do?" Steve wanted to know.

"Well," was the reply, "I'm a lawyer."

"But what kind of work does a lawyer do?" Steve persisted.

The attorney did some quick thinking.

"It's like this," he replied. "A lawyer helps people who are in trouble."

Steve's eyes opened wide as he looked up at the attorney in stark wonder.

"Like God?" he gasped.

A Good Idea Belongs to Everyone

I appreciated the following editorial in the *Evening Tribune*, December 12, 1946. The credit was really due a truck driver who came to my office to complain that he had jackknifed his truck on an overpass in town and couldn't see why the city or the state highway department or someone couldn't have those approaches sanded.

In bad weather, of course, we sanded all the surfaced streets, including the overpasses. But overpasses are a peculiar problem. If the humidity and temperature are right, ice will form on the roadway of an overpass when the highway approaches at both ends of the overpass are dry. Yet, we couldn't afford to assign a man with a truck the sole duty of watching the overpasses and sanding them when they needed it.

I asked the trucker, "If we put out sand barrels and keep them filled, will drivers be willing to spread the sand when it's needed?"

"Hell, yes," he replied. "You put the sand out there; we'll put it on. We don't need it very often, but when we do, it's bad."

"The next time you come through here," I said, "there'll be sand barrels ready for use."

He thanked me and left, but I had a feeling he doubted anything would be done, that I was just easing him out. From the fact that the newspaper later checked with me about this, I guessed he went from my office to the newspaper to register the same complaint. The editorial read:

---§---

A City Service

Without any trumpet blasts or other bally-hoo city workmen have placed a number of sand barrels about the city. The sand is to be available for use by anyone when streets and sidewalks become iced and slippery. It will no doubt help reduce accidents.

The idea came to City Manager Harlow from a truck driver who said he sometimes had trouble negotiating local hills when the pavement is covered with ice. So Mr. Harlow gave instructions to have the sand barrels set out.

Here's an example of the type of city service which some of the more cynical of us had thought was a thing of the past. It is gratifying to know we have a city administration that is responsive to the small needs of the citizens and alert to suggestions submitted.

The moral obviously is: If you have ideas for civic improvements, be they big or small, then speak up. It's when everyone takes an interest that city government is at its best.

Always Another Mountain to Climb

The June 25, 1947, office mail included a form letter on a Fargo, North Dakota, city commission letterhead. It said simply, "The city commission invites you to submit an application for the position of city manager of this city."

I didn't know that Fargo's manager, who had gone there from Kenosha, Wisconsin, had left. I telephoned the mayor to acknowledge and thank him for the invitation and to tell him I was not interested in changing jobs.

"Even if you're not interested," Mayor Dawson said, "would you be willing to come and talk to us? We have some problems we think someone from the outside could give us some suggestions about. We would pay your expenses, of course."

This was not an unusual request, and we set a date for me to fly up to Fargo in about a week.

The mayor and another city commissioner, a local banker, met my forenoon plane. Starting at the airport, we toured the city until late afternoon, observing and discussing problems as we drove. At lunch we had met several businessmen and were joined by a third commissioner, who accompanied us on the remainder of the tour.

We inspected street improvement work, talked about Fargo's special assessment practices, discussed the need for expanding the water treatment plant, and made a hurried trip through the large municipal auditorium and discussed its financing. The commissioners asked my opinion on one item after another: Should they be financing street improvements through special assessments instead of a general tax levy? What did I think of the practice of having street improvement districts end in the middle of a block so that paved streets ended in the middle of city blocks? Were the new mechanical mixing chambers now on the market as effective in treating water as the older type of mixing and settling basins? What should be city policy on charging private operators, the airlines, and the National Guard for use of the airport? How important was a long-range plan for the city? What should be the relation between the city and the Chamber of Commerce? How should the city go about solving the downtown parking problem? What salary should they expect to have to pay to get a qualified city manager? I gave specific answers when I could. To some questions, I presented the pros and cons. On others, I had no opinion.

From time to time we stopped at an office to meet a business associate or friend of one of the commissioners. I noticed that the commissioners' descriptions of these individuals contrasted with what was emphasized in Albert Lea. In Albert Lea I had been given a quick description of what the individuals had done or were doing in the community—former city councilman, member of Jobs, Inc., on the zoning board, and so forth. In Fargo, the standard description was, "He's made a lot of money," with an added word about where or how he made it.

At about 5:30 p.m. the group dropped me at a hotel, saying they would pick me up for dinner at 6:30.

I expected there would be six of us for dinner—the five commissioners and myself. Instead, we drove to the country club, and after I was introduced to some of the commissioners' wives in the foyer, I was escorted into a private dining room where some twenty men were seated around a large table. I was introduced to all of them—bank presidents, merchants, the power company manager, attorneys, and another commission member.

During and after dinner, these men put more questions to me. To several of their questions I had to answer simply, "I don't know"—especially about matters peculiar to Fargo. It was necessary also to make clear that many of my responses were opinions only, since I lacked facts on which to make a sound judgment. By nine o'clock or so, they had pressed me for opinions on such a wide range of subjects that they and I were ready to call it quits. I bade them goodbye, with the hope that our day together had been of some value to them in their efforts to improve their city government. I did not expect to see them again.

Arrangements had been made for one of the commissioners to drive me to the hotel. Having been together much of the day, the commissioner and I were now on a first-name basis. As we started into town, Commissioner Toussaint asked, "Well, Roy, what do you think of our city?"

"I liked what I saw," I said, "but I get the impression you have some problems."

"Yes, I suppose we have. But I guess we're not much different from any other city on that score. Most cities have had to let things run down during the war, and now have to catch up. It's going to be painful, because I don't suppose people are going to want to pay for the things they demand."

I agreed.

There was a rather lengthy pause, then the commissioner said, "Roy, the other commissioners have authorized me to offer you the city manager position. This group you met tonight included almost all the important business leaders. They have agreed we should invite you to come here as our city manager."

Perhaps I should have suspected something like this from some of the questions asked during the day and the fact that they had assembled a group of business leaders for our evening meeting. But I was taken completely by surprise. I had gone to Fargo just as I had gone on invitation to a number of other cities to counsel with them about some of their problems. I was merely following a practice I had observed about most city officials, that they would drop whatever they were doing to try to help a fellow city official with a problem. My visit to Fargo had been part of this pattern.

I reiterated what I had told the mayor over the telephone, that I had no interest in a job change. We had a lot of exciting things going on in Albert Lea, my family was settled, and we were very happy there.

Commissioner Toussaint responded that he understood all that, but he wondered if from the point of view of my family and my own career I ought not to reconsider this opportunity. He pointed out that Fargo was a bigger city with bigger challenges than Albert Lea.

"It won't be easy," he said, "but we're willing to pay for that."

I felt uncomfortable with this turn of events. I had been in Albert Lea less than a year and a half. Most of the citizens and all the council members had been supportive and cordial. It never entered my mind that we would be at Albert Lea less than four or five years. We had bought a home and had settled into our neighborhood and church and civic activities with the expectation of being there a long time.

"Well, Roy, what salary would it take to get you to come?" the commissioner persisted.

I repeated what I had said during the day—not what it would take to get me or any other manager, but what I thought the job in a city Fargo's size and with Fargo's problems was worth. This figure was $10,000, two-thirds more than I was getting in Albert Lea. Commissioner Toussaint responded that he thought a man ought to expect to start out a little bit low. He continued to press me about my availability until I said I would consider the position if they would pay moving expenses in lieu of a $1,000 first-year difference and the city would go to $10,000 automatically at the end of one year.

He said, "I'm willing to accept your figure, and I think the other commissioners will, although it's a little higher than we expected to go."

We had a cordial parting at the hotel, and I went up to my room, to lie awake a couple of hours, wondering if I was doing the right thing to even consider a change.

Back in Albert Lea, Agda and I went over the whole matter in detail. We weighed the pros and cons as best we could. On the one hand, I disliked leaving a community that had been so good to us after such a short period of service. On the other hand, having four children, I could see good use for additional income, and I wondered if I turned down this opportunity whether another one as good would be available, even in five years. After several days of soul-searching we decided that if the offer came, we would accept it.

The first sign that the Fargo City Commission was prepared to offer me the appointment on the terms I had stated to Commissioner Toussaint was a call from the Fargo newspaper. The reporter wanted to know when I would start work in Fargo. I replied I had had no offer; therefore I had no comment. He said the commission had met and decided to offer me the position and again asked if I was going to accept. I declined to make a statement because it seemed to me out of order to publicly announce acceptance of a position I had not yet been offered. However, the next day I received a telegram from Mayor Charles Dawson saying they were offering me the job on terms previously discussed and asking when I could report for work.

On receipt of the mayor's telegram, I asked immediately for a meeting with the Albert Lea City Council and our city attorney and presented the matter to them. They were most generous in expressions of regret at our leaving but added their opinions that I should not pass up this opportunity.

I hoped we could make the change with a minimum of lost motion for Albert Lea. I knew that another man with much the same background as mine had been runnerup when I was appointed. He was now manager of a Chicago suburb. I suggested, therefore, that they might want to consider him in preference to going through a lengthy process of advertising the position, screening applicants, and making a choice. They accepted the suggestion and authorized me to offer him the position on their behalf. In short order, we had made arrangements for Warren Hyde to succeed me. He was able to come to Albert Lea for a few days of orientation. A month later he reported for work.

In addition to the support I received from the citizens and the city council, one of the highlights of my Albert Lea experience was the extraordinary help from the media—radio station KATE, owned and managed by former Mayor Ed Hayek; the *Community Magazine;* and especially the *Evening Tribune.* The newspaper fulfilled the pledge it had made editorially the day before I assumed office. At that time, the editor had written, in part:

"This newspaper would be turning its back on its duty to its readers and the community if it should beforehand pledge blind support to Mr. Harlow in all his designs and all his works. That it cannot do. We must continue in our role as watchdog of the public weal, as the saying goes, and as such we must be free to criticize when we feel it necessary to do so.

"But we can and do pledge him our full cooperation in conveying fairly to the public his views on all municipal affairs. As a newspaper that is perhaps the greatest contribution we can make towards the success we all want him to have. But also in other ways this newspaper stands ready to assist him.

"We sincerely hope Mr. Harlow will like Albert Lea and its people, that he will feel challenged by the city's problems, and that when the time comes he will tackle those problems with vigor."

The editor, Trygve Ager, covered many municipal activities in person. He was a quiet, thoughtful man, who confined his editorializing to the editorial page. His reporting of municipal affairs was so accurate in context, perspective, and emphasis that often after a council meeting, when Agda asked what had taken place, I replied, "Read the *Tribune* tomorrow. Tryg was there, and he'll have it all, exactly as it was."

The *Evening Tribune's* editorial of July 23, 1947, following the announcement of my resignation, was more generous than I deserved. But it did describe the kind of local government I believed then—and believe now—the people of America are entitled to from their public servants. This is the editorial:

THE EVENING TRIBUNE

Published Every Day Except Sunday by The
Albert Lea Publishing Company
Paul C. Belknap, Publisher

Established 1897
Entered as second class matter Nov. 1, 1893, at the post-office at Albert Lea, Minn., under Act of March 3, 1879.

The Associated Press is exclusively entitled to the use or re-publication of all news dispatches credited to it or not otherwise credited in this paper, and also the local news published herein. All right of republication as special dispatches herein are also reserved (July 25, 1917). Anonymous communications will be rejected.

Subscription Rates

Delivered by carrier salesman in Albert Lea:
One year, $13.00; Six months, $6.50; One week, 25c.
Delivered by mail in Freeborn and adjoining counties:
One year, $8.00; Six months, $4.50; Three months, $2.50; One month, $1.25.
Delivered by mail in all other zones:
One year, $10.00; Six months, $6.00; Three months, $3.00; One month, $1.25.
Single copies mailed to any address in United States 10c.
All Subscriptions payable in advance
Member Associated Press Audit Bureau of Circulation

A Bible Thought for the Day
Prov. 13:14: The law of the wise is a fountain of life, to depart from the snares of death.

—S—

Mr. Harlow's Resignation

Just as sick men call out for a surgeon to come and make them well so are cities all over our country summoning experts in administration to come and help them work their way out of political jungles and financial morasses. Such a call has now reached the ears of Le Roy F. Harlow, Albert Lea's city manager, and he has decided to respond.

Albert Lea isn't exactly free of municipal problems, either, and the incontrovertible fact is that we as a city could make good use of Mr. Harlow's keen abilities for at least another year or two. Therefore it is with deep regret that we accept the news of his decision to leave us.

More outstanding than anything else during the nearly seventeen months that Mr. Harlow has been active here has been the close cooperation between him and the city council. It has resulted in numerous significant forward strides—too many to mention here.

To the credit of Mayor Ostrander and the city councilmen it must be said they early developed respect for Mr. Harlow's extensive knowledge of municipal problems and his skill in coping with them, and they have consistently given sympathetic consideration to his recommendations. On Mr. Harlow's side the cooperation has been no less hearty. On those rare occasions when the council has acted counter to his recommendations he has unhesitatingly accepted the final verdict and carried out the council's wishes to the letter.

Mr. Harlow is especially well fitted for the painstaking tasks that await him in Fargo, a city which has only recently adopted the council-manager form of government and where municipal affairs are said to be "in a mess." Given the kind of cooperation from the Fargo city council that he has been receiving in Albert Lea he can be counted upon

to get the new system properly established and functioning smoothly.

Opponents of the council-manager form of city government like to resort to use of the word "dictator" in describing the man who heads up the city administration under that system, but so far as Mr. Harlow is concerned it would be almost impossible to find a more inappropriate term. He has an unshakable faith in democratic procedure and a profound respect for the will and wisdom of the people. Ever since his coming to Albert Lea he has demonstrated his faith by pursuing a policy of letting the public in on all the facts and by turning the full light of publicity on all problems of city government.

His procedure has always followed the fixed pattern: This, he says, is the situation; these are the facts; here is my recommendation; what are your wishes in the matter?

Summing it all up it can be said that Albert Leans have for seventeen months been treated to a demonstration of democracy efficiently at work, and that's as good a definition of the council-manager form of government as we know of.

It is because we dislike seeing this work interrupted that the announcement of Mr. Harlow's resignation evokes regret. And yet, in all fairness, we cannot begrudge Mr. Harlow this chance to better himself financially, and particularly the chance to test his skill and knowledge against the more difficult problems of a larger city.

Our guess is that even Fargo will have trouble in holding onto him for any great length of time. He seems marked for even bigger and more challenging tasks.

Before he leaves Albert Lea he will lay before the council a proposed budget for 1948. That budget is certain to contain many an important recommendaion that will deserve the careful study of the council and the public alike. It will represent an advanced phase of Mr. Harlow's program for improving and revitalizing the city government's services to the people. It will also represent the wants of the people as they have made known since adoption of the 1947 budget.

"Serving you—the taxpayer" has been Mr. Harlow's motto from the beginning, and it has become the motto of all departments in the city administration. Never once has he betrayed it. He has worked from early in the morning till late at night, always giving the best that was in him to his job. Certainly his diligence is deserving of the recognition and reward that has come to him, and his advancement should serve as an inspiration to other public servants, be their present duties big or small.

It's still too early to say goodbye to Mr. Harlow—thank goodness! But we do say: Congratulations!

Fargo, North Dakota

Welcome to Fargo

After the end of World War II the businessmen of Fargo organized the Greater Fargo Association and got the voters to adopt what the brief, two-page state law called the "City Manager Plan" of city government. The new government became effective May 13, 1947.

Although Fargo had had a city manager for a short time, the city government had reverted to the commission form before I was appointed. Charles A. Dawson, an independent insurance executive, was serving as fire and police commissioner and mayor; E. E. Simonson, a banker, was finance commissioner; Fred C. Hagen, a department store shoe manager, was water commissioner; and the other departments were assigned to William H. Toussaint, a former county agent now active in farm loans and insurance, and to Leo C. O'Brien, a Western Union Telegraph Company manager and an active member of the Junior Chamber of Commerce.

I reported for work on September 19. On September 23 the board of city commissioners addressed a letter to the heads of all city departments and offices. Signed by all five commissioners, it read as follows:

"The board of city commissioners has appointed Mr. LeRoy F. Harlow to the position of city manager. Upon his assuming office on September 19, 1947, the administrative control of all departments and offices, which control has heretofore been exercised by the several members of the board of city commissioners, was transferred from the board to the city manager. . . .

"We ask that matters affecting the administration of the affairs of your department be taken up hereafter with Mr. Harlow rather than with the individual members of the commission.

"The board of city commissioners will serve as the policy-making body of the city government and will continue its keen interest in administration of departmental affairs, working through the office of the city manager."

"Unavoidably Detained"

I called our first full staff meeting for 9:00 a.m., November 1, and all the department heads arrived promptly except Police Chief Lloyd Jester. We waited about ten minutes for him, then began. He came in a few minutes later, explaining that an important matter had come up requiring his immediate attention.

I used the meeting for two purposes: one, to give our key people my views on the importance of city service and their jobs in our community; and, two, to forewarn them of some possible realignment of offices and departments and some procedural changes. I asked for their suggestions and cooperation and informed them we would probably meet rather frequently the first few months—perhaps weekly—in order to coordinate our efforts during the period of change.

A few days after that first staff meeting, I happened to meet one of the commissioners on the street. In the course of the conversation he asked, "How are you getting along with Jester?"

I responded that things were going all right and inquired how he happened to ask that question. He said the first manager had had a little problem because Jester came late to the meetings and the manager had objected.

At the next staff meeting after everyone had arrived and to avoid singling out anyone in particular, I asked that all try to be on time thereafter. I pointed out that there were fifteen of us at the meeting, and if we had to wait only ten minutes we were wasting the equivalent of more than two hours of one person's time. But my soft sell was not very effective. The police chief continued to come late to the staff meetings and often left early on the excuse that he had to take care of some pressing matters.

Spelling It Out

Because of the brevity of the state law concerning the city manager plan—quite unlike Albert Lea's carefully drafted and comprehensive city charter—I took two steps to flesh it out into a workable basis for operations. First, I asked the city attorney to draft an opinion for the state attorney general's approval, spelling out in more detail how the plan of government was to function, and second, I used the model city charter of the National Municipal League as a guide in other details. The attorney general issued an opinion in the exact form drafted by the city attorney. His opinion plus the state law and the model charter were the bases for my next move to carry out the program I understood the city commission had in mind—reorganizing the structure of city government.

My analysis of our organizational structure and operations revealed essentially the same problems we had had in Albert

Lea—too broad a span of control after the administrative responsibilities were transferred from five commissioners to one city manager; unbalanced workloads; and some illogical groupings of departments, probably based on the preferences and interests of individual commissioners rather than on standard and proven organizational principles.

On May 13 I submitted a reorganization plan to the city commission. The plan reduced the number of people reporting to the city manager from about 13 to the heads of nine departments: fire, police, public works, water, sewers, airport, health, law, and finance.

The city commission unanimously adopted a resolution establishing the office of the city manager and the nine departments. The resolution did not describe the divisions within the departments because the commissioners said they did not wish to concern themselves with organizational arrangements below the department level. I spelled out the divisional structure and responsibilities in the annual budget message, and also prepared a pictorial organization chart showing departments and divisions, which was distributed throughout the city organization and to the public.

By letter to each department head I delegated to them authority to appoint and remove all employees within their departments, subject where applicable to Civil Service rules.

Taxes Are Not for Tippling

One of the chores the commissioners were glad to turn over to me was the monthly auditing of "claims against the city"—bills, most of which were from outside vendors, but some of which were reimbursement claims from employees. Under state law with the commission form of government, every claim had to be examined and approved in writing by the commissioners. Inevitably, the task was handled in a perfunctory manner, partly because the part-time commissioners could not be fully informed about the minutiae of departmental operations and thus were in no position to judge the correctness or propriety of most of the claims.

This responsibility had required several hours of their time every month. They would stop in at the commission chamber at odd times, when they could get away from their offices and places of work for an hour or so. Sitting at the commission table, often talking about other matters, they would go through

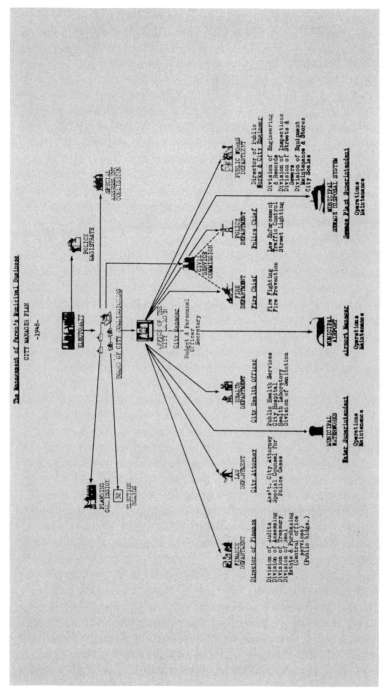

The Management of Fargo's Municipal Business

CITY MANAGER PLAN
-1948-

Organization chart, City of Fargo, North Dakota, 1948.

a tall stack of claims, now and then examining one but more often simply glancing at a document, signing it, and going to the next. I sensed that in addition to disliking having to take the time for this legal chore they had worried a little at signing their approval of so many things they were not sure about.

The first time I audited the bills, I came on a simple one-sentence request from the chief of police for $300 to reimburse him for expenses of his attending a conference of the International Association of Chiefs of Police in Duluth, Minnesota. There was no detailing of the item as required by law; furthermore, the amount seemed excessive for five days, at a nearby location (these were 1949 figures).

I asked the Chief to give me a breakdown of the $300, which he did in a memorandum dated October 28, 1947. He listed mileage, hotel, and conference charges. Included in the latter was "Entertainment, as chairman, North Dakota, IACP — $112.50." I asked him what was included in the entertainment item, and he explained that it was for liquor and snacks, adding that it was necessary to throw this kind of a party for the other police chiefs around the country so he could count on their cooperation on cases. I responded that it was hard for me to believe that this was necessary to gain the cooperation of other police departments on professional business, that in any case I was going to seek commission policy on this kind of use of city funds.

I did ask the commission to meet informally in my office, and I presented the situation to them. I said I would carry out their policy if this practice seemed appropriate to them, but in my judgment the administration would be in serious trouble if it became publicly known that taxpayers' funds were being used to purchase liquor. They were emphatic in their reaction: It was their policy *not* to use city funds for this purpose. They directed me to pay the chief what he claimed this time but to make plain to him that this was not to happen again. I did as instructed and informed the chief of the commission's stated policy.

"I Meant to Pay it Back. . . ."

During my college years and after, when I was trying to get a foothold in city management, I occasionally read or heard of a local official being sentenced to prison for some misdeed. Later, it came close to home when I learned that a streets superintendent I had known slightly while working for the city of Ames was in prison for padding payrolls, and also when an auditor for the federal Social Security Board, with whom I officed in Nebraska, told me his experience—that on the average, in a state with 100 counties you could expect that every year at least one county official would be discovered misusing public funds and probably would be sentenced to the penitentiary.

In small governments, where officials run one-man offices, it is especially easy for this kind of activity to go undetected. But even in larger places there are numerous situations where controls are lax and opportunities for dishonest activity may tempt people so inclined. For instance, a street superintendent who hires a lot of casual labor, sends in a weekly payroll, and later in the week picks up the checks to give to the men at quitting time can be tempted to add a few names to the list. Or a treasurer, short of personal cash, can borrow temporarily from the till, fully intending to replace the money soon. He does it once; it was so easy he's tempted to do it again when things get tough. It's only a matter of time until he's caught, maybe five or even ten years later. Occasionally, the official himself will bring the situation to a conclusion—with a bullet in his brain.

When I became a city manager, I tried to build in procedures that might at least reduce, if they could not eliminate, the temptations and the ease of padding payrolls and of "borrowing" money and city equipment. I took such steps in Fargo.

My devices were not so sophisticated as those now available. For example, to avoid payroll padding I required all employees to make out a job application with a person centrally responsible for personnel administration. This can be a part-time responsibility of a clerk, and it gets a record on each employee that can be checked against the payrolls submitted by the departments.

More important, at irregular intervals and without notice, I would walk into the finance office on payday morning and instruct the finance director to have one of his assistants take the checks to a particular department and personally hand out the checks to the persons listed on the payroll. Checks not issued were to be brought back to the finance department and held until called for by the payee in person.

This second practice was awkward and bothersome. All crew members had to come in off the job, and the finance department lost the services of a person for perhaps half a day. But it was done only once or twice a year, and the time lost seemed to me worthwhile.

Instead of an annual financial audit made after the close of the fiscal year, I have preferred to put the outside auditors on a retainer basis so that they can come in at any time and conduct a partial audit. I think they are likely to do a more thorough job, and the cost may not be much greater, if any.

As to loss of public equipment and supplies, clear, nonerasable markings, an inventory control system with periodic physical counts, a central storeroom, and strict prohibition against private and personal use of public property—except for designated emergency purposes—are helpful.

All in an Arbitrator's Day

There was much less cohesiveness and cooperation within the Fargo city government than in Albert Lea. Perhaps this was attributable to Fargo's being a larger city and the fragmentation and compartmentalization of autonomous units characteristic of the commission form of government, or perhaps simply to the personalities who were with the city while I was there. Whatever the reason, I was involved frequently in trying to resolve interdepartmental tension and conflict. Although the employees' advisory council worked well together once they became acquainted, they were unable to generate interest in having all-employee parties and picnics and gave up trying. Their principal contribution—that gained general support—was studying and comparing several group hospitalization plans, then making recommendations to the employees.

One example of an effort to share responsibility and to develop teamwork evolved out of a major fire in the downtown area. The fire started in a multistoried building at an hour when there were a great number of shoppers crowding the streets. Their presence created a severe traffic problem, preventing fire trucks from being strategically located.

The fire and police departments had been under the same commissioner and were accustomed to cooperating in setting up barricades and rerouting traffic during the first hours of a fire. However, the fire department was unable to completely extinguish this particular fire during the night. They still had nearly a block barricaded off when the stores started to open in the morning.

The police department began to receive complaints from

business places in the same block. They wanted the plank barricades and ropes removed so that customers could reach their doors. The police department suggested to the fire department that since the fire was under control the size of the restricted area could be reduced. The fire chief said no. He wanted his men to have all the room they needed for maneuvering equipment, particularly if they had to respond to another call. Moreover, he pointed out that although the building was gutted the walls were still standing and were a major hazard.

The two chiefs were unable to settle the question and brought it to me. Although basically they wanted to cooperate, each felt so strongly about his own position that neither felt able to give in to the other.

After listening to the two sides—one for untying traffic and the other for maneuvering fire equipment and keeping watch on the hazardous wall—it seemed to me an element had been overlooked, namely the engineering aspects. Just what were the chances that the wall would collapse? If it did, what would be the radius of the hazard? From a building safety and building economy standpoint, would the replacement building use the old walls, or would they have to be taken down? How long would either pedestrian or vehicular traffic be restricted by the existence of the destroyed building?

These were technical questions. In addition, I hoped we could use this occasion to make a policy decision, so that if in the future we faced a similar situation we would know who was going to do what. I called two other officials into our discussion, the city engineer and the building inspector. After outlining the current specific situation for them, I added that I hoped we could arrive at a policy and a procedure to handle future emergencies of this kind.

The engineer and building inspectors surveyed the situation and gave us their judgments on the nature and extent of the hazard to the public. Barricades were adjusted accordingly.

Out of this meeting, we eventually developed a policy. Thereafter, at the start of a fire and as long as it was raging, the fire department had complete authority to determine what areas it wanted blocked off and what traffic lanes it wanted kept open. The police department would comply promptly and fully. When, in the judgment of the fire chief, the fire was under control and offered no danger to nearby property, the fire department would relinquish its authority over the area. Normally, at this time the police department would take over and decide the location of barricades and direction of traffic movements; however, if the fire was under control but in the judgment of the public works director a hazard to the general public from a weakened structure existed, his department would have authority and would assume responsibility for barricading, enclosing, or otherwise securing the hazardous area. Finally, when the fire was under control and no unusual building hazards remained, but there was need for additional, semipermanent barricades, the police department would designate the restricted area and the location of barricades. The public works department would set the semipermanent barricades and leave them in place until requested by the police department to remove them.

Bite the Bullet, Borrow, or Save?

Perhaps it was because he was an insurance executive that Charles Dawson was appalled at the age and condition of the fire department's equipment he found when he became fire commissioner and mayor. (The first thing I remember seeing in his business office was this powerful message: "We don't insure ashes.") Replacement of fire equipment was high on the mayor's "catching up" list.

Before I went to Fargo, the commission had started to modernize the fire department. Among other things, they ordered a new aerial ladder truck to replace the nearly thirty-year-old hook-and-ladder unit still equipped with fragile, wooden ladders. Delivery time on the new unit was eighteen to twenty-four months, and it cost about $30,000.

Tragically, before the new aerial truck was delivered, a young fireman was killed in the line of duty. The unfortunate accident was traceable to the financial dilemma Fargo faced, along with many other cities, and which we tried to correct, at least in part.

The circumstances of the fireman's death were these: The wooden extension ladder was so old, weak, and brittle that the fire chief was afraid to put a man on it. But the department needed some way to fight multistory fires. They rigged a hose to the wooden aerial, with the nozzle at the top end. In this way they could raise the hose several stories high and play water on a fire from that position.

One weekend a severe fire broke out in a major warehouse and truck storage building. In desperate need of all the firefighting force they could mobilize, the department moved in the old ladder truck with the hose attached. They ran it up its full length to hit the fire from above, but the hose got tangled. They sent the young fireman aloft to free the line. At the moment he reached the top of the ladder, a sudden change in water pressure sent a surge through the hose. It whipped the ladder backwards, breaking it off some 10 feet from the top. Down came ladder piece, hose, and man, hurtling fifty feet to the ground. The young fireman was dead on arrival at the hospital.

It was a sad duty the mayor and I had, calling on the bereaved widow and the brave young fireman's grim-faced mother to express the community's regrets and condolences.

The financial dilemma was part of the question that is as old as taxes: Who pays, and when? To modernize a fire department all at once is costly business. The cost of the one aerial ladder truck was equal to about one mill on the tax rate, other needed equipment might total two or three mills.

To add that much to a tax bill in one year might well be political suicide for elected officials. But how do you pay for such equipment when it is needed? In general, there are three choices. One is the pay-as-you-go method. In this, you "bite the bullet" and raise the tax rate (assuming there is not a state or charter-imposed tax rate ceiling that makes the increase illegal). A second choice is to borrow the money to pay for the capital equipment, either through a bond issue where the amount of interest is known or through installment payments where the interest is hidden in the cost. The third way is to accumulate a reserve by small amounts over a period of time, so that when a piece of equipment must be replaced the city has part or all of the cost on hand.

Each alternative has its good points and its bad points. For example, pay-as-you-go avoids the cost of interest that a bond issue requires and gets the money from current users or beneficiaries of the new capital equipment. But it imposes a sudden, large tax increase on the current taxpayers and lets future users and beneficiaries escape paying a share of the cost. On the other hand, the building of a reserve saves interest cost (in fact, it can be invested and can earn interest) and avoids a sudden jump in the tax rate. But it takes the money from taxpayers who may never get the benefit of the items purchased with their taxes, and it deprives them of money they might invest for their own benefit. Perhaps the worst feature of the reserve approach is a practical political one: few politicians are willing to put an extra tax burden on the voting public with nothing to show for it, especially if it means building up a reserve of money that a later administration can spend and then take credit for the improvement. This is expecting too much altruism and public understanding. But we tried it.

North Dakota's cities were prohibited by state law from carrying money forward from one year to the next. To get an exception to this, we drafted a new statute for legislative consideration. The State Legislature passed the new law, permitting a city to accumulate a cash reserve to purchase fire equipment. The amount of the annual contribution to the reserve was determined when a major piece of equipment was purchased. The estimated salvage value was subtracted from the cost. This net cost was then divided by the number of years of estimated life of the equipment. The quotient from this calculation was the amount to be placed in the reserve each year for the estimated life of the equipment. Under the law, money could be spent out of the reserve only for new fire equipment.

Had the city of Fargo had such a cash reserve at the time its old hook-and-ladder became too dangerous to put a man on, they probably could have replaced the unit. And two Fargo families might still have a husband, father, and son.

Little Things Can Mean a Lot

I doubt that many citizens are aware of the devotion to a job that can be found in city government service. It may be found in any department but is especially characteristic of workers in the public safety and public works and utilities departments, so critical to the existence and functioning of a community. Men and women in these unnoticed, humble jobs sometimes have a dedication to efficiency and economy that approaches missionary zeal. One such public servant was superintendent of our sewage disposal plant.

The plant was out on an open plain a mile or more north of town. On my first visit I was impressed by how spotlessly clean the entire plant and grounds were. As the superintendent showed me around, I noticed that the lighting was dim in several corridors. There were bulbs, but they were not all burning. I asked if they were burned out. No, the superintendent replied, he had merely unscrewed them to save electricity. If more light was needed to do cleaning or maintenance work, the men would screw them back in.

The plant included several sections at various locations. There was the pump station and settling basin at one location, filtration beds at another, and so on. Going from the main pump house to the filtration building, we had to walk across some seventy-five feet of open space.

I asked the superintendent how many men he had on the night shift and how often the men on night shift had to cross this open space on their rounds.

He replied that during the winter months they needed only one man at night, and he made hourly rounds.

"Is that man in touch with any other city office during his tour of duty?" I asked.

"No," he answered.

"Isn't there some danger that a man might fall down the stairwell in the pump house, or be overcome with gas? Or he might stumble or have an accident crossing this open space during a blizzard. If anything like that happened, how would he get help?"

"Frankly, I never thought of that possibility."

Thinking about it a moment more, I asked, "How would you feel about putting a covered passageway between the two buildings?"

"Oh, I'm afraid that would be too expensive."

"How much do you think it would cost?"

Based on the distance to be covered, and assuming a tile structure to match the buildings, the superintendent gave me a quick estimate. It would run some thousands of dollars.

"Instead of building a structure," I suggested, "what would you think of simply laying two or three lengths of large steel culvert pipe from door to door. It doesn't make much difference how it looks. What we're interested in is providing safe and protected passage for you and the men as you pass between buildings during North Dakota winters. Will you look into the cost of doing it that way?"

He said he would get a figure for me.

Then I offered another suggestion.

"What do you say we make arrangements with the police department to have your night man call the department about every hour? If your man doesn't call in, the department can have a patrol car check on him."

This, too, was agreeable.

We instituted the call-in system the next day. And within a week the superintendent had figures on an above-ground tunnel.

It would cost a fraction of what a tile structure would cost. We agreed to go ahead with it; his men would do the work.

As insignificant as these suggestions were, and as unattractive as the corrugated steel culvert pipe was, I felt relieved of another "what-if" tension whenever I passed the disposal plant thereafter.

New Board, New Problems

A few weeks after my appointment in September 1947, the banker member of the city commission resigned because of the press of private business. The remaining commission members appointed Oscar Kjorlie, another leading businessman and highly regarded member of the Fargo community, to fill out the banker-commissioner's term. This continued the 4-1 majority on the commission from the Greater Fargo Association, the businessmen's "party" in the nonpartisan political alignment.

As the April 6, 1948, election drew near, ads began to appear for James P. Dunn, credit manager for a local plumbing firm, and Sam Dahlgren, a naturopath. The ads were sponsored by Fargo Taxpayer Friends and spotlighted the growing city budgets. The ads asked:

"Has your income gone up 29% in the last two years? Don't you think the city's budget should be based on the taxpayers' ability to pay? Don't you have to base your own budget on your income?"

Over the radio, Mr. Dunn and Mr. Dahlgren added this complaint: "I'm tired of two-toned whistles and white gloves in the police department. I hope you're tired of them, too."

When the votes were counted, businessman Kjorlie and Junior Chamber of Commerce man O'Brien were out. The 4-1 majority of Greater Fargo Association representatives and those who favored the council-manager plan had become the 2-3 minority. Although commission votes were often unanimous, the political and philosophical lineup was Dawson and Toussaint versus Dahlgren, Dunn and Hagen.

The two new commissioners were suspicious of all that was going on in City Hall. They went back over old vouchers showing city payments to vendors. They rode with police officers on patrol, a practice that irritated the police chief. They joined Commissioner Hagen in asking for a variety of detailed information about both the general administration of the city, the operation of departments, and the performance of individual employees.

Three weeks after the election and the change in the composition and philosophy of the commission, I sent a letter to each of the five commissioners, suggesting a meeting at an early date "to discuss informally the relationship between the governing body and the city manager . . . in order that there may be complete understanding of the function of each."

I pointed out in the letter that North Dakota was not a "home rule" state and, therefore, the city manager plan was not fully and clearly set out in a single document.

I added, "In order that the city government may operate within the spirit of the council-manager plan, which was adopted by the voters in 1946, the impartial Model City Charter of the National Municipal League is being used as a guide wherever necessary. In addition, the attorney general has been consulted on some questions. A copy of one impartial opinion of the attorney general is attached because the information contained therein may be helpful to the members of the commission, and you may want to have a copy on hand. Copies of the Model City Charter are on file in the city manager's office."

Only Commissioner Dunn responded to my letter. On one of his numerous visits to my office, when I asked him about having the meeting I had suggested, he said, "We can have that meeting any time." But the meeting was never held.

Why Annexation?

The city of Fargo could not escape the annexation issue. Walled in on the east by the Red River, an adjacent state, and a rival city; with the municipal airport northwest of town; and with the bulk of highway traffic moving east and west on U.S. Highway 10, there was only one direction for Fargo's industrial development to go. That was to the west, where the two transcontinental railroads that passed through the city crossed each other.

The city had cooperated with the Chamber of Commerce-sponsored Fargo Industrial Development Corporation to assemble dozens of scattered parcels of property into a single tract. This tract was the foundation of an industrial park on the west side. And the city and the FIDC had succeeded in getting the Great Northern and the Northern Pacific railroads to start constructing an interchange track to facilitate movement of cars between the two.

Already an unplanned, unsightly, and uneconomic ribbon development was strung along Highway 10 to the west, beyond the city limit. Red Owl Food Stores of Hopkins, Minnesota, the state Wool Growers Association, and other firms were establishing warehouses and other facilities outside the city. The city government had to act or watch its economic lifeblood drained by parasitic fringe developments. But to suggest annexation was to embark on a rough journey, over many political roadblocks and legal hurdles.

Annexation is a complex and controversial subject. It pits against each other two directly opposite points of view—that of property owners, and sometimes renters, who want to have property near a city but not in a city and that of city officials who see a need for their city to expand its boundaries to reduce present problems and avoid future problems.

With the occasional exception of planning authority and control of water shed or milk shed areas, a city's jurisdiction rarely extends beyond its own boundaries. For instance, a city does not have law enforcement power beyond its own boundaries (except if police are in "hot pursuit" of a suspect). Even if a city is adversely affected socially, economically, and politically by what goes on in the surrounding unincorporated area or in a neighboring municipality with which it has a common boundary, it cannot levy taxes, administer elections, or enforce police, building, plumbing, or electrical codes beyond its borders.

In some states a city may reach out and annex territory merely by ordinance or resolution. In others, annexation proposals are subject to decision by special commissions. Perhaps the most common arrangement is to require approval of a majority of the voters of both the city and the territory proposed for annexation. In this last arrangement the law gives veto power to the voters in the unincorporated area. In the past, some state laws even permitted one city to "lasso" another city by annexing a strip around the other city, thereby foreclosing it from annexing territory outside its boundaries.

Although some may quarrel with the following brief presentation, I believe it is a reasonably accurate description of the points of view not only of the businesses and individuals who locate outside of city limits but also of city officials.

A business may locate outside a city to avoid traffic problems. For example, freight truck lines frequently have their terminals in the unincorporated areas. This enables them to acquire relatively cheap land for their sprawling warehouses and parking areas. Their huge tractor-trailer combines can get on and off the highways without going through congested intown traffic. This benefits the city, too, by reducing the traffic congestion the trucks would otherwise create.

Other businesses may also locate outside the city to reduce their own problems and by so doing are a help to the city. Examples are the nuisance industries—those with smoke, odors, and noise, as well as traffic. These businesses choose to be outside the city for convenience and safety and to avoid trouble with their neighbors. Their first consideration is not avoidance of regulation, taxes, and general community responsibility that goes with being inside the city.

For other firms, however, the decision may be a self-centered, economic one. By locating outside, they get cheaper land. (City land is usually higher because of proximity to built-up areas and existing improvements such as streets, sewers, water, and the like.) They escape city taxes, too,—an advantage over their competitors inside the city. (The advantage is not total, because local taxes are deductible from state and federal income taxes.) Also, they may save on building and operating costs by avoiding city building, plumbing, electrical and fire codes, and land-use regulations. This latter advantage probably is the factor of greatest concern to city officials.

Similar economic reasons motivate the housing developer who puts up homes outside the city and the people who buy outside the city. The city may set a minimum for lot sizes and street widths. It may require a developer to reserve a portion of his property for park and playground use. Before it will accept a subdivision plat, it may require the developer to put in streets, street lights, drainage, sewers, and utilities before he sells a lot.

In the unincorporated area, the developer may escape all this. He may be free to put on his land as many houses as he can find room for. Unless the local government with jurisdiction over the unincorporated area—usually a county—has and enforces a building code, the builder may be able to build with narrower footings, shallower foundations, greater distance between wall studdings and floor and ceiling joists, and cheaper materials. The electrical wiring, too, may be lower grade if he doesn't have to meet a city electrical code. He may even skip the kitchen and bathroom vents that a city plumbing code would require. Not all builders will cut this many corners, but some have done every one of the things just mentioned. Outside the house, if the developer can leave off the costs of drainage ditches and pipe, street grading and surfacing, the sidewalks, playgrounds, and other conveniences to the purchasers of his houses, he can sell for less than his competitor in the city.

The do-it-yourself carpenter-plumber-electrician who builds where there are no regulations has the same advantage over the city home builder or purchaser as the developer enjoys.

Frequently, businessmen and builders who oppose annexation for the reasons we have just seen are joined in their opposition by farmers, ranchers, and officials of adjacent local governments.

The farmers and ranchers know that historically city land has been valued higher than agricultural land. They fear their land will be reassessed and their tax bills will increase astronomically.

The governing bodies of adjacent rural school districts, special drainage districts, and the like fear that the city will so gerrymander the boundaries of the annexed territory that high value properties will be taken into the city, leaving the local unit deprived of a major part of its tax base. Where the units whose territory is being considered for annexation have long-term debt, both the people in the city and the officials outside may become concerned. The city people will want to know if they are going to have to assume debt for facilities they have never benefitted from; the special district people will fear being left with the total debt but a greatly reduced tax base to meet the debt payments.

Turning from the reasons businessmen and home builders may locate outside the city limits, let's see how the same picture looks to the city officials. First, there is the simple question of fair play. They may view the businessman, developer, or do-it-yourselfer as a kind of parasite—one who wants all the advantages that a city provides but is unwilling to pay a proportionate share of the cost. They note, for example, that if the people were sincere in their allegations that they get no advantages from the city they would locate many miles from the city. But they don't; they snuggle as close to the city as they can without getting across the line that makes them liable for city taxes and subject to city regulations.

City officials observe that these close "neighbors" add to the traffic, health, and even sometimes crime problems the city is continuously wrestling with. They see them also using the parks and playgrounds, enjoying city-sponsored and managed cultural activities, and depending on the expensive city airport, without paying what the city taxpayers pay for these conveniences and privileges. The city officials feel this because their voters are pressuring them for better service at less cost, while some of what the city officials have to spend money for is services for nonresidents.

Then there is the problem of double taxation. People living in the city have to pay the same taxes to the county as the people living in the unincorporated area of the county. These city residents pay for their own services with city taxes; at the same time, part of what they pay to the county goes for services the county gives to people living in the unincorporated area but which the county does not give to residents of the city. Since city officials are often blamed for the total tax bill paid by their voters, they get the blame for the double taxation.

The city officials watch business and industry locate or relocate outside the city and take with them, of course, part of the tax base. They compare what is happening in their city with what happened in other cities that failed to act in time to stop the drain of their tax base and self-supporting citizens. They see the handwriting on the wall. It points not only to the filling up of the vacant land surrounding the city with new industrial plants, commercial establishments, and homes, but also to the spread of blight, vacancies, and social problems within their own boundaries.

Next, they see these outside areas nearly as thickly populated as the city. They know that some of the people outside will eventually start agitation for some kind of government. A few will want it to protect the majority from the thoughtless and inconsiderate acts of the few in the community who think they should still have the independence they had when the unrestricted area was first settled. Others will want fire and police protection, sewers instead of septic tanks, and a dependable water supply.

They also know that likely a business leader or a delegation from the unincorporated area will one day approach the city with what to them seems a fair and generous proposition. They will offer, for example, to pay the city a substantial amount, maybe $300 to $400 a run, if the city will extend its fire protection service to the unincorporated area. To guarantee the city payment, they will offer to have a rider put on their insurance policies. Then, if a home or business is destroyed and there are no resources or inclination to pay, the insurance company will pay the city.

These neighbors from just across the city limits will ignore the important fact that over the years the city taxpayers have paid for the fire stations, the several pieces of $20,000 to $50,000 equipment, and the water system; that each year the city taxpayers have paid several hundreds of thousands (maybe millions) of dollars in salaries and other expenses to maintain the fire department, and that now the neighbors want to "rent" on a pay-as-used basis. The neighbors close their minds to the fact that there would be no trained, equipped fire department to fight anyone's fires if over the years the city taxpayers had said what the people in the unincorporated area are now saying: "I'm not going to pay anything for a fire department. Why should I? I may never need it. If I have a fire, I'll pay then, and gladly; but why should I pay if I don't have a fire?"

The city officials know that if they reject such an offer they probably will be accused of being unneighborly or uncooperative. Worse yet, to reject this offer and also give notice that there will be no fire service outside the city limits unless the beneficiaries of that service pay their full share along with everyone else is viewed as unconscionable by nonresidents and also by some residents. The officials may have learned that in a calm discussion of city financial problems, double taxation, and annexation, local taxpayers may agree it is unfair for anyone to deliberately locate outside the city—perhaps just across the city limit line—to escape city taxes and expect the city to respond in case of fire. But in an emergency, when they see a man's house burning down across the street from the city limit line and the city fire department standing by and doing nothing, they are likely to expect—or demand—that the city officials make an "exception."

City officials know that if outside development continues to the time when the residents in the unincorporated area must have city services and must choose between forming their own municipality or annexing to an existing city to get them the situation may have gone too far. By then it is too late to have streets that are wide enough, that don't dead-end where they ought not to, that line up with other streets, and that are soundly constructed from the base to the surface. By then the area asking for annexation will have streets and drainage systems that were built just to "get by." Lots will be small, and houses will be crowded next to one another. The houses may be below safe standards. Second purchasers might not know what went into the construction and might inherit sagging floors and ceilings, bathrooms that hold odors, and wiring that can't carry the load.

This was the situation we faced in Fargo. Instead of being ahead of the oncoming problems, we were getting farther and farther beind. So we initiated annexation proceedings. We were taken into court. I presented maps that showed the city's annexations had been well within the limits prescribed by law, that they were reasonable, and that the current proposal did not single out high value areas and leave a small school district with an inadequate tax base. I argued for a "balanced" community, for permission to zone so that the area would not be so scrambled we could never get it right again, for discontinuation of the flight of valuation from the city, and the elimination of unfair competition. Above all, I argued, we are all part of the same economic and social community.

The court approved our annexation proposal.

How Does Your City Serve You? Let's Count the Ways

I don't know if Mayor Dawson and the other commissioners included a citywide reappraisal of property on their list of what Fargo needed to "catch up" after World War II. But a discussion with the city assessor and a brief review of assessment figures showed that assessments had not increased at the same rate as the market. This was especially true of land values.

A comprehensive reappraisal of the thousands of parcels of property in even a small city is a large undertaking. Consequently, cities often engage outside appraisal specialists who have the time, as well as the broad experience, objectivity, and expertise to do the job. I felt we should have such a reappraisal in Fargo to bring our figures in line with changes in market value and the value relationships among various properties. I hoped to get public backing for the project.

I thought a widely advertised public meeting to discuss property assessments might give us a feel for our major problem areas and might also provide the hoped-for support for engaging out-of-town professional appraisers. We held the meeting. It did not do all I had hoped it might, but it provided me an opportunity to draw some public attention to what the citizens were getting for their city taxes. It also produced complaints from a source I would not have expected.

The assessor announced through the press and radio that on a certain night, at a well-known meeting hall, he would hear all citizens who had objections to their assessments. At the appointed time nearly a hundred people showed up. Notable by their absence were the substantial property owners, those with large commercial and industrial holdings. I never knew whether this meant they thought they were getting a break and had better not stir up the waters or that the meeting was meaningless and nothing could be done. They may simply have been disinterested. In any case, almost everyone at the meeting was an individual home owner.

The assessor gave a brief introductory talk, outlining the steps he went through to arrive at an assessed value for a property. He explained that his office had a separate card for each property. The cards carried detailed information, with land and improvements shown separately.

He said since land values were determined primarily by location and land use he assigned various front values to each parcel of land. If the land was near high-value areas, it was assigned a higher front-foot value than if it was farther from a high-value area. If the property was zoned for commercial use, it had a higher value than if zoned for residential use. If it was located at the corner of a block instead of in or near the center, a percentage of value was added for "corner influence," and so forth.

He said all buildings had been measured, and the square and cubic footage was recorded on the card. The type of construction was also shown—frame, brick, stucco, or other. Additional items of value—extra bathrooms, fireplaces—were recorded. He said he assigned a unit value for each type of construction, multiplied this unit value by the number of square or cubic feet in the building, added an amount for extras, and arrived at a value for the improvements.

He explained that the total real value of land and improvements was not the assessment on the property, that he applied an "assessment ratio" to the actual value so that the assessed value was about 50% of the actual full and true market value.

He acknowledged the difficulty of being absolutely fair and invited the taxpayers to review the books if they felt they were not as well treated as their neighbors. He promised to discuss with them the reasons for differences, such as cubic footage, number and value of extras, depreciation of older, larger buildings, and the like.

Knowing that many of the people there came to complain about their taxes, not just their assessments, he closed his remarks by explaining how the tax bill was determined. He made clear he had nothing to do with how much tax money the city got. His job was only to see that every taxable property in town was on record. The amount of taxes they paid was the assessed valuation he set multiplied by the tax rate set by the city commission.

He did a good job. He was careful, accurate, and pleasant. When he completed his explanation, there was a moment of quiet talk in various places among the group. Then one man put up his hand.

"My taxes are too high," he said. "With the cost of everything going up, four kids in school and a sick wife, I just can't afford it. Now you tell me you don't have anything to do with taxes. *Somebody* must have something to do with them, because they've sure been going up. Every year they get bigger. We've got to put a stop to this somewhere. That's why we're here; to get some relief."

The assessor looked at me. It was obvious he preferred that I respond to the gentleman.

I said, "I suppose we all feel the same way. I don't like to pay taxes either. But as long as you and I insist that the city do things for us, we have to pay for those services. You said, 'The cost of everything is going up.' That's right. And the city's costs are going up, too. We have to pay more for help than we used to, and practically everything we buy has gone up—cars, trucks, asphalt, typewriters, chemicals, uniforms, paper, and paper clips—everything."

"Well, if that's the case, we'd better quit having so much service. In fact, I don't know that I'm getting any service from the city. I never see a policeman, unless I park my car over time."

This brought vigorous nodding of heads.

Spurred by this support, he went on excitedly. "Just what are we getting for our taxes? You talk about service. All it seems to me we get are demands from the city: Shovel your walks! Turn off your water! Don't park here! Pay your taxes, or we'll penalize you! Where are all these services you talk about?"

The man had triggered the crowd. They were getting angry, ready to explode from pent-up frustrations. And I had no choice but to answer him—and them.

"I understand how you feel," I said. "It does seem that all the city government does is restrict our freedom and demand more money. But there is another side to this picture I want to show you, if you are willing to listen.

"There are things wrong with this city government, no doubt. I don't know of any organization of human beings that can't be improved. And we who happen to be responsible for this one are sincerely interested in hearing and trying to do something about every one of your legitimate complaints. I hope, of course, that in addition to your complaints you'll have some specific, workable suggestions for correcting what is wrong.

"This can be a profitable evening for all of us, if we can talk rationally, factually and unemotionally. Now, what are your wishes? Do you want to simply unload all your complaints and accusations, or shall we spend a few minutes getting the full picture and some of the important facts out in front of us, so we can look at the whole problem objectively?"

To their credit they were willing to sit still long enough to give me a chance to answer the man who claimed his taxes kept going up but who could see no services from the city.

I started this way: "This gentleman over here asks where are all these city services I'm talking about. Let's see, then, if together we can find them. We're going to just walk through an ordinary day in the lives of all of us, to see where the city government touches our lives. Let's start with when we got up this morning, and deal with the very ordinary but necessary things of everyday living.

"My guess is that the first thing you did after getting out of bed this morning was to go to your bathroom. Perhaps you ran some water into the sink to douse your face. Maybe you took a drink. Well, right there is where you ran into the first city service. You didn't have to go out on the back porch to pump the water, like we did when I was a boy. It was right there at your fingertip. It had been right there all night, in fact every day and every night, all year long. The water was there in all the quantity and pressure you needed. If it wasn't, you have a legitimate complaint and we want to hear about it. The city has a plant and men that work around the clock, every day of the year, drawing water from the river and from wells, straining it, purifying it, delivering it through underground pipes right to your very bathroom and kitchen. This is one of the city services you pay for through your water bill.

"One other thing about that water. You probably took a drink of it. You never worried a moment whether it was safe to drink. Yet when the water you drank first entered the city's plant it was dangerous to your health. Living as we do, side by side with thousands of other people, and with industrial plants near by, that water probably carried enough impurities and germs to make you dangerously sick—with typhoid, jaundice, or diarrhea. But because the city strained and purified the water, you drank it out of the tap without a second thought. Thousands of other people did the same thing this morning, without a single reported case of sickness due to impure water.

"We're still in the bathroom. Probably you let the excess water go down the drain. I suppose you used the toilet and flushed the waste into the sewer. You didn't have to walk out in the cold to a miserable, smelly outhouse. You didn't have to give a thought to disposing of the waste. The city took care of it for you, quietly and unnoticed. Yet the sewer system that runs from your house out to a larger sewer in the street, and from there to a big main sewer that carries all that waste to a final resting place at the sewage treatment plant, cost millions of dollars to build and costs thousands of dollars a year to maintain and operate. Incidentally, your share of that cost is about two cents a day.

"Most of the services the city gives go directly to you, but not all of them. Many of the services you get are the quality they are because the city regulates the private company or individual serving you. For example, you undoubtedly used electricity or gas for half a dozen things this morning. In many cities these, too, would have been supplied by the city government. In our case, a private company does this, but under a franchise granted by the city that requires the private utility company to give you prompt and adequate service, twenty-four hours a day the year around.

"Did you or the children have milk for breakfast? Did you worry whether any of you might get undulant fever or tuberculosis from sick cows that gave the milk you and your family drank? Or, did you look to see if the container the milk came in was clean? Probably not, yet these are ever-present dangers to us. That's why the city inspects and regulates every source of milk delivered to us at our homes or in the stores. This service, by the way, is paid for from taxes. It costs you about one-tenth of a cent a day.

"Of course, you and I probably had breakfast at home. However, many hundreds of people—single individuals, men who got down to work early, people staying in a hotel or traveling through town—ate in a restaurant. I suppose if we were to ask them if they worried whether they would get a disease from the person who used a glass or utensil fifteen minutes before they did, or whether the ham and eggs were clean, or the cooks and waitresses were carrying a disease they could spread, the answer would be no. The reason they could eat in a restaurant without a worry is that the city regularly inspects all our restaurants. It holds classes in sanitation for the people who handle food. More than that, it inspects the bakeries and food storage warehouses to be sure the products used in the restaurants are clean and pure. I can tell you, these are some of the reasons why, on the average, a baby born today will live to be sixty-five instead of forty as was the case when our parents were born.

"Ladies and gentlemen," I continued, "I think I see some of you are tired already of hearing about city services, yet I've hardly begun. So let me hurry through a number of services you may or may not have thought about. Then, if any of you want more details about any of these, I'll be glad to give you what information we have on them.

"I mentioned gas and electricity. Either of these could destroy your home. Gas could escape and kill you by asphyxiation or explosion, or you might be electrocuted or your house burn down. But this is not likely because of city inspections when your home was built to see that there was proper venting and adequate wiring.

"When you looked out the window this morning, there was space between your house and the neighbors. You could see the sunrise, and a little of some green areas. This wasn't always the case. In many cities, you'd look at a house one foot away; in fact, in some, your neighbor's wall and yours would abut each other. But because of zoning regulations by the city, you have more open space.

"As you stepped out of the house, you were able to avoid walking in the mud because of a sidewalk the city had built. You drove to work over a paved street that the city had paved. For your safety and convenience, a few blocks down the street you came to a traffic signal light. If it weren't for that light—which, incidentally, cost about $2,500—you and the hundreds of other motorists using that intersection would waste a lot of time fighting your way through. During a year's time, there would probably be many bent fenders and much cussing at that corner. Then as you proceeded, you unconsciously watched warning signs along the way—'Slow, Dangerous Curve,' 'School,' 'Pedestrian Cross-walk,' 'Railroad Crossing.' You may have noticed there were stripes down the street to mark the center line. Maybe the lanes of traffic were separated by other lines so you could more quickly pass through the crowded city where you make your living, your children go to school, and your family buys the things it needs. Crosswalks were marked. All these things are done by the city.

"Perhaps you parked your car in a public parking lot that the city provided, or perhaps you had a bad time finding a place to park. That's one of our toughest problems; but you parked as close as you could to your office.

"You didn't notice, but no thieves or vandals had molested your place of business. Every hour or so during the late hours of the night, a police officer 'rattled' the front door—as they call it—checking to see if it was secure. Had he found it unlocked, he would have notified you; if he had found anyone in there who didn't seem to belong, he would have risked his life to protect your property.

"If you took an elevator to your office, you didn't hesitate to go up in the elevator. You knew it wouldn't fall fifty feet into the basement and kill you and the other people on it. You could feel safe because the city had inspected it when it was installed and continues to make periodic inspections. When you got off the elevator, you walked over floors that were steady and firm. They held up your weight and that of the heavy furniture and equipment in your office because the city required the building to be built with an adequate factor of safety.

"You had hardly sat down to your desk, when you heard a fire siren outside your window. Three pieces of equipment flashed by, each with a group of trained, uniformed men aboard. Those men were on a twenty-four hour tour of duty. When they go off, another group comes on for twenty-four hours. They are riding trucks that cost from $15,000 to $30,000 each, loaded with the latest means of fighting fires and saving lives. They were notified, by an alarm system that the city installed and maintains, that some citizen's property was in danger. They were off to they didn't know what. Maybe it was a warehouse full of household goods or a garage full of cars. Maybe an oil or gasoline storage tank had caught fire. Let's hope, if it was that, the city has required the owner to build dikes around his tanks so the flaming oil won't get into the sewers used for carrying storm water and spread the flaming petroleum over half the city.

"When they got to the fire, it wasn't any of these; it was a rest home for old people. There were fifty aged fathers and mothers, maybe yours, caught on the second floor. The firemen didn't hesitate a moment to risk their lives to save these people.

"If the city water department had checked the water pressure at the nearest fire hydrant, we could be sure there was enough water to throw on the fire and hopefully control it before anyone died. If there was not a hydrant near by, or the pressure was not enough to fight this fire, we'd be in trouble.

"What's more, your fire insurance rates could be higher than they need to be, because the fire underwriters set your rates by the quality of the water system, the fire department, the building inspection, and half a dozen other items for which the city is responsible.

"Before the snow comes this winter, maybe you and your family will be having picnics in the city parks, using the tables, benches, and fireplaces put there by the city. All summer the children have been using the playground equipment; maybe they've even learned crafts and some skills from a playground attendant hired by the city.

"When the snow does come and piles up on the streets, the city will do its best to keep the streets open so your life can go on normally. Sometimes we get behind—when nature dumps it on faster than we can get it off. But rarely do you have to wait more than a few hours to have your street open so that fuel and food deliveries can be made to your home, and a police car, fire truck, or ambulance can reach you if you need it."

I paused at this point. "I guess there's no use going into more detail. You folks get the picture. In fact, you can probably add to the list of city services I've touched briefly. When you go home tonight, I hope the streets are lighted well enough to help you see your way better, whether you're walking or driving. The city arranged to have those lights put in for your convenience and safety.

"Please let me add just one more comment," I said. "The services I have listed are paid for mostly out of taxes. But please keep in mind when you get your tax bill that it includes your property taxes for the school district, the county, maybe even a special district or two, and the state. Less than 20¢ of every tax dollar you pay goes to the city.

"Thanks, folks, for listening!"

There was a moment of silence, then a spontaneous burst of

applause. I asked if there were any questions. There were none. I said the assessor and I would stay after, in case anyone had a particular problem he wanted to discuss.

Seven or eight people stayed back as the others left. Several of those leaving were smiling. A number of them shook my hand as they said goodnight. When the crowd had thinned, the seven or eight came up to me. A spokesman said, "Harlow, that was a pretty good speech, but our taxes are still too high."

"That could be," I said. "Of course, whether or not something is too high depends on our standard of measure, don't you think? Take in your business, for example. You may feel that the wages you have to pay to get good help are too high, and the prices you pay for materials are too high, as you say. But if your business is run as efficiently as it can be, and you are meeting competition and getting your share of the possible business, then probably the costs aren't too high. They are in line with your competition, and you'll probably stay in business. Of course," I acknowledged, "you can cut the cost of running any business—by 50 percent if you wish. The only catch is that you won't any longer be in business. The same holds for the city. Assuming we are operating as efficiently as we can, if we reduce expenditures, we are actually reducing services; we are cutting into the business. If we carry that far enough, the city will no longer be able to do the things I mentioned a few minutes ago. Just as in your own business, if you reduce expenditures far enough, you'll be out of business."

Then I added, "By the way, what businesses are you folks in?"

The spokesman replied, "I'm with the Army, in charge of the recruiting office here."

That surprised me. "Oh," I said, and turned to the next couple. "What about you?"

The husband said, "I work for the Bureau of Reclamation." The wife added, "And I'm a typist at the Weather Bureau office."

This was interesting. "What about the rest of you?" I asked.

One fellow worked for the Soil Conservation Service, another for the Air Force, and another for a federal lending agency. Every one of them was a federal employee.

"With federal taxes what they are—and every one of you supported by taxes—I'm a little surprised you think city taxes are too high. You must know how much federal income tax you

165

pay through withholding, not to mention the many hidden federal taxes on a lot of things we buy. When you get home tonight, I'd like to suggest you get out your local tax bill and compare it with your federal income tax. My guess is you pay about as much federal income tax in three months as you pay in city taxes on your house in one year."

I might as well have talked to the wall. Ignoring my point, the spokesman said, "You people at City Hall are wasting our money. I won't say you're crooked—although I'm not too sure about that—but you're sure spending more than you have to."

With effort, I managed to keep from flaring up at the insinuation as I replied.

"All I can say is that we will welcome your specific suggestions for doing things more efficiently and more economically. Your broadside blasts—these generalizations that we are spending too much—don't help much. Let's be specific. What services do you want us to discontinue? Playgrounds? Traffic lights? Snow removal? Fire protection? Police patrols? What shall we reduce or eliminate?"

Without hesitating, he continued. "There are a hundred ways you could save tax money."

"All right," I said, "maybe there are. But we haven't found them. You say they are there. I ask you to show them to us. We want to know. If there are really opportunities to cut costs, we'll do it. Now, what do you suggest?"

A woman cut in, "He's right. Our taxes are too high. Ours went up ten dollars this year, and what are we getting for it? Nothing but higher pay for all those people down at City Hall who don't do anything all day."

Others, who had been silent to this point, chimed in. "We can't take it," I heard one man say. "It's confiscatory. If taxes keep going up, we'll have to move out."

They kept on for five minutes. Soon they were talking to each other and anybody else around, as much as to the assessor and me. I listened a moment, tried again to get some suggestions for reducing costs, but didn't make a dent. Finally I left them, walked over to shake hands with another couple who had waited patiently to ask how much their assessment would be increased if they put an addition on their house. Out of the corner of my eye I saw the federal employees make their way out the door. They were still arguing with each other that city taxes were "terrible," that "somebody has to do something about it."

A Standing Offer

North Dakota had a so-called "liquor divorcement" law that prohibited the sale of liquor in eating establishments. Restaurateurs got around the law by having a bar next door. Their patrons could step out the door and enter the bar. Inconvenient to be sure, but reasonably handy.

One day the police chief and I were discussing our liquor ordinances. I related an experience we had had in Albert Lea and how the city had dealt with it. A young sailor and a girl friend got into a brawl in one of the taverns. One of them was killed. The public became upset when they learned that the tavern continued to operate after the incident as though nothing had happened. When I was asked about it, I pointed out I had no authority to close the place; licensing was the exclusive function of the city council. As a result of the incident, the council amended the ordinance to empower the city manager to suspend an intoxicating beverage license (not revoke it) in an emergency until the council had time to meet and act on the matter.

The chief thought this would be helpful in Fargo, so I took it up with the commission. They thought it was a reasonable protection for the community and adopted the necessary amendment to the liquor control ordinance.

I never used the authority. In fact, on one occasion when the chief asked me to suspend a license so that he could get at a man who was causing the police a lot of traffic problems, I declined to do so. I told the chief the authority was intended for emergency situations involving the liquor traffic, and I was not justified in using it for other purposes.

I was surprised, therefore, when State Senator Shure came to my office one day and asked what arrangement I had about my salary. Was it provided for by ordinance, commission resolution, simple motion by the commission, or was there merely a verbal understanding?

I told him it was by resolution, and getting out a copy, I handed it to him, then asked the reason for his question.

He didn't answer immediately but read the resolution, then said, "That's good. This is all right."

I pressed him for a reason for his inquiry. After all, Senator Shure (who was in his late sixties and had been a state senator for several terms and before that city attorney for twelve years or more) didn't go out of his way to ask a question like that without a reason.

He hesitated a moment. "I suppose I may as well tell you the reason. I just hope it won't interfere with the work you're doing. The liquor dealers in town are afraid of the suspension power now in the liquor ordinance. They think they can't operate without violating the law, and they are afraid that with the suspension power you have, you may suspend them any time and put them out of business.

"They don't think they can get this commission to repeal that provision, and they don't think they can get the commission to fire you. Consequently, they have made a standing offer of $2,500 to any commissioner who will vote to reduce your salary. Their plan is to get the commission to reduce you from $10,000 a year to $200 a month. They assume that if the commission did this, you would quit."

I thanked the senator for letting me know what was going on, and he left. As far as I know, they never got any takers. But as things eventually turned out in Fargo, I have since wondered if the liquor dealers may have had some impact on relations between the commissioners and me.

Cats, Dogs, and People

Fargo was enough farther north and farther west than Albert Lea that the winters were longer and colder, and the growing season was shorter than in southern Minnesota. Consequently, in March all the Fargoans who could afford it were still in Florida, but most of the populace was in Fargo straining to break out of doors. The first day the thermometer crept above freezing, they were out raking lawns and pulling up dead flower stalks, though they had to work around five-foot piles of soot-covered snow at every driveway and hack through hard pack in the shady places behind each house. Camilla Ross, writing to the editor of one of the Minneapolis newspapers, could have had Fargoans in mind when she wrote:

> *Little does it matter if it's only ten degrees.*
> *Little does it matter if there's snow mixed in the breeze.*
> *If just one ray of sunshine breaks through the darkened sky,*
> *These Eskimos are overjoyed, "Spring is here!" they cry.*

Soon the dog lovers and the garden lovers would be at it again, respectively challenging and upholding the city ordinance that required dogs to be tied up during garden season.

The first challenge of the season came when a woman telephoned me at the office. "Mr. Harlow," she said, without a word of introduction, "it's simply awful how your police department treats man's best friend. Do you know what they're doing? They've told me to tie up my dogs and keep them in my yard. I won't do it!"

I recited the city ordinance provisions, but she knew them better than I did. She had them memorized. To get her off the telephone, I told her I would talk to the chief and see what we could do.

She didn't wait for me to confer with the Chief. Within the hour she was outside my office, demanding loudly to the secretary that she see me right away, that this was an emergency. Again, she didn't waste a moment getting acquainted. Seating herself on the edge of the chair in front of my desk, she began her sweeping criticism of the way people treat "nature's dumb things that are unable to protect themselves." She was furious at the police for picking up stray dogs and putting them in the pound. "Have you seen that place where they are keeping these poor creatures?" she demanded. I had to admit I had not inspected the dog pound.

"Well, you ought to," she said. "It's a disgrace to the city of Fargo. I'm a charter member of the Humane Society, and we're going to see that something is done about it."

I thought this might be my opportunity. I said, "We would be glad to have the Humane Society take over the handling of the animals as they do in many cities."

"You're trying to trick me. You know I don't believe in penning dogs up. The trouble with you is, you don't love animals."

"That's not so," I said. "I do love animals. In fact, when I was a small boy my dog Rusty was my constant companion. We did everything together. We lived in the country, and he could wander around without disturbing anybody.

"Here in the city, when spring comes, a lot of people want to get outside to work in their gardens. They don't want some great big dog racing across their lawns, tearing up or knocking down whatever they've worked hard to fix up. Then, too," I went on, "mothers with small children want to take their children out, or let them play on the sidewalks. But some mothers are afraid to. Big dogs come along and jump up on the mothers, knock the children off their feet, and . . ."

"Oh, children!" she interrupted. "Kids! They're the ones that ought to be tied up! It's not natural for pets to be tied up, or put in cages."

"Do I understand you," I asked, "that you think children should be tied up or kept in the house and that dogs should be allowed to run at will, going about wherever and whenever they want?"

"That's exactly what I think," she glared. "If the children are bothered by dogs, let their parents put fences around their yards and keep the children inside. But don't expect to keep dogs—or cats—penned up. Nature never intended her creatures to be treated this way."

I could do no more than shrug my shoulders and say half-heartedly, "As I said I would, I'll talk to the police chief and see what we can do to relieve the tension out in your neighborhood."

I did talk to the chief. I wanted to know what he thought about trying to get the Humane Society to take over the dog catching and pound operation. He doubted the organization could do it, even with a subsidy from the city.

He said, "Actually, most of the members of the Society are very reasonable. But there are a few who are so unreasonable and aggressive that the other members have lost interest."

The chief and I having agreed there was nothing we could do for the lady, in view of the ordinance provisions requiring that dogs be kept on leash during the garden season months, I asked if he would have one of the officers stop by her place and tell her our decision.

Next morning the chief stopped in my office. "Well, we delivered the message to your dog-lover friend," he said. "Apparently she likes cats a lot, too," he added, obviously trying to get a rise out of me.

"So?"

"Yep. My man got there just at supper time. She and the cats were having supper together. He counted them. There were 13 cats, and she and they were all eating at the same table!"

Gambling Again—the Easy Way

On his return from New York where he had attended a national conference of mayors, Mayor Dawson gave us a report of his being propositioned by a slot machine syndicate. He said that while he was in his hotel room, he received a telephone call from a person he'd never heard of. The man said he would like to talk to him about an important business matter that would benefit the city of Fargo. Would the mayor be able to see him at some convenient time? Learning that the caller was in the hotel, the mayor invited him up to the room.

The man came promptly. He was a tall, good-looking, well-dressed man in his early thirties. He passed the time of day a few minutes, then turned to the purpose of his call. He began by a description of Fargo. The mayor was surprised by his intimate knowledge of the city—its population, economics, and habits. He knew the names of several prominent citizens and their reputations. He was especially knowledgeable about the city's finances, noting the difficulties Fargo was having raising enough revenue to do even part of what the citizens were clamoring for.

He moved steadily toward his point. He said the group he represented had thoroughly investigated the town. They were satisfied it would pay to "open up" Fargo to machine gambling. He supported his proposition with more facts and figures. He had estimates of the annual take, based allegedly on their experience in other cities. Also, he had cost figures for capital investment and for servicing the machines. He said the group was prepared to make a generous split of the profits with the city and with designated city officials if that was the way the city wanted it. The city could count on 50 percent of the take after expenses. Based on their estimates, this could make a substantial contribution to the Fargo budget. In other words, they were ready to go into partnership with the city of Fargo and its officials.

As Mayor Dawson related this incident, I noted how much this man's approach resembled that of the punchboard representative who had come to see me in Sweet Home, Oregon. The Oregon visitor also had had an impressive knowledge of our needs and our finances, and his estimates of return to the city, if accurate, looked very good against the total city budget.

Mayor Dawson dismissed his New York visitor without a second thought. He had not taken the time from his business to run for office and spend the effort he did on city business to bring open gambling to Fargo. He was determined the citizens of Fargo would have the clean, efficient government he and his running mates on the businessmen's ticket had promised them.

Nevertheless, the mayor recognized how attractive the proposition could be in some city situations. Having been mayor a couple of years, he saw the squeeze the city was in between demands of the citizens and their continued resistance to paying for those demands and the rising costs due to inflation. He could believe now that other harassed officials might succumb to the enticements of that easy way of escaping the bind, at the same time providing the open town some citizens might want.

Read the Fine Print

The city of Fargo had a large airport operation. Hector Field served Northwest Airlines on its east-west flights and Mid-Continent Airlines on its north-south flights. It was also the home base of the North Dakota Air National Guard and of several private crop-dusting operations and other private flyers.

These users were constantly pushing for more room, better facilities, and various kinds of help from the city, all of which cost money—lots of money. This led to the only source of that kind of money—federal airport funds. Late in 1948 I started gathering the large amount of data and other information needed to back up an application for a federal grant.

I had a special interest in applications for federal grants. My master's thesis in public administration at the University of Minnesota was titled "Federal Supervision and Control of Municipal Public Works Construction." I had dug into the regulations and practices of the Roosevelt era Works Progress Administration (WPA) and Public Works Administration (PWA). Before that I had worked for the PWA, reviewing local government grant applications. I knew that every now and then a local government signed an application without reading the small print and later regretted the way they were contractually bound. I decided to read every word of the agreement before recommending it to the city commission.

In its several pages of standard provisions (often called "boiler plate" provisions), I found nothing unusual or adverse to the city's interest. Then I came on a brief passage, buried in a main paragraph. It said that the "sponsor" (in our case the city of Fargo) ". . . will not exercise or grant any right or privilege which would operate to prevent any person, firm, or corporation operating aircraft on the airport from . . . purchasing off the airport and having delivered on the airport without entrance fee, delivery fee, or other surcharge for delivery any parts, materials or supplies necessary for the servicing, repair or operation of its aircraft. . . ."

I could hardly believe what I read. We were barely staying in the black with $63,000 annual revenue, of which $28,000 came from our sale of gasoline and oil. If we agreed to such a provision and lost our gasoline and oil revenue, we would be cutting off the economic lifeblood of our airport operation. Could it be that this was what dozens or maybe hundreds of other cities had agreed to when they got federal airport assistance?

Noting that the agreement I had before me was of recent date, I got hold of the previous contract form to compare the two. Sure enough, this was a new provision. When the district Civil Aeronautics Administration representative made his next call, I pointed out this newly added provision to him. He hadn't noticed the change in the new form.

"I guess they did that down in Washington," he said.

I told the city commission of my finding and recommended we hold off on the application. Next, I telephoned Carl Chatters, executive director of the American Municipal Association, and told him what I had come across. He immediately recognized the implication of this provision for all the cities in the country. We decided to enlist the help of the National Institute of Municipal Law Officers to get the agreement changed and to seek whatever other help we could get.

I arranged a meeting with our U.S. Senator Milton Young, to tell him what the provision meant to us and to solicit his help in getting CAA to change the requirement. Also, I wrote the Civil Aeronautics Administrator, Del Rentzel, of our concern about this provision and what it meant to our airport and perhaps to others around the country. As for our situation, I wrote:

"Much as airport improvements are needed here, it would be foolhardy for the city to trade a major source of revenue in exchange for help in adding to our capital plant. We would be increasing our costs of operation at the same time we reduced our income."

Carl Chatters and Charles Rhyne, general counsel for the National Institute of Municipal Law Officers, followed up my letter by arranging a meeting with Rentzel. The city attorney and I flew to Washington to meet with him. Before we went in for our appointment, one of Rentzel's staff informed us that the administrator had already conferred with the Air Transport Association and the petroleum industry representatives on the subject. We went into the meeting feeling we had two strikes against us already.

Rentzel showed no interest in changing the regulations. They had already been printed and circulated. Although he did not

RED RIVER VALLEY FORECASTS:
Fair tonight and Thursday, cooler north tonight, low 35-45; cooler Thursday, high 70-80.
(Details on Page 18)

THE FAR

Established 1878   Entered as Second Class Matter
Postoffice, Fargo, N. D.   Price Five Cents   FARGO, N. D., WEDN

CITY WINS AIRPOI

Exclusive Gas Sale Is Assured

The city of Fargo has been victorious in a long controversy with the federal government over the city's right to exclusive sale of gasoline at Hector airport under the federal aid program.

The decision will affect every federal aid municipally-owned airport in the country.

City Manager LeRoy F. Harlow last night received a telegram from Carl H. Chatters, Washington, director of the American Municipal association, saying:

"CAA regulations announced today remove restrictions on right of cities to regulate dispensing of gasoline and oil at federal aid municipal airports. Glad we won."

The decision will enable the city to complete application for 50 per cent matching federal funds for airport improvements, including a new administration building, while retaining its major source of revenue.

Information from Charles S. Rhyne, general counsel for the National Institute of Municipal Law Officers, indicates that Fargo was the only city which had protested the form of the CAA agreement containing the restrictions against the exclusive rights.

* * *

Harlow and City Attorney E. T. Conmy, Jr., went to Washington last December to confer with D. W. Rentzel, CAA administrator. Following that, with the refusal of CAA to remove the restriction from the agreement, Sen. Milton R. Young of North Dakota and

say so, we assumed the airlines and the petroleum people favored the regulation as printed in the agreement.

Having made no progress with the CAA, I asked Senator Young to seek the help of Pat McCarran, senator from Nevada and known as the "father" of the Civil Aeronautics Act. In the meantime, the American Municipal Association's *Washington News Letter* of December 15, 1948, carried this news item: "The issue of gasoline and oil sales is still warm. Fargo, N. D., recently made clear to the CAA in an informal hearing that the city will not accept federal aid for airport construction unless it is permitted to dispense all gas and oil put in planes on its field."

FIGHT WITH U. S.

Sen. Patrick A. McCarran (D-Nev), a leader in the senate on airport matters, backed Fargo's plea. The city was supported by the municipal association and the municipal law officers institute.

In a letter to Rentzel last November, Harlow set forth the city's position in refusing to sign the proposed sponsor's assurance agreement which would permit the city to participate in the federal air program, because of the restriction clause.

The city took the position, Harlow wrote, that "We are not interested in sharing with one or more private operators the profits from gasoline and oil sales."

The agreement which Fargo opposed provided that the sponsor "will not exercise or grant any right or privilege which would operate to prevent any person, firm or corporation operating aircraft on the airport from . . . purchasing off the airport and hav-

ing delivered on the airport without entrance fee, delivery fee or other surcharge for delivery any parts, materials or supplies necessary for the servicing, repair or operation of its aircraft. . ."

* * *

The net profit from operations of Hector airport for the year ending June 30, 1948, Harlow pointed out, was $1,345.35. Income from airport operations totaled $62,797.53, of which $28,044.30 was from the sale of gasoline and oil. In 1947 the airport showed a net loss of $6,324.02, with income from gasoline and oil sales of $17,897.97.

Much as airport improvements are needed here, Harlow said, "It would be foolhardy for the city to trade a major source of revenue in exchange for help in adding to our capital plant. We would be increasing our costs of operation at the same time we reduced our income."

Senator Young presented our story to Senator McCarran. Later Senator Young told me the substance of their conference. He told Senator McCarran he thought CAA's new regulations ran counter to the spirit of the Civil Aeronautics Act. Senator McCarran agreed; he said the Civil Aeronautics program was never intended to put any city out of the gasoline and oil dispensing business.

On May 10 I received a telegram from Carl Chatters. It read: "CAA regulations announced today remove restrictions on right of cities to regulate dispensing of gasoline and oil at federal aid municipal airports. Glad we won."

We were able to proceed with our application for federal airport funds.

Cut Our Taxes but Not Our Project

I was asked to attend an emergency meeting of the Chamber of Commerce, an unusual request because I was not usually included in Chamber affairs. On arrival I found about thirty men assembled, most of whom I didn't know but who were introduced as leading farmers in the area.

Without introductory preliminaries, a speaker embarked on an impassioned protest against federal government spending. After some twenty minutes reciting facts and figures on the rise in expenditures and in the national debt, he closed his presentation with a strong statement of his conviction that "we have to do something about it." Several others took turns rising and making concurring statements. Finally, one man made the suggestion that the Chamber send telegrams to the members of the North Dakota congressional delegation in Washington, urging them to do everything possible to reduce taxes. This was approved unanimously by the group, and I thought the meeting was over.

But there was more to it. Almost immediately another individual rose to his feet and began to recite the steps that had been taken locally to get federal appropriations for a dam needed in the area. He described the spring floods that repeatedly inundated farmlands and even killed some livestock. Others joined with statements of their first hand knowledge of why a dam was needed.

After reaching a point at which speakers were repeating themselves, someone said, "I think we've talked enough. Everyone knows we need that dam, and we haven't been able to get it. It's time we stopped talking and started acting. I suggest we appoint a delegation to go to Washington and present our case in person to the Corps of Engineers, to the Bureau of Reclamation, to our senators and congressman, and to whoever else we need to see to get some results."

I was startled by this turn around. Here the very same group that less than ten minutes before had been deploring federal expenditures was about to send a delegation to ask for the expenditure of more federal money. Leaning over to the fellow next to me, a stranger, I whispered, "Isn't this kind of inconsistent—to vote one minute to wire our congressional delegation to reduce taxes and then the next minute to vote to send a delegation to Washington to get an appropriation for our area?"

"I don't see that it is," he said. "This is different. We need this dam; we need it bad. If Uncle Sam doesn't spend the money here, he'll spend it someplace else; so if we can, we may as well get our share."

That silenced me. The question went to a vote, the chairman called for and got some volunteers, and they were given instructions as to whom to see and what to ask for. The meeting adjourned.

This was the second time as a city manager I was dumbfounded by what seemed to me stark, illogical inconsistency. In Albert Lea someone had got word that a new Veterans Administration hospital was to be built someplace in the Upper Mississippi region. A meeting was called to discuss how Albert Lea might get the hospital. The group in attendance included several of the community's loudest complainers about high taxes and high federal expenditures. But there was not a single dissenting voice to the motion to do everything possible, including sending telegrams, preparing descriptive materials, and sending a delegation to prevail on the Veterans Administration to choose the Albert Lea site.

At the Albert Lea meeting I was asked to authorize the delegation to say the city would extend water service free of charge to the suggested site, which was a mile or so out of town. Before responding to the question, I asked for a moment to consider the other side of the whole proposition.

I said, "This is not an unmixed blessing, you know."

I pointed out that not only were we talking of making an expensive water extension which the whole community would have to pay for, but presumably the hospital would bring in a good-sized staff. This would add to the general burden of the city and especially the schools. If these staff members bought or rented homes in the city, they would pay some taxes, but not anywhere near enough to pay the cost of the added service. It was more likely they would live in government houses, which would be tax exempt. Unlike bringing in a private, tax-paying plant with a number of tax-paying employees, this operation would pay little or no local taxes.

A local grocer took immediate offense at my remarks. What kind of talk was this, he wanted to know. Anybody could see the whole town would benefit if a new hospital were located in Albert Lea. Just think of all the people who would have relatives in the hospital and would come to see them every week.

I quietly retired, without committing the city to install the water line. I guess some other city outbid us for the project.

Competition Is Great . . . but Count Me Out

My experience tells me there are essentially three ways local officials can save taxpayers' money:

1. Systematize work procedures and methods for maximum efficiency of production;
2. Guide and help employees perform at greater efficiency through directing them, training them, facilitating their work, and providing inspiration and incentives;
3. Manage the purchase, control, and use of goods and contract services.

I have observed that, paradoxically, although number 3 provides the most precise measure of how much is saved and where, it also generates the greatest resistance. I want to describe my Fargo experience because it illustrates the kinds of pressure that can converge on a lone official trying to protect the people's pocket book.

First, let me put the situation in perspective. Municipalities buy cars, trucks, parts, tires, gasoline, grease, and oil. They buy uniforms and work clothes. They need food and medical supplies. They pay for heat, power, and insurance. They spend millions for asphalt, cement, gravel, steel, lumber, and other construction materials. And they are continually in the market for desks, chairs, files, paper, ink, printed materials, and other office supplies. From cranes and construction projects to paper clips and toilet paper, local governments are among America's largest consumers of goods and services.

Studies show that in most situations, centralizing the purchase of these goods and services will save 10 to 15 percent of their costs. In Fargo our total expenditures for these items ran about $350,000 a year. Conservatively, by investing $5,000 a year for centralized purchasing, we could make a net saving of $30,000 to $35,000 a year—one mill on the tax rate. This saving was possible simply because, although our division and department heads were specialists in water treatment, police and fire protection, airport management, laboratory analyses, and engineering, they were not specialists in purchasing. They could not keep track of new products coming on the market, of seasonal changes in supplies and prices, or of the opportunities for discounts and tax exemptions available to local governments. They could not know what the other departments were buying that might be pooled with their own needs for quantity discounts—or what the other departments had on hand that they might use instead of buying. Moreover, it was a waste of their time to listen to the stream of salesmen wanting to sell their wares to the city.

With these benefits for the city in mind, I recommended to the city commission that we set up within the finance department a central purchasing division under a purchasing agent. The division would prepare specifications in cooperation with the using departments and would buy all supplies, materials, and equipment for all city departments. Also, the purchasing agent would handle contracts for services and would inventory and manage the land and buildings the city owned. The commission approved unanimously.

I appointed a longtime assistant to the city auditor as our first purchasing agent. Unfortunately, almost immediately thereafter the city auditor died unexpectedly. The new purchasing agent was the logical successor to this important position; so I appointed him city auditor, and he was confirmed by the city commission as required by the city manager plan law. This left vacant the purchasing agent's position. I was unable to fill the vacancy for several months.

By November I had located a Fargo resident with experience in governmental purchasing. Donald E. Bloese went to work for us on December 14. He began writing the operating procedure for the centralized purchasing system, setting up a small office with necessary forms and files. In addition, I had him visit several cities in the Midwest to observe their central purchasing operations. He spent two days in Milwaukee, Wisconsin, where he received special and useful counsel from city purchasing agent Nicholson, then president of the National Institute of Governmental Purchasing. On February 1 we put central purchasing into operation.

The new program was not entirely free from problems. At a staff meeting of department heads and their assistants a week before we planned to get underway, Police Chief Jester took the floor and declared that the plan spelled out in detail by the purchasing agent was a "Rube Goldberg" invention and one which he, the chief, found it impossible to understand.

It was not long after that that an irate individual presented himself at my office door and demanded to know, "What in hell's going on around here?" He said he was the district sales manager for one of the chemical companies that supplied chemicals for our water purification plant. He wanted to know how come the last order for a certain chemical had not gone to his firm. He had driven up from Minneapolis to find out. I replied that we were buying on a bid basis and perhaps his company had not submitted the lowest bid.

"Wha'd ya mean, bid?" he asked. "We've got a deal. I made it with Fred Hagen. We were to get all the business."

"Commissioner Hagen is no longer the water commissioner," I said. "The city has changed to the council-manager form of government, and I now have responsibility for that department."

"I don't give a damn what you've done. All I know is we had a deal, and I'm going to find out about this." With this he left.

That wasn't the only flak I ran into while Don Bloese was with us. For instance, the mayor and I were walking back to our offices from a service club luncheon one day. The mayor had been sitting next to his good friend, Larry Hamm, head of the largest office supply and equipment firm in both Fargo and the state and chairman of Fargo's fire and police Civil Service Commission. "Larry tells me the city's now buying paper from some cheap New York outfit," the mayor said.

I didn't comment. I knew the purchasing agent had advertised for bids on paper, specifying both quality and quantity, and that a representative of a firm across the street from City Hall had come over to ask if we really meant that we wanted bids—that he had never been able to get any city business before. I also knew that Larry Hamm's firm had not submitted the low bid and had not been given our order. As I recall, the "cheap New York outfit" that got the order was the Burroughs Corporation, almost a household name in American business since the turn of the century.

The mayor's comment alerted me that sooner or later I'd have to fight for our policy of seeking the best price we could get on city purchases, even after we had met the legal requirements for giving preference to local vendors.

State law gave a preference to residents over nonresidents. Cities were required to purchase goods and accept bids from North Dakota resident bidders if the resident bidder's proposal was not more than 5 percent above the lowest bid of an out-of-state firm. We went further than that; we added more than a 5 percent differential on the assumption that we would get better service from local merchants, although that was not always the case.

But even our strict compliance with state law plus additional preference did not satisfy some gasoline vendors, and it didn't satisfy Larry Hamm. The gasoline vendors argued that if a company had its headquarters out of state, even if its service stations were in Fargo, they were nonresidents; therefore we should not buy from them on a competitive basis.

Larry Hamm telephoned to make a bitter complaint because we had given our order for two files to someone else. He wanted to know why his firm didn't get the order. The purchasing agent had talked to me about this, so I had the facts in mind.

"Larry," I said, "we invited bids on those files. The bids came in. For the identical file—same manufacturer, same catalog number, same color—everything the same—there was a 30 percent spread between your price and the other man's." Then I gave him the exact figures.

He said, "You're forcing me to give a larger discount than I think I ought to. You're chiseling."

"Larry, we can't force you to do anything. We simply ask for bids, and we accept the lowest one for equal quality goods," I replied.

"This is taxpayers' money, and they don't want you to spend it this way. They want you to pass the business around," he said.

"I'm not sure the taxpayers would want it passed around if they knew the facts," I said. "I made an analysis of our purchases over a period of a year. We know that only 20 percent of the businesses in town—I'm not talking about professional people or anything like that; I'm talking about the fellows in the merchandising business—only 20 percent of them received from the city of Fargo more than twenty dollars last year. In other words, for all practical purposes 80 percent of the merchants in town don't get a penny from the city. Why? Because they happen to be in the type of business we don't use. For example, George Hoenck has a fur store. We never buy fur coats. And the ladies' ready-to-wear stores. We never buy ladies' ready-to-wear. But we happen to have to buy office equipment, trucks and tractors, and so on.

"It seems to me that the 80 percent of the merchants and all the other taxpayers are entitled to know that when they put a dollar down here in city tax money, we're going to get the most we can for that dollar."

"Look," Larry said, "I've been in business here for forty years, and I've seen them come and go. If you give business to that fellow who is willing to undersell, he's going to go broke in a little while. He'll soon be out of business."

"That's a very interesting statement," I said. "I know you are for the American free enterprise system—free competition. You are opposed to paternalistic government; I've heard the speeches you give on that subject. Yet now you're telling me that when one of your competitors is willing to sell for less—because of better merchandising or for whatever reason—I should say to him, 'Joe, if you offer your item at this price, and we buy from you, you'll soon be broke. Therefore, I'm not going to accept your bid.' "

"Well," Larry said, "I see I'm not getting anyplace with my argument."

"I guess I'm not getting anyplace with mine either," I replied, and we hung up.

I kept in close touch with Bloese, to be helpful where I could and to encourage him, knowing the change would be difficult. He was a conscientious and agreeable young man who did everything possible to cater to the needs and wishes of the department heads. They responded in kind, except for the police chief. Despite my specific request that insofar as possible the departments consolidate their monthly supply requirements, the chief sent three and four officers at a time to the purchasing agent, each with a requisition for a single roll of Scotch tape, a box of paper clips, and other small items. He gave several salesmen orders for merchandise, then sent them to the purchasing agent for confirmation of the order.

Despite these difficulties, Don Bloese was making progress. We were catching up on the payment of bills, had eliminated duplicate payments (made previously because of inadequte record keeping), and were realizing some substantial savings. Because we had no system for servicing vehicles, except in the fire department and street division, each department took its vehicles to be serviced wherever and whenever they wished. The purchasing agent was negotiating for a standardized preventive maintenance program that promised substantial savings as well as better service.

Then one day in early April, Bloese did not come to work. I asked Dwight Ink, our budget and personnel officer and my principal assistant, to check. Dwight called Mrs. Bloese, who reported she thought Don had gone to the office.

When we didn't hear from Don in an hour or so, I called Mrs. Bloese. By this time she was very upset. She had heard nothing from Don and had no idea where he was. When I asked if she could explain his actions, she said, "Mr. Harlow, has Don told you the problems he's been having with the police department?"

I replied I knew he was having some problems.

She said, "Every night this week he has walked the floor most of the night, saying over and over again, 'I've got to work it out with Jester; I've just got to get it worked out with Jester.' Don has worried me, he's been so nervous and tired."

I tried to reassure her, telling her we would start a search for Don, and I would call her back.

I asked Dwight to do everything he could to locate Don—find out who some of his friends were, where he might be.

At noon Dwight called in to say he had not located Don but thought he was on his trail. He had seen some people who had seen Don around.

Later that afternoon Dwight called again. He was at the bus station. He had arrived there in time to see Don leaving, but too late to speak to him.

We kept in touch with Mrs. Bloese but didn't hear of Don for several weeks. Finally we got word. Don had reenlisted in the army. He was at Fort Riley, Kansas.

I immediately began a search for a successor to Don Bloese. After interviewing several candidates, I appointed Harold Conway, a disabled World War II paratrooper retrained by the army for purchasing work, who was living in a nearby small town. He was an exceptionally fine and able man. He knew purchasing procedures and markets and had the ability to get along with department heads, vendors, and the public.

He moved his family to Fargo and went right to work. Although we had lost some time due to Don Bloese's sudden departure, it looked as though we were finally on our way with the purchasing program. But Bloese's troubles had not all been inside City Hall, and neither were Conway's to be.

Harold Conway started work as purchasing agent in late June. The following July 13, during the city commission's budget hearings, the commission had a lengthy discussion about the function and need for centralized purchasing. Finally, on a 3-2 vote, they decided to continue it a year to determine whether the savings made it a profitable operation.

On July 27, after the budget passed the Board of Budget Review and the last person had been heard, with no protest or comment of any kind on the central purchasing program, the commissioner alignment changed, and by a 2-3 vote the city commission cut out all funds for the purchasing office.

This was a blow. Although we had had only three months of actual operation, we had realized the following savings:

- On office supplies, a 10 percent discount on some items, and on carbon paper and typewriter ribbons, 40 percent;
- Office equipment, a 10 percent discount, standard to government offices, if requested;
- By purchasing chlorine for the water department in carload lots, for which we had plenty of storage space, instead of month-by-month, we dropped the price from 14¢ a pound to 10½¢ a pound. The saving: $980 per year;
- The purchasing agent had negotiated a new price for sand, from $2.25 per yard to $2.00 per yard, for a saving of $200 in one month;
- He obtained a 25+10 percent and a 20+10 percent discount on tires and tubes;
- The estimated savings on printing was 20 percent;
- A 26 percent discount was obtained on electric lamps.

In total, during July the city spent $13,000 at a saving of $2,100 or about 14 percent. And that was only the start; but it was also the finish of the central purchasing program.

Dissension in the Ranks

Most city affairs ran smoothly. We were busy arranging for expansion and modernization of the water filtration plant, installing a new position classification and pay plan, improving the airport, working on employee needs through the employees advisory council, surfacing streets, extending water and sewer lines, evacuating people from flooded areas, occasionally having to resolve departmental and interdepartmental problems, and trying to answer a range of citizen complaints—barking dogs, potholes, speeding cars, and street lights.

The one point of serious disharmony within the city family and with the public was the police department. Although the police chief was always prompt for our personal conferences, he usually came late and left early from our staff meetings. Citizen complaints irritated him. When complaints came to my office, I dictated a memorandum to the affected department and asked for a report of action taken. Whenever practical, I assigned the complaints to other departments, but unfortunately most of the complaints were the kind that only the police department could handle, so he got the bulk of them.

The chief had a quick temper. I first observed it a couple

weeks after I went to work in Fargo. He had asked me to take a drive with him to inspect some bad traffic locations. We were driving along, talking, when suddenly he stopped the car, leaned across me, livid-faced, and bellowed through the open window on my side at a taxi driver, "Hey you! Get that car out of there! *Get That Car Out of There! GET THAT CAR OUT OF THERE!*"

The cab was on a portion of an extra long driveway in front of a store. The driver tried to explain he had driven up there at the direction of his passenger, to make it easier for the passenger to get out. The chief paid no attention. He was almost hysterical. "I ought to cite you in!" he shouted again. *"GET THAT CAR OUT OF THERE!"*

At another time, I got the brunt of his temper. It was winter and had snowed most of the night. The chief called me at home before office hours to tell me the streets were not yet cleaned of snow. I had just had another call, telling me a radio station had reported that Moorhead's streets (across the river, on the Minnesota side) were open but Fargo's were still blocked.

I said to the chief, "Yes, I understand a radio station has reported Moorhead's streets are open, but ours are not. Did you give the radio station that report?"

"Do you mean to ask me that question?" the chief retorted.

"Yes, I am asking you that question."

"All right for you, Mr. Harlow. *All Right For You! ALL RIGHT FOR YOU!*" and he hung up the telephone.

I never confronted the chief about the incident, attributing it to his probably being tired and irritable. But I had a reason for asking. The chief frequently criticized and belittled the streets division men. For instance, at one time we were considering putting prisoners to work on the streets and sewers, figuring on getting something out of them instead of having them fed, housed, and lying around in jail while tax-paying city employees were working in rain, heat, and cold. I talked to the public works director about this. He checked with his men and reported to me they objected to riding on trucks with prisoners. They thought their friends and acquaintances, seeing them in that company, might think they were prisoners too.

At the close of a staff meeting, I mentioned the men's feelings to the chief. In the presence of most of the division and department heads he responded substantially as follows: "What the hell. Most of those damn guys you've got down there at the street department aren't good enough to ride on the same trucks with the prisoners."

I wanted to know if the chief was using the radio station to get in another jibe at our streets crews.

On another occasion he blew up at the budget and personnel officer, saying, "We were getting along all right until you came along and started sticking your nose in."

The Ag College homecoming snake dance incident was one that irritated a number of townspeople. The night before the homecoming game at North Dakota Agricultural College, the college kids organized a snake dance and wound their way through the streets, in and out of buildings, all in the spirit of good fun. Unfortunately they included the police department in their line of march. I was not there, but as I got the story, their leader was carrying a stick, like a baton. When they got into the station, a duty officer tried to turn them around and head them back out. In the confusion or skirmish, the leader poked an officer with the stick. The chief described the students as a mob and charged the student leader with assault on a police officer.

Next day the chief appeared at the college president's office just before the homecoming parade was to begin. He insisted on seeing the president immediately. Although the parade was organized and everyone was ready to move (including the governor of the state), the chief held up the whole proceeding while he lectured the college president on his failure to control the student body.

There followed an exchange of letters to the editor. Finally, the city commission directed the city attorney and me to meet with the president, to make apologies, and to try to cool off the situation as best we could.

President Longwell was gracious, but said, "Never in my life have I been addressed by anyone as that man addressed me."

There continued to be various little incidents: people telling me in person or telephoning to complain that the chief had "bawled them out"; his reluctance to go along with the other departments in using a standard city letterhead, insisting instead that he needed a special insignia on his department's letterhead; failure to let me know when he would be out of town so that I would know who was in charge of the department; calling the local citizens "blockheads," "square-heads," "clod-busters," "self-satisfied and selfish businessmen," and "hicks"; and threatening to quit the Fargo safety council because "they make a bunch of ridiculous suggestions nobody can put into effect."

One occasion of the chief's being out of town without my knowing where to reach him was particularly embarrassing. He had not told either the city attorney or me that he had prepared a detailed plan for a corps of citizen informers. The plan called for supplying selected citizens "known to be of good reputation" with U.S. postal cards. Whenever they observed a traffic violation, they were to fill in the car's description and license number and the nature of the violation and mail the card to police headquarters.

Maybe the plan had merit, but much of the public didn't think so. The chief released details of the plan to the press and radio and gave a local doctor credit for the idea. Immediately the proposed setup was tagged a local "Gestapo." The doctor credited with the idea denied ever suggesting such a thing. The department and I had to take the heat; the chief could not be reached.

Decision Making Is a Lonely Business

All of these incidents, as well as those involving the exaggerated expense account for the Duluth trip and the damage to the central purchasing and other interdepartmental relations, were irritations, and they were exasperating; however, they could be tolerated. But now we experienced a rapidly accelerating series of events that pointed to deliberate dishonesty and a collapse of police department morale. These situations forced me to make some complex decisions involving the police chief and, ultimately, my own service in Fargo.

In brief, the events were these: first, discovery that the chief had again used city funds to purchase liquor, this time attempting to cover his misuse of funds by arranging that the restaurant and bar owner who supplied the liquor and also provided meals for city prisoners would inflate the number of meals until the excess meal charges equalled the liquor costs; second, finding that the chief's report of yearly departmental activities did not add up to the claims of records made and national police figures surpassed; third, the chief's move to fire a long-service officer, ostensibly because the officer failed to issue enough citations, although the officer's duty post and shifts made it virtually impossible to observe violators (of significance, this was the officer who refused to sign for more prisoners' meals than there were prisoners); fourth, the chief's posting bulletins to "all hands" in the department, stating the city manager was dissatisfied with the officers' performances and intended to reduce

July 6, 1949

From: Chief of Police

To: All Hands

Subject: General Information Bulletin

The monthly police reports prepared by the different bureau heads and submitted for filing with copies to the City Manager are not reflecting a work load that should be expected of a Department this size. The analysis is as interesting as the opinions and conclusions of the readers, and therefore, is given to you.

Taking the most recent month, namely June, the traffic citation and parking violation score sheets, which are official and have now become part of the official files of both the Police Department and the City Manager's office, reflect that the following officers issued no tickets of any nature or description in the month of June:

R. Gilbert
J. Lysaght

It shows that the following officers issued only one ticket of any nature or description in the month of June:

R. Bush
N. Christensen
J. Pavek
J. Strong

The following officer issued only two tickets in the month of June:

E. Knutson

Then starting at that point the amount of tickets increases from four to the top scoring which was naturally held by the car marker. It would be, and it is, difficult for me to explain the Police Department's position to persons of authority when it is realized the above score is an indication that the officers are either not on the job or not willing to produce. There is no denying the fact that if a man really wants to work his beat, he can observe more wrong parkers than is indicated by the above score, and furthermore, if he happens to be a car man he could certainly see more violations than is indicated in the 30-day period described.

In discussing this with the Department heads I find that there are a certain few who have made light of or found fault with, or criticized some

General Information Bulletin issued to All Hands by Chief of Police, City of Fargo, North Dakota, July 1949.

the force, a statement diametrically opposed to what I had said to the chief on the subject; fifth, officers coming to me in groups, at my office and home, to describe conditions and the state of morale in the department, such as: officers being required to use one another's high-collar winter overcoats, despite the soil from others' breathing, sneezing, and colds; in below-zero weather, a traffic officer being ordered not to leave his post at an open intersection for a straight 7½ hours, and to hand- and arm-signal every vehicle that crossed the intersection; the city's ammunition priority being used to purchase $1,800 worth of ammunition, largely on behalf of a private sporting goods store; officers having to go around in pairs because of fear of violence by the chief and arranging for another officer to of the younger officers for displaying courage and ambition. As a matter of fact, I am informed on good authority that one of the officers most recently accepted under Civil Service made the statement that "I used to issue citations but was called down for it by some of the old-timers, and I don't do it anymore." It is not hard for the City Manager or myself, or anyone else on the Force to figure out who may be critical of initiative by simply studying the personnel list of this Department starting with Evenkaaum at the top and going down twenty-three places to Wallace Gwynn at the bottom, the latter being employed on this Department May 20, 1946. Whoever it is that has been discouraging this young officer therefore, must have been hired between May 1, 1921 and May 20, 1946.

Starting with John Pavek, who was hired on November 7, 1946, to the last man hired by this Department, I am the one who hired those people and gave them their jobs. I was the one who gave them their raises and their uniforms and their six 8-hr. day week, and their vacation periods and all those things that are now enjoyed by the Department that were not enjoyed by other members of the Police Department in the years prior to my taking office. I can guarantee one thing--that the men I hired were properly screened and personally instructed by me wherein, among other things, they were told that they should conscientiously perform their sworn duties to the best of their ability, and should the time come when they could not conscientiously perform their duties to the best of their ability, or found that they must be dishonest in any way, shape or form, they were to do the honorable thing and hand in their resignation to me personally.

I, therefore, feel that it is a rank injustice for anyone who considers himself an authority on Police work to indicate by word of mouth or any insinuation that these young officers should lay down on the job for any purpose whatsoever.

For the information of the Police Department personnel, you may be interested to know that the Department is to be cut from three to five men and that cut is due this month. You should know that I am not going to cut from the payroll any man who has a personnel record, quarterly marks, and work record which indicates that he is doing his job conscientiously and to the best of his ability and pursuant to the instructions I have given, but I am willing to cut from the payroll forthwith anyone who is failing to do what is expected of him, or who is a trouble maker, or a complainer, and who is in any way attempting to injure any member of the Department as a whole through his actions, associations, comments, or any other form.

This communication is straight from the shoulder, and although some may feel that the remarks may be broad and not include them, it should be understood that the person whom the shoe fits must put it on, because I know who they are and I am willing to accept their resignations as soon as the same can be made out and handed to me which may assist me in picking out the 3 to 5 men that are to be out from this payroll.

My commands have been simple. They have requested simply that you do good Police work in a manner that will be a credit to the Department and which will bring favorable comment from the public, and that you be

accompany the second-in-command when he was to meet with the chief.

I concluded that for the preservation of the department and the well-being of the community, the police chief's services had to be terminated. But in what manner? Here were some of the factors to be considered.

- Under state law, the city manager was the appointing and removing authority, subject to civil service provisions. Therefore I had to check the legal removal procedure with the city attorney and must follow it to the letter.
- As to the advisability of giving advance notice or the opportunity for the chief to resign rather than be dismissed: repeatedly, the chief had stated, "They're after me in this town," never indicating who "they" were. If asked to resign, he would either refuse or do so with a lot of noise. He would

loyal to your Department and all the members therein. I shall not at this
time engage in the matter of singling out the individuals hoping that they
will single themselves out and be honorable enough to do the proper thing.

In closing let me point out those people who, I feel, are doing
exceptionally good work, in order that you may use it as a yardstick.

(1) The Detective Bureau has been carrying a load with exceptional success which load should be carried by at least two more persons
in their complement.

(2) The Traffic Sergeant has been carrying a load that is
commendable.

(3) The I. D. Bureau and the File Clerk together with the
stenographic help receives my highest compliments.

(4) The Duty Officers have carried their burden against the odds
that have been enumerated in this report and indicated above.

I shall expect to hear this memo quoted to me in the very near
future by persons other than members of this Department because in all
other memos the outsider had learned of the memo and the information contained therein, and the reflections on them within a matter of hours after
the memo has been posted. The readers will bear in mind that I always
learn who told which gives me the ammunition and the power I need as the
administrative officer to continue operating a Police Department which not
only has gained a good reputation in this State, but is now recognized
throughout the States as probably one of the most efficient Departments
in the country today.

There is nothing secret about this memo and I don't particularly
care who knows it, but as in all family affairs, none of us appreciate our
neighbors knowing our personal affairs unless, of course, it is something
of common knowledge. Therefore, this memo is not made public, nor is it for
publication, nor shall the personnel of this Department repeat its contents
to anyone outside of the Department itself. Be assured that the authorities
upstairs will know of its contents because a copy is being made for the City
Manager and it will not be necessary for anyone to be quick in informing
other members of the City government as to its content.

It would be far better if the men would take to heart what has
been said and buckle down and go to work, and assisting the Department in
going forward maintaining its good name and reputation that has been built
up in the last three years.

L. G. Jester
Chief of Police

likely carry a martyr's campaign to the public through newspapers, radio, and speaking engagements, saying, "I told you
so; I told you 'they' were after Jester," with the aim of
shifting attention from his unbecoming conduct.

- If the chief were dismissed, with the dismissal to be effective
at some later date, he would have the same opportunity to
carry a martyr's campaign to the public.
- If Jester were permitted to resign, a potential employer of
his, unless he checked the circumstances of the chief's leaving
the Fargo municipal service, might take upon his community
the same kinds of problems the chief had created in Fargo.

In addition, there were a number of miscellaneous considerations.

- The mayor had selected Jester for the job; he felt the chief had done a good job; and they were rather close hunting companions and social friends. Furthermore, although the law spoke of dismissal power, because of conflicting provisions of law that had never been resolved, the possibility existed that the city manager had only power to suspend, and the chief had right of appeal to the civil service commission. If, on hearing his appeal, the civil service commission ruled that the city manager dismissed the chief for racial, religious, or political reasons, the civil service commission could overrule the manager and restore the chief to his office.

- Our civil service commission was a three-member board, with one of the three positions vacant. The chairman was Larry Hamm, the office-supply man I had offended when we put city purchasing on a competitive basis. The other member of the commission was an employee of Hamm's at his office supply business.

- The city commission was divided on many issues two to three. Part of the campaign of the two new commissioners had been criticism of the police department's two-toned whistles and white gloves. One of these commissioners had been the first to hear of something wrong concerning the prisoners' meal tickets. The other had said to me after hearing the chief, "It's obvious that the chief of police has lied about the meal ticket matter." If I consulted the commission about a contemplated dismissal action, the commission would likely divide on this issue too.

I decided to take the following action.

- To avoid the risk of precipitating a serious split in the commission with continuing and destructive results throughout the organization, I would take the action and the full responsibility for initiating for the chief's dismissal without consulting the commission beforehand.

- To keep to a minimum the adverse effect on the chief of the dismissal, I would list in the dismissal notice only enough charges to justify dismissal, and I would make them general rather than specific.

- To forestall the chief's successfully undertaking a diversionary campaign while still in office, I would make the dismissal effective immediately.

In preparation for carrying out my decision, I drafted, typed, and signed a letter that I would personally deliver, notifying the chief that he was dismissed as of 10:00 a.m. Monday, August 1. The closing paragraph read: "A copy of this notice shall be filed immediately with the civil service commission of the city of Fargo, as required by law. As you know, the law permits you to file, within five (5) business days after delivery or mailing of this notice, an appeal for a hearing before the civil service commission."

The Reaction

On Monday morning I invited the chief and my assistant to my office. I handed the letter to the chief and then later had Dwight Ink deliver a copy to Chairman Hamm of the civil service commission. I sent a memorandum to the second-in-command in the department, advising him of the dismissal and asking him to notify all members of the department. I issued a written statement to press and radio that both Jester and the civil service commission were free to disclose the contents of the dismissal notice and that detailed information supporting the reasons for dismissal would be submitted to the civil service commission if Jester asked for a hearing. In the afternoon, I appointed the night captain acting chief.

When word of the dismissal reached the publisher of the morning and evening papers, he telephoned me to say he wanted a copy of the dismissal notice. I declined to give it to him, on the ground that this information would come out in the hearing. I said if Jester preferred to avoid publicity, he could do so by not asking for the hearing; that it was up to Jester or the civil service commission whether the reasons for his dismissal were publicized further; it was not appropriate for me to do so.

This angered the publisher, and he threatened to take action against me. His evening paper reported: "Lawrence W. Hamm, chairman of the civil service commission, said the reasons for the dismissal would be withheld for five days, during which time Jester can appeal. Hamm said the decision was made to insure 'fairness' to Jester." But by 9:00 p.m. first Jester, then Chairman Hamm, made the contents of the dismissal letter available to the paper.

Also that evening we had an emergency at home. Our oldest son, Steven, who had been listless for two days, became feverish and started vomiting and complaining of severe stomach pains. We called the doctor. At 10:00 p.m. the doctor ordered Steven to the hospital for an emergency appendectomy. By midnight the surgery was over, and we were assured Steven was sufficiently out of danger that we could return home.

Agda and I fell exhausted into bed only to be shocked out of our sleep by the telephone two hours later.

A liquor-loaded voice at the other end asked, "Are you the city manager?"

"Yes," I replied.

"I'm a friend of Jester's. I just got into town. I wanta tell you, you ought to have your throat cut, and your guts dragged around the streets of this town. Dya hear me? You ought to have your throat cut, and your guts dragged around the streets of this town."

I didn't say anything. After all, what is there to say to such a suggestion, at that hour of the night, after a long, hard day?

After a moment of silence, the caller yelled, "Why don't you say something? Ain't ya got no guts?" Then he hung up.

More Facts

The mayor and three commissioners were at the Tuesday morning commission meeting. Led by the mayor, they took turns sharply criticizing me for dismissing the chief. That evening, under an inch-high banner headline, HARLOW STAKES JOB ON CHIEF FIRING, the paper reported the meeting, published one of Jester's bulletins, and said Jester would appeal his dismissal.

The next day I was served a "Demand for a Bill of Particulars" by Attorney Bergesen, representing Jester. This was the former Speaker of the State House of Representatives who had tried to get the state law on council-manager government changed or repealed.

The press quoted Jester as saying most of my charges were false and that he was removed without warning or opportunity for a hearing or a chance to resign.

I had two pleasant surprises. One was receipt of three or four letters from citizens and a telegram from a Minot city alderman, supporting my action. The other was a telephone call from Senator Shure. I knew he had opposed adoption of the council-manager plan, so I did not know what to expect. It was reassuring to have him say he knew the chief was going to have to be dismissed sometime, that the way I did it was the only way it could be done, and that he would help me any way he could; all I had to do was call.

More letters arrived the following day, some anonymous, but all favorable. I also received a reply to a telegram I had sent to

RED RIVER VALLEY FORECAST:
Fair and warmer tonight and tomorrow, low
tonight 50 to 60; high Wednesday 85 to 95.
(Weather Details on Page 14)

THE FARG

AND DA

Established 1878   Entered as Second Class Matter
Postoffice, Fargo, N. D.   Price Five Cents   FARGO, N. D., TUESI

HARLOW STAKES J

Will 'Stand Or Fall' On Police Case

In the face of criticism by Mayor Charles A. Dawson and several city commissioners, LeRoy F. Harlow, Fargo city manager, told the commission today that he will "stand or fall" on his action Monday in dismissing Lloyd G. Jester, chief of police.

"We are probably going to have to decide here what form of government Fargo is to have," he declared.

The session was tranquil and there were no raised voices, no interruption by one disputant of another, or anything to indicate any break in friendly relations between the commission and city manager.

He pointed out he acted fully within authority given him by statute; that he is satisfied he acted with good cause and that the reason he did not consult with commissioners was that the proposal might prove embarrassing to Mayor Charles A. Dawson, who appointed Jester.

He also was concerned by the possibility of a split on the issue within the commission which might prove detrimental to the city's interests, he declared.

"The commissioners might have disagreed; I don't know," he said. "I had given the matter long consideration and I had

made up my mind the job had to be done no matter how disagreeable."

* * *

He pointed out provisions of the city manager form of government which give the manager the responsibility of hiring and dismissing appointive employees.

"I am sorry that you should have taken the attitude at the beginning that I as city manager am wrong. The ordinance was passed by the commission, providing steps for dismissal, for a hearing and for a disclosure of facts.

"I am working for you. If you are dissatisfied with my actions as manager you can dismiss me as I dismissed the chief.

"I choose to stand or fall on my action."

He declared that if the officer involved had been "someone who had received less publicity and attention," the commission probably would have been satisfied with his action and would have accepted the action without comment.

"There has been too much stress on the importance of any one city job," he said. "What is needed more is teamwork. Lack of teamwork is primarily the cause of this change."

* * *

As to the details of the charges against Jester, Harlow said, he would prefer to discuss them privately with the commission. He mentioned several instances of alleged lack of teamwork, however.

He said that in his opinion Jester's handling of employees has been harsh and marked by violent language.

He cited an instance in which

194

O FORUM

BLICAN

Evening Edition

ENING, AUGUST 2, 1949   1   Fourteen Pages   Vol. 71, No. 222

B ON CHIEF FIRING

certain health department employees had objected to riding in trucks with jail inmate laborers and quoted Jester as having said: "Those damn guys aren't any better than the prisoners."

Such acts by Jester, Harlow said had been "untactful and demoralizing."

Outside of an airing of views on the question there was no action taken by the commission, except to make plans to fill the vacancy on the civil service commission within a week.

* * *

Mayor Dawson opened discussion on the Jester case by declaring "I don't believe he should have been dismissed."

Criticizing Harlow for failure to consult in advance with the commission, he contended that neither corruption, dishonesty or lack of ability appeared among the charges.

"The dismissal was a shock to all of us," he declared. "By consulting us in advance, the city could have avoided a lot of furore and a bad reputation.

"I was dumfounded by the dismissal," said Commissioner Fred C. Hagen.

"The commissioners should have been advised," Hagen said. "We, too, have a responsibility to citizens. A frank discussion with the commissioners would have been better.

"I was embarrassed. I knew nothing of what was going on."

Commissioner W. H. Toussaint said "You will have an awful time justifying a dismissal on the

charges. As to the dismissal itself, it seems to have been well known by others not commissioners. It seems to have been common knowledge at Park Rapids, Minn., Sunday."

Toussaint said he learned Fargo tourists passing through Park Rapids had heard the story at that place.

While declaring he is not in a position to discuss the merits of the dismissal, Commissioner James P. Dunn also criticized Harlow's failure to consult with the commission.

"I am not questioning Harlow's authority," said Toussaint. "But the charges should involve morals or integrity for a dismissal of this kind. Maybe there is something I don't know about.

"Jester has done a good job and the charges don't seem to justify his dismissal on short notice."

Harlow declared the problem has been on his mind for a period of time.

"The situation has gradually been getting worse," he said. "I seriously considered consulting the commission. But I came to the conclusion that it would result in a split in the commission and an unfortunate situation in the commission itself by which nothing would be gained and something might be lost.

"It's a difficult job to discharge a man. I don't like it. He has a right to protect himself, his family and his reputation. I will be glad to discuss the details and circumstances with the commission."

195

Dunn pressed Harlow to explain what matters he felt it necessary to discuss with the commission.

"You don't feel an obligation to consult the commission on administrative matters, yet you feel it necessary to advise the commission on policy," Dunn said.

Harlow replied he saw it as his duty to provide information for the commission for its use.

"But you have no obligation to consult with me," he declared.

"If the commission is to be consulted on appointments and dismissals, that means wiping out of the city manager plan."

Jester Says He'll Appeal Dismissal

Lloyd G. Jester, who was dismissed yesterday as Fargo's police chief, said today he will appeal to the city civil service commission the dismissal order served upon him yesterday by City Manager LeRoy F. Harlow.

Jester has retained A. R. Bergesen, attorney, and Bergesen said an appeal is certain but that he has not had opportunity to review the case.

Six reasons, of which "any one or more . . . is deemed sufficient cause for dismissal," were presented by Harlow in the letter of dismissal.

Contents of the dismissal letter were made available to The Fargo Forum last night by the ousted chief shortly before 9 o'clock.

Harlow, in announcing the dismissal, said it was up to Jester or the civil service commission to release the letter if they so wished.

Lawrence W. Hamm, chairman of the civil service commission, said at first the letter would be withheld five days "in fairness to Jester," but released it to the press about 15 minutes after Jester had made his copy available.

*   *   *

In his letter to Jester, Harlow said, "As police chief of the Fargo police department you have:

"1. Wilfully failed to co-operate with other administrative personnel of the city administration, and aspersed the character and reputation of such administrative personnel with a resulting loss of efficiency of the administrative service of the city government;

"2. Conducted yourself personally, and in writing, in a manner unbecoming a police officer, by the use of harsh, profane, violent and or insulting language to your subordinates, to the city manager, and to private citizens;

"3. Oppressed your subordinates, the members of the Fargo police department, by the issuance and enforcement of verbal and written orders which

(a) Prohibited police officers from conversing, whether upon chance meeting or as prearranged and whether on duty or off duty, with certain citizens ot this city;

(b) Prohibited police officers from discussing outside the police department the contents of a general information bulletin, which contents were declared elsewhere in the bulletin to be not secret;

(c) Served as veiled and open threats of dismissal of police officers who failed to issue to the public so-called "citations," or tickets, in sufficient number, when such number was not stated and when the duties and period of work of certain officers made compliance virtually impossible;

(d) Stated that the city manager had indicated dissatisfaction with the performance of certain officers, and had expressed a desire that certain actions be taken, when as a matter of fact the city manager had at no time so expressed himself to you or to any other person;

"4. Wilfully and knowingly disobeyed a direct order from the

196

city manager by ordering and or permitting charges for intoxicating beverages to be made against city appropriations by your subordinates;

"5. Failed to exercise the prudent judgment required of a police chief in your relations with the administrative officers and heads of other political subdivisions and institutions, despite the necessity of close co-operation and harmonious working relationships if the public interest is to be properly served;

"6. Failed as chief of the Fargo police department to prevent the morale of the city's principal law enforcement agency, the Fargo police department, from reaching a point which is so low as to endanger this city and to interfere with the proper and necessary enforcement of law and order."

---

the FBI in Washington the day the paper carried the story of Jester's dismissal. The paper had called him "a former FBI agent," which I doubted. Mr. Notesteen, assistant special agent in charge of the FBI in St. Paul, telephoned to say: "Jester was never on the staff of the Federal Bureau of Investigation—was never with the FBI. He attended the FBI Police Academy as a police officer, but that's a long way from being with the FBI." Then he added, "This is not the first time we have had this problem. We have tried to get the paper to quit saying Jester was with the FBI, but evidently they haven't stopped."

With this information, I decided to call the city of Albany, California, where the paper reported Jester had been chief of police before going into the navy. I talked to the mayor. He remembered Jester. I told him the action I had taken and briefly why. He said that sounded like Jester. Although he didn't remember much about him, the mayor said, "There's one thing I do remember—he treated the men like animals."

The Tension Increases

The next three months were dramatic, but hardly ones we would care to live through again. The district court returned Jester to the position of police chief. This made it awkward for the men in his department as well as other city employees who had to work with the police department. Our four-year-old Christine came home from playing with a neighbor youngster. "Mother," she asked, "when are they going to burn up Daddy?" She had heard the neighbors saying her daddy was going to be "fired." Several people whom Agda and I had considered close acquaintances, if not friends, now found it convenient to cross the street to avoid meeting us when we were downtown. We moved out of our home, thinking that doing so might make it more saleable. A neighbor who, with his wife, had been in our home several times and knew what we paid for it, came to me to say, "When you get down to half what you paid for your place, I'll buy it."

On the other hand, we had many letters, telegrams, and telephone calls from both local and out-of-state people, offering encouragement, support, and help.

At my first opportunity to reply to the commissioners' unanimous criticism of my action, I prepared a written statement that read in part:

"We act according to what we believe, and I believe that the first prerequisite for administrative responsibility in public office is integrity. Honest mistakes, honestly made, can be tolerated and excused. But regardless of technical ability, the man or woman whose conduct has demonstrated beyond a question that he is not honest is, in my opinion, unfit to fill a public office. When the person in responsible charge of the organization has satisfied himself of this fact, it is not his choice but his duty to take necessary action. The degree and extent of evidence of dishonesty is not of major importance. There are those who hold that unless a man has already committed a heinous crime he should not be removed from office. It is foolhardy to wait for a catastrophe when you are convinced that it will come if no action is taken. The time to stop dishonesty in government is when it is first detected, not after it is well established."

To almost the end of the episode, the picture was confused and full of details that have little general interest. Perhaps it would be helpful to list in chronological order newspaper front-page headlines of the period. They give an overview of the sequence of events. Here they are:

The Fargo Forum
Monday Evening, August 1, 1949
JESTER FIRED AS POLICE CHIEF
City Manager
Gives Notice
In Person

The Fargo Forum
Tuesday Morning, August 2, 1949
CITE REASONS FOR JESTER OUSTER
Police Chief
Is Fired By
City Manager

The Fargo Forum
Tuesday Evening, August 2, 1949
HARLOW STAKES JOB ON CHIEF FIRING
Will "Stand
Or Fall" On
Police Case

The Fargo Forum
Wednesday Evening, August 3, 1949
No Warning
Of Dismissal
Jester Says

The Fargo Forum
Monday Evening, August 15, 1949
COURT ORDER REINSTATES JESTER
Chief Back In Job
Pending Hearing On
Injunction Aug. 30

The Fargo Forum
Friday Morning, October 14, 1949
JESTER RESIGNS AS CHIEF OF POLICE
Letter To
Commission
Raps Harlow

The Fargo Forum
Wednesday Morning, October 19, 1949
COMMISSION ASKS HARLOW TO RESIGN
Fargo City
Manager
Says 'No'

The Fargo Forum
Wednesday Evening, October 19, 1949
DRAFT CHARGES AGAINST HARLOW
Manager
Refuses
To Resign

The Fargo Forum
Friday Evening, October 21, 1949
HARLOW SUSPENDED BY COMMISSION
Jorgenson, Acting
Manager, Urged To
Let Jester Resign

The Fargo Forum
Friday Morning, October 28, 1949
COMMISSION REINSTATES HARLOW, 4-1
City Manager Denies
Lack Of Cooperation
Before Large Crowd

The Fargo Forum
Friday Evening, October 28, 1949
HARLOW BACK IN CITY MANAGER POST
4-1 Commission Vote
Reinstates Him After
Hearing On Charges

Public Hearings—the American Way

I doubt that anyone was more surprised than I at the outcome of the hearing on my dismissal.

Jester's lawyers had not only succeeded in getting their client
reinstated; they even got a court injunction that prohibited the
civil service commission from holding a hearing on the Jester
matter. Mayor Dawson had telephoned me at home the evening
of October 17 to tell me the commission intended to ask for my
resignation. He suggested I resign because that would "look
better on your record." At the regular commission meeting the
next day he made a "loss of confidence" statement, declaring
he had lost confidence not only in me but possibly in the city-
manager form of government. He expressed the opinion that
"the National Association of City Managers, or whatever it is
called, has as one of its objects to create in city managers the
idea they are dictators." The commission had followed with a
3-0 vote to ask for my resignation. It was either resign or be
suspended and dismissed. I declined to resign.

In the meantime, Senator Shure had found that other com-
mitments would keep him from assisting me as he had offered.
He did say, however, that some citizens who wanted to see the

matter cleared up had offered to pay attorney's fees if I was willing to see the case through. Senator Shure had already asked Attorney Murphy, a former state assistant attorney general, if he would be willing to represent me.

Agda and I met with Murphy to discuss the procedure if I chose to request a hearing, as permitted by law. He made his position clear from the outset. "I'm not entering upon any crusade," he said. "Some people have offered to pay me to defend you. That is the only reason I am interested. My advice to you is to forget the hearing and get another job. I know from my experience as assistant attorney general that you'll never be reinstated to your position by the same body that removed you. Those men who fired you certainly aren't going to turn around and put you back in office."

I told Murphy I felt no bitterness toward the commission members. I said I subscribed wholeheartedly to the principle of council-manager government which gives the council absolute authority to hire and fire the manager, with or without cause, and I did not want anything done which would cause trouble for the commission. I would go through with the matter as the only way to bring out the facts, which had never yet been presented to the public.

Murphy said that was my decision, but he was not going to merely sit at the hearing. He was going there to defend his client.

The evening of the hearing, the paper carried a brief front-page item, "Shift Harlow Hearing to Courtroom." The reason given for the change from the small city commission chamber was that "interest of citizens indicates a considerable attendance."

Agda was depressed. She recalled the words of an ex-city manager who was my supervisor at the U.S. Bureau of the Budget. When I told him of my interest in a city-manager career, he had said, "When it's all over, all you'll have to show for it will be headlines and ulcers."

It was a lovely fall evening, and on our walk to the courthouse I tried to raise Agda's spirits by observing, "We can be grateful we live in America, where to disagree with the commission only means losing a job, not being sent to a concentration camp or Siberia."

The Cass County Courthouse occupied a city block next to the block occupied by the Fargo High School. As we approached the courthouse, I saw that cars were parked around both blocks. I remarked to Agda that I wondered what was going on at the high school. But as we turned up the walk to the courthouse entrance, there were people lining both sides of the walk, at the doors, and inside the first floor foyer. As we moved past them, several greeted us quietly, "Good evening, Mr. Harlow, Mrs. Harlow." Evidently the cars parked around the high school belonged to people who had come to the hearing.

At the second-floor courtroom the corridors were packed, and so was the courtroom itself. Every seat was taken; all the wide, deep window sills were being used as seats by spectators; and the jury box was filling. The thought that came to my mind was that people just naturally like to see bloodlettings and executions.

A gentleman gave Agda his seat. The five city commission members, the city attorney, the city auditor, and Murphy were seated at a large table behind the rail and in front of the judge's bench. I walked through the gate and took a chair beside Murphy.

Surprise!

Mayor Dawson called the meeting to order. The seven charges were read, mostly that I had "arbitrarily and obstinately refused to cooperate with the city commission."

Murphy uttered only a few words, but they were crucial. "Let the record show that Mr. Harlow denies each and every matter and thing contained in the charges. Where is your proof?"

This move took the three signers of the charges totally by surprise, as it did me. They and I apparently had thought alike, namely that they would listen patiently while I responded to their charges; they would vote to make the suspension permanent, and it would be all over.

The second surprise came when Commissioner Toussaint spoke. He said, "You're limiting this charge to the Jester case. The only way Mr. Harlow could have cooperated with the city commission on the Jester matter was to have withdrawn his charges against Jester and allowed him to remain in office. . . . Insofar as the Jester case, the charge is true. Otherwise, the charge is false. I can't go along with it."

The third surprise came when the audience began applauding Commissioner Toussaint, and another when one of the commissioners who had voted out the purchasing program said he had made an error.

It took me about 1½ hours to answer the charges. When I finished my presentation, I tendered my resignation. The mayor attempted to delay a decision, but Commissioner Toussaint moved "that Harlow's resignation be denied and that he go back to work tomorrow morning and do his job."

The vote was 4-1, but the instant there were three yes votes, the audience burst from their seats and surged forward, cheering and shouting. Old people with tears in their eyes embraced me. Young businessmen were slapping me on the back. Other earnest people were shaking my hand. Over the heads of the crowd, a political science professor from the North Dakota Agricultural College was waving at me. He had called at my office a few weeks before to study how an administrator reacts under stress. At that time he had given me this advice: "Harlow, you seem to think if you do the best you can and the people know the truth, it will turn out all right. You're too optimistic. You've got to be practical. Being right isn't going to feed your wife and your five kids." Now, he was waving and shouting, "Harlow, you've made an optimist out of me!"

Later, Agda told me she overheard Attorney Murphy remark, "Before tonight, never in forty-two years did I ever know of a reversal in an ouster case."

Any Skeletons in *Your* Closet?

For days after the hearing I received congratulations by telephone, letter, and in person, some from individuals who had avoided speaking to me during the past couple of months. The Sunday, October 30, newspaper carried the following editorial:

Commission, Manager Off To Fresh Start

The Fargo city commission has given City Manager LeRoy F. Harlow a vote of confidence—a clean bill of health on the charges which that same body had preferred against the manager.

The audience at the hearing was solidly pro-Harlow. Those who wanted to see Mr. Harlow fired might contend that the hearing room was "packed" with Harlow supporters, but there is no law against Americans demonstrating their support for any person by cheers and applause. And it is significant that the Harlow supporters were there in force, while nobody in the audience did any cheering for the opposition.

But even assuming that the audience was sold on Harlow ahead of time, the important thing is that he sold himself to the judges—the city commission, a majority of which had filed the ouster charges and had been openly hostile to Harlow for some weeks.

With those odds against him, Mr. Harlow girded himself for battle. He argued that he had been right in seeking to dismiss Police Chief Lloyd G. Jester; he was righteously indignant that he should be the "goat" because he had done what he thought was right.

Mr. Harlow made a magnificent showing,

a masterful argument, and got results.

He won the ball game and he's entitled to the fruits of victory—co-operation from the city commission, and from the public generally, in carrying on a difficult assignment.

The charges against Mr. Harlow in no way attacked his integrity, but ran mostly to allegations of stubbornness and lack of co-operation with the city commission.

In his dealings with the commission, he may have been a little short on diplomacy, at times, but on the other hand, the commission itself has certainly intruded into the city manager's territory, as outlined by state law, on several occasions.

The Fargo Forum does not take seriously the charge that Harlow's actions have "created unfortunate and unfavorable publicity for the city of Fargo," quoting from the charges.

Certainly this city is big enough and has enough substantial assets so that a public airing of a government family squabble isn't going to impair the community. A row of the sort we've had shows a healthy interest in city government administration, which in our book is better than the lethargy with which many communities contemplate their government.

Now that the atmosphere is cleared, this is the time for Fargoans generally to do everything they can to make the city manager form of government a success.

In voting to reinstate Mr. Harlow, two of the commissioners, Mayor C. A. Dawson and Fred Hagen, voted against the charges they had preferred. In doing so, they admitted they were wrong, which, generally, is a pretty hard admission for any person in public life to make.

Mr. Harlow, by consenting to continue as city manager even after his vindication, demonstrates he is willing to wipe the slate clean and not have any hard feelings as the result of the ouster attempt. If the commission adopts the same attitude, then the commission and the city manager are off to a fresh start on the job of giving Fargo a city government of which it can be proud.

But the city commission meeting on the following Tuesday took a different turn. Mayor Dawson made a lengthy statement to all present, lashing out at what he called the "hooliganism" of the audience at the hearing. He closed by speaking directly to me that as far as he was concerned I was back on a "probation principle." After the meeting, one of the commissioners told me the mayor had been booed when introduced over the loudspeaker at the preceding Saturday's college football game, which may have helped to account for his attitude.

Two weeks later, at a meeting of some Chamber of Commerce and city officials, one of the group asked me to stay a minute after the meeting to talk "about something else." The "something else" was that the liquor dealers were determined to get rid of me; that one of them had offered $2,500 to any commissioner who could bring this about. The plan was to either get me fired or get my salary cut to $1,000 a year so I would quit.

His story was essentially the same as what Senator Shure had told me some months before.

A week later the owner-operator of a local business college called me on a business matter. When we finished talking business, he added this puzzling remark: "I have watched with interest—as have many others—recent events, and I like the way you have handled yourself. This is particularly significant because in politics, and in a sense that's what you are in, you

204

don't always find people about whom it can be said, as a party said about you the other day, 'There just isn't a single thing in that man's personal life that you can put your finger on.' " Then he added, "And he isn't a friend of yours, either."

This was something new. It now looked as though not only would there be no letup from the liquor interests, but possibly some others might be trying to pin something on me.

The most challenging employment opportunity that had developed while I was job hunting after the commission suspended me and I was sure I was out at Fargo, was that of director of a new, legislatively created commission of private citizens to study and recommend improvements in the Minnesota state government. Its official title was Minnesota Efficiency in Government Commission, later dubbed by the press Minnesota's "Little Hoover" commission. The commission had a year to do its work. When I was offered the directorship at the same salary I was receiving in Fargo, I accepted. One final Fargo headline:

The Fargo Forum
Tuesday Morning, November 22, 1949
HARLOW RESIGNS CITY MANAGER POST
To Head New
Minnesota
State Agency

Richfield, Minnesota

The range of local government administration
How to figure your local property tax

New Challenges

Although my task with the Efficiency in Government Commission was to direct a comprehensive study of the policies, organization, and operations of the more than 100 state departments and agencies, my interests still centered in local government. For instance, I was pleased to accept an invitation to present a description of American local government to a delegation of Japanese local officials touring the United States under U.S. State Department sponsorship. Also, knowing the commission would go out of existence shortly after filing its report with the legislature and governor, I began actively seeking another city-manager post about three months before I finished writing the report.

During that time I received a call from a party identifying himself as a member of the Richfield, Minnesota, Taxpayers Association. He said the association was promoting the council-manager plan in that Minneapolis suburb and would like to have me address a public rally on the issue before the upcoming election, to describe to the public the basic ideas of the council-manager plan and how it was intended to work. I accepted the invitation.

After completing its report, "How to Achieve Greater Efficiency and Economy in Minnesota's Government," the commission members decided they should have someone around to explain their dozens of recommendations to the legislature and to the public, and they extended my contract to April 1951. They completed their work ahead of schedule with enough money left over and turned back to the state treasury to earn the commission a "thanks are in order" editorial in the *Minneapolis Star* on April 18, 1951.

In the meantime, the Richfield voters approved the new government for their municipality. At the suggestion of Professor Clarence Ludwig of the League of Municipalities, the Richfield village council engaged me to make a comprehensive administrative survey and lay out a step-by-step plan for the change from a mayor and board of trustees government to a council-manager government. Also, I was to be the acting village manager on a part-time basis, to sign checks and generally keep the governmental wheels turning. So for the next few months I was on three jobs—director of the Little Hoover Commission, director of what we called the "Administrative and Personnel Survey of the Richfield Municipal Government," and—during my spare time—acting village manager of Richfield.

It took me until July to complete the survey and the fifteen chapter report, with its more than 100 recommendations. The report was representative of comprehensive administrative surveys, with provisions for changing from one basic form of government to another. It considered such subjects as the following:

- Services rendered by the Richfield municipal government
- Principles of council-manager government
- The job of the council
- The job of the manager
- The relationship between council and manager
- The organization problem
- Recommended overall organization for Richfield
- Organization for financial administration
- Organization for personnel administration
- Organization for line operations
- Independent boards and commissions
- Financial management
- Personnel management
- Legal services
- Police services
- Fire protection services
- Public health services
- Public works
- Parks and recreation
- Liquor store operations
- Planning and zoning
- The space problem
- Staffing requirements
- Council procedures affecting administration

The survey report included policy documents, organizational charts, procedural charts, and operating forms. Later, I learned that Professor Ludwig used the report as a reference text in his course in municipal administration at the University of Minnesota.

After I completed the survey, the council invited me to stay on as full-time manager. Because I had known the Little Hoover commission assignment would be temporary, we had lived in rented houses. Now we bought a home in Richfield near the Minneapolis-St. Paul airport. The family and I were glad to be settled in this pleasant and growing Minneapolis suburb.

To our disappointment, my service in Richfield was brief, but

I think the experience revealed the kinds and the range of governmental challenges that face citizens and local officials living and working on the fringes of rapidly expanding urban complexes. Of course there were the basic problems of providing water and sewer services to a city of nearly 20,000 people, all of whose residents were using individual wells and septic tanks. There was an urgent need for planning, and for subdivision regulations. Because the huge Minneapolis-St. Paul Airport was carved out of Richfield originally, we had to develop practical working relationships between our residents and the Metropolitan Airport Commission. To add to the challenges, a tornado struck the main business section the weekend I went to work full time, leveling several business places and bursting several residences at their corners. In sum, the Richfield experience ranged from the disappointing and frustrating to the amusing and the satisfying. Let me touch on a few of the situations, starting with the administrative and personnel survey.

Growth Pains

My relations with individual councilmen and all the employees were pleasant, and the survey went smoothly. But the council meetings were disappointing. They probably were a picture in miniature of what happened after World War II wherever developers built and sold thousands of homes on what was formerly farmland at the outskirts of large cities. The newcomers who wanted all the amenities of city living clashed with the old-timers who wanted things left as they were. The only subjects the two groups agreed on were (1) that taxes were too high, and (2) that they distrusted and were determined to have nothing to do with the residents and officials of the "big city" next door—Minneapolis.

The mayor was a man whose father's farm had once covered a large part of what was now Richfield. The mayor still farmed the "home place." A couple of other council members were local businessmen. The former board of trustees had exercised some foresight by attempting to get through a multimillion dollar sanitary sewer project to meet the exploding growth—ten-fold in ten years. This effort failed, largely because the new voters did not trust the old board of trustees or the consulting engineers that the board had employed.

Council meeting after council meeting ran past midnight, some into early morning. The councilmen seemed set on arguing every minute detail of each item on the agenda, in a kind of endurance test. When there were no items to argue, they argued over past actions of the former board of trustees, some of whose members were now on the village council.

Some council meetings were attended by so many citizens it was necessary to drive the fire trucks out of the fire station onto the driveway apron and set up for the council meeting in the fire hall. Then the councilmen played to the gallery. It often seemed that the needs of the entire community and what was good for all the people was of little or no concern to any of the councilmen.

But perhaps this is to be expected. Although elected officials are supposed to represent all of the people, the fact is they are most sensitive to the wishes of those who support them for office, or who reside in their districts.

Not "Assessable"

Richfield was not the only Minneapolis suburb with severe growing pains. At least a dozen others faced similar problems of increasing public needs, low tax base, wasteful competition to get more industry (to bring in more taxes), and duplication of services, personnel, facilities, and equipment.

With the hope of improving the situation, someone arranged a meeting of suburban officials to explore ways in which the suburbs could cooperate and help one another. In opening remarks at the meeting, some officials expressed hope that this unofficial association of officials might be made permanent. If it had been, it would have been a forerunner of the "councils of governments" that have been virtually required since the mid-60s by the federal government as a prerequisite for federal aid to local units.

At the meeting I suggested that one way the suburbs might help one another would be to adopt a uniform personnel ordinance, because recruiting, hiring, and retaining qualified personnel was one of our major problems. With a cooperative program, instead of each government recruiting candidates, preparing and administering examinations, and maintaining its own list of eligibles, and instead of candidates having to apply for municipal employment in many places, we could have one agency to whom all applicants would apply. This agency could hold examinations in several locations for the convenience of candidates, but it could maintain a master list of eligibles from which all the suburban governments could draw qualified applicants. I thought this might also reduce the pirating of employees then going on among the competing governments.

Along with the pool of candidates from which we could all draw, I thought a uniform pay scale would make it harder for employees to continue to play one government against the other by pointing to one or more governments that pay more, thereby getting their own pay brought up to or beyond the high one and keeping in motion the game of leap-frogging compensation.

Having made the suggestion, I was asked to draft the model ordinance, which I did. It was presented at the next meeting of the suburban officials. But neither the uniform personnel ordinance nor the few other suggestions offered at the meeting were adopted, and there were no further meetings of the suburban officials during my time in Richfield.

During the administrative and personnel survey I interviewed the chief building inspector to familiarize myself with the procedures followed in administering the zoning ordinance and the building, plumbing, and electrical codes.

He was showing me his files when I noticed that several of them contained originals of letters to contractors and others. That was unusual, since we usually think of files as containing file copies. Curious about this, I asked if someone had failed to mail these letters and they had gotten back into the files by mistake.

"No," was the reply, "we always mail the carbon copy to the addressee and keep the original in our files. That way our files stay neat and clean; carbon copies mess up our files."

I made a mental note to check the legality of this unique practice and also to find out, if I could discreetly, how the recipients of carbon copies of letters felt about this kind of secondhand treatment.

At about the same time, in order to get background on Richfield as rapidly as I could, I scanned the past three or four years' issues of the local newspaper. It was clear that taxes—especially special assessment charges to cover the cost of new streets, sidewalks, curb and gutter, drainage, and others—were the hottest issue in town. Both the village assessor and the consulting engineer who calculated the share of improvement costs to be charged against each "benefited property" were under continuing attack.

The consulting engineer was an independent, licensed professional. He was not a part of the municipal government, hence he was outside my survey. But the assessor was a vital part of the government. His performance could either enhance or damage the public's view of it. Therefore, I made a special effort to get to know him and to understand his procedures. This was not easy.

I asked him to tell me about his major problems. One of them, he said, was the difficulty of setting proper values on property that "is not assessable."

I asked, "Why is any property not assessable?"

"I don't know; it just is," he replied.

"But there must be a reason. Is it owned by a tax-exempt organization? Does it have homestead exemption? Is some political influence being applied to keep it not assessable?"

He said he didn't know, so I dropped the subject and we turned to other matters.

But what he had said about some property not being assessable troubled me. I wanted to make as few personnel changes as possible. At the same time, here we had a man in a key position, who could make or break the new form of government and any administration. He was obviously conscientious and seemed to be competent. Yet on this delicate point about tax exemption, or maybe tax evasion, he was woefully ignorant.

I met with him again. We went over the same subject. I got the same answers. He was red-faced and perspiring. I was baffled. Finally, I said, "Bring me a map please. Maybe if you show me on a map where these parcels are located, I can figure out what you're telling me. I certainly haven't been able to get it through my head from our conversation so far."

He brought a map showing the boundaries of all the streets, blocks, lots, and other parcels in a certain section of town. On it he pointed out three or four blocks in which properties were "not assessable." I asked who owned the properties in those blocks. He didn't know offhand, but he would look it up in the records.

"Never mind," I said. "Just show me, specifically, in these blocks which parcels are not assessable." He took a pencil and marked some parcels. Each was in the center of a block.

Suddenly it dawned on me what he was trying to tell me. All the parcels he marked were located at the inside of a block—an unusual situation, but probably left that way for a neighborhood tot-lot, playground, or little park—and none of them had access to and from a street. "Oh," I said, "you mean these parcels are not 'ak'sess-a-ble.' They can't be reached from the street."

"That's what I said. They are not 'a-sess'a-ble.' " Although we continued to pronounce the words differently, from then on we were able to communicate.

A Knowledgeable Citizen—a Willing Taxpayer

Rarely does a local government official have an opportunity to explain, unhurriedly and completely, to an individual citizen or group of citizens any of the complex, fundamental facts of local government—how the local government was created and its relationship to the state government and other local governments, the election process, the powers the local government has and doesn't have, what it does, how it operates, or how it is financed. Individuals usually come to the city hall or courthouse to get a particular service, to support or oppose a specific issue, or to register a request or a complaint. They don't have interest or time to listen to a lengthy explanation of complex subjects. Similarly, groups such as service and civic clubs, PTAs, professional societies, and even political clubs usually try to squeeze a talk by a local government official between a meal and club business. Consequently, citizens with neither interest nor time to get a full explanation and a real understanding of these topics continue to have, and often to spread, their incomplete or wrong conceptions about local government.

During my years as a manager, I recall only twice when I could explore one of these topics without restraint of time or disinterest. One was the meeting in Fargo with the group that had come to complain about assessments and taxes and gave me an opportunity to list the services they were getting for their money. The other was a conversation with a Richfield taxpayer. He came in to complain that he had moved to the suburbs from Minneapolis to get away from high taxes, and "now they're getting as bad here as they are up there." He stayed long enough for me to explain the tax system.

His was such a recurring problem—of citizens paying taxes without understanding what the money goes for or how their share of the bill is figured—that I want to summarize our nearly two-hour conversation.

I don't remember his name, so I'll call him Mr. Olson. Mr. Olson faced me across my desk. He was well-dressed, looked prosperous, and probably was retired.

"Mr. Olson," I said, "you have the same concern about taxes that a lot of other people have. However, most of the others just grumble and complain; they don't give us a chance to explain what's happening."

"Well," he said, "I'm willing to listen to what you have to say, but I can tell you now that I don't expect to agree with you."

"I can appreciate that. I hope you won't be offended if I take you through a kind of basic course in local government taxation. I'd like to do so because it is amazing how many people pay local taxes without knowing what they're paying for or how their tax bill is figured."

"Go on," he said modestly. "You won't offend me. Besides, I don't have anything else to do, and I might learn something I ought to know."

I began by telling him how many other governments were taxing his property besides Richfield's. There was the county, the school district, and some special districts. Also, there was a special assessment district. He wanted to know what a special assessment district was, and I said I'd explain that before we got through.

I asked him what services he could think of that he got from local government. Fire, police, schools, and parks were what came to his mind. I added a number of others.

Then we went to taxes, which was the subject he had come in to talk about.

"So that I won't be taking your time unnecessarily," I said, "let me ask: Do you know how local government property taxes are figured?"

"No, I can't say that I do."

"Then let me explain by first pointing out that property taxes are really a simple matter, made complicated and confusing by three little-understood facts. First, as already mentioned, is the fact that the taxes on your property pay for several governments, not just one government; the second is that the value assigned to your property for tax purposes is not the same figure you would use if you were selling your property; and, third, tax rates are often figured in 'mills,' which is a term that mixes up our arithmetic."

I asked him to picture a layer cake, each layer a different thickness. Each layer of the cake represented the tax needs of one of several local governments being supported by his taxes— the thickest layer being the school district because it placed the biggest tax burden on properties, and a thin layer representing a special district that levied a small tax.

"The slice of the tax cake that is your share of the whole cake is your tax bill," I continued. "The size of your slice is determined by the value assigned to your property by the assessor. The value an assessor puts on your property is called its 'assessed value' or 'assessed valuation.' If each of the governments your property is supporting has its own assessor, as sometimes is the case, your property may have several different assessed valuations. Are you with me?"

"So far, I am."

So I went on. "The assessed value, or valuation, of your property is almost never the same figure you would be paid if you were willing to sell your property to someone who was willing to buy it. The selling price is the property's real value, often called its 'full market value' or 'full and true value.' To arrive at the assessed value, the assessor multiplies what he considers to be the real value by a fraction or percentage that is called the 'assessment ratio'; or he may simply assign an assessed value to the property that he thinks is in line with his assessed valuation of other properties. Either way, his decision can be pretty arbitrary. So long as he treats similar properties of equal real value essentially the same, the courts rarely interfere with his decisions."

At this point my visitor interrupted. "Why do they choose an assessed value that is different from the full, true value? Wouldn't it be a lot simpler to just use the real value and let it go at that?"

"A good question," I replied. "I've never been an assessor, so it may be unfair for me to express an opinion. But I've worked with enough of them that I think I see some possible reasons why they don't use full, real value.

"For one thing, an assessor's figures are subject to challenge by taxpayers before boards of equalization and in court. If the assessor departs from an established base and begins to make changes, his new figures are open to challenge. So the tendency is to keep assessed values approximately where they have been in the past, with only gradual change and then often across the board so that the relationships remain quite constant.

"Another reason for using assessed values which are different from full and true values may be the indirect, or secondary benefits under certain circumstances. For example, state financial aid to school districts and other local units may be based on a formula that includes assessed value as one of the factors. If the governments with low assessed values get more outside aid than those with high assessed value, the units will strive to keep their assessed value low. Or, in states having homestead exemption on the first few thousand dollars of assessed valuation, the lower the assessment ratio, the higher the true value of a property that qualifies for homestead exemption.

"Another reason may be political and psychological. For instance, I found some years ago in Massachusetts that it was politically unpopular for a government to have a tax rate over a certain figure. So, in order to allow the local government to collect more taxes without raising the tax rate, the assessor applied an assessment ratio that was not less, but was more, than the full and true value of the property.

"Another example of a political and psychological reason for applying an assessment ratio to the real value of property in order to get a low assessed value applies where an assessor has to get elected to office. Suppose that the assessor came to your home to appraise it for tax purposes, and you knew you could get $20,000 for your home any time you wanted to sell it—in fact, just recently you had been offered $20,000 for it. Now suppose that after the assessor measured the house, noted the kind of construction, added amounts for extras that make it more valuable—for instance, a fireplace—and reduced the value because of age and depreciation, he said to you, 'How would you feel, Mr. Olson, if we put the value of your home at $7000 for tax purposes?'

"How would you feel? Would you feel pretty good toward the assessor? Pretty nice fellow, isn't he? Would you probably vote for him next election? Don't answer. You and I know his 'reducing' the value of your home for tax purposes would be popular, and he might get reelected many times.

"Yet, the fact is his setting an assessed value different from your property's real value is of no benefit to you, unless as I said before there is homestead exemption, or state aid, or a state-wide tax, or maybe a tax rate ceiling. Even then, if he gives all the people he hopes will vote for him the same 'tax break' he gave you, and he probably would, you will pay your share of the total tax bill no matter what assessed value he establishes for your property. The local government tax-setting body would simply increase or decrease the tax rate to produce the number of tax dollars they need.

"This brings us to our discussion of the third little-understood fact about how tax rates are figured and why they are figured in 'mills.' But I've taken a lot of your time. Shall I stop here, or do you want me to go on?"

"No, don't stop now," Olson said. "I'm learning some things I've wondered about for years but never understood. I wonder how many taxpayers know what you've been telling me?"

"Too few, I'm afraid. I'll try to hurry through the rest of this."

I went back to the layer cake. I said each of those governments figures how much money it would have to spend for services it provides. Each estimates how much it will receive from charges it makes for some services, fees, fines, grants—any source except property taxes. The difference between what it figures it will spend and how much nonproperty tax revenue it expects to take in will be the amount it will have to get from taxes on the properties within its boundaries.

To simplify our example, I said, "Let's take any one of those governments and see what happens. The pattern is the same for all of them. The assessor adds together his assessed value figures for your property, your neighbors' properties, and all the other properties—both real estate (land and structures) and personal property (whether used for residential, commercial, industrial, or agricultural purposes) within the boundaries of that government. Let's assume that he comes up with a total figure of $50,000,000 of assessed value. Let's assume also that after the governing body of that government subtracts its estimated nonproperty tax revenues from its estimated expenditures it needs $2,000,000 from property taxes.

"The basic formula for determining the amount of taxes produced is the assessed value times the tax rate. Put another way, the tax rate is the amount of taxes needed, divided by the total assessed value. In our example, then, the tax rate will be $2,000,000 divided by $50,000,000. The resultant rate is four cents.

"Had the needs of the local government been much less than $2,000,000 and the total assessed value much more than $50,000,000, the answer might have been less than one cent. This would have been awkward to state. But you may remember from school days that one tenth of a cent was called a 'mill.' So, if we talk of 'mills,' 'mill rate,' or 'millage,' it is easier to deal with fractions of a cent. Therefore, in many places tax rates are stated in mills per dollar of assessed value. In our example, the tax rate would not be stated as 'four cents,' although that is what it actually is, but it would be stated as 'forty mills.' In some parts of the country, tax rates are in dollars and cents instead of in mills.

"Mr. Olson, if you look closely at many tax bills you will see a listing of all the local governments being supported by taxes against the property billed, and the tax rate of each government. This is the layer cake we talked about. In fact, the bill may show more than one tax rate under a single government, indicating that one government is taxing the property for several different purposes. When you add all the mill rates together, that total is the tax rate applied to the assessed value of the property. The tax due is that total mill rate multiplied by the assessed value of the property.

"So much for how tax rates are established, and how your tax bill is figured. Any questions?"

He didn't have any questions, and I thought I had better stop at this point. Experience had taught me that the best way for a local official to bore someone is to start explaining the tax system. First they yawn, next they look at their watches, then the sensitive ones get glassy-eyed. The nervier ones interrupt in the middle of a sentence to say they just remembered they had an appointment and were already late for it.

But Olson was different. Instead of looking for an excuse to get me to stop, he seemed to be hungering to understand something that had been a mystery to him. I've since thought that maybe he was getting the thrill that comes only a few times in a person's lifetime, when suddenly something that has long been an unfathomable mystery to him suddenly penetrates, and he grasps the concept. Whatever his reasons, Olson urged me to continue.

Apologetically, I said, "I've taken so long on this I haven't yet answered your questions about what is a special assessment district and why Richfield's taxes are approaching those in Minneapolis. Shall I try to do that now?"

"Go ahead."

"O.K., special assessments first. Some of the things a local government does may benefit only part of the community. For example, the people in one neighborhood may want sidewalks, but the people in other sections of town don't want them. Sidewalks cost money, and the only place the city can get money for this purpose is from the people. But since only a few people want this improvement, it would be unfair to charge all the people.

"I've used a simple example, sidewalks. But the same situation would exist if only a few people wanted curb and gutter, a surfaced street, or street lights.

"To get what they want in their neighborhood and what they are willing to pay for, these people can petition the local governing body to create what is called a 'special assessment improvement district.' The area that is expected to benefit from the proposed improvement is marked out on a map. That is the district. The cost of the improvement in that district is distributed among the several properties in that limited territory in proportion to the benefit each property receives from the improvement. Here, the charge to the property is not based on the assessed value of the property but on its share of the benefit. Benefit varies from property to property, depending on such factors as location, front footage, nearness to the actual improvement, and other considerations.

"Determining relative benefit among properties—called 'spreading the benefit' or 'assessing the benefit'—can lead to some hot arguments, especially from some people who did not want the improvement but were outvoted by their neighbors, or on whom the local government imposed the special assessment improvement because they felt it was needed whether or not the people wanted it. But I won't take your time to go into that.

"Let me close with a response to the comment you made when you came in this morning. Apparently you expected taxes to be much lower in this new suburb than in the old city. Is that right?"

"That's right. That's what everybody out here thought."

"Well, then, just three or four quick points, which I think you can verify from your own experience or observation.

"Vacant building lots up in the city cost more than what you paid out here. Is that right?"

"Yes, quite a bit more. But what was worse, they were smaller than lots out here, and a new house would be real close to the other houses."

"Right. But were the paved streets, curb and gutter, sidewalks, street lights, and sewers already in at the city lots?"

"Yes they were."

"How do the people where you're living now like driving on dirt streets, with no drainage?"

"They don't. They're yelling to get out of the dust and mud."

"Well, there's the first reason taxes are going up in the suburbs. The people want the same improvements they can get in the city. The lots are cheaper out here because they don't include those conveniences. And you said the lots out here are bigger. How much bigger?"

"Oh, half again as big, I'd say—at least. Lots we saw in the city had fifty-foot frontage and were shallow. Lots out here seem to start at about seventy-five feet, and some are wider. And they're deeper."

"Well," I continued, "it requires 50 percent more sidewalk, curb and gutter, and sewer line for a seventy-five-foot lot than for a fifty-foot lot. And if the street is wider than some of the older streets, it takes more material to surface it. Do you remember the Thirties?"

"Yes."

"Do you remember the W.P.A.?"

"Yes."

"Do you remember the hourly rate for common labor those days?"

"I think about fifty cents."

"That's the second point. Just figure how much more it costs a local government today to build these improvements than when they were built under W.P.A. or by the city at depression-level wages.

"A third point. Do you know of any factories or large office buildings in Richfield?"

"No."

"Neither do I. Yet they are the backbone of the property tax. The industrial and commercial properties have high value but relatively low service requirements. But since bedroom suburbs like Richfield don't have much industrial and commercial property, most of the tax burden falls on home owners who can't pass the burden on to customers or renters.

"One final point. From your observation, would you say the people in the suburbs are older or younger than the city residents?"

"Oh, younger—definitely."

"Then who have the most school-age children, the people in the suburbs or in the city?"

"There are sure a lot of little kids in our neighborhood."

"Are the children going to school in older buildings that were built when labor and materials were cheaper than they are now?"

Without Fear or Favor

"I'll say not! They're in the most modern, fancy buildings I ever saw. Furthermore, I think I see your point."

With that, we closed our conversation. I thanked him for being such a patient listener. He said, "When I get home, I'm going to get out my tax bills and study this over myself. I think I know where to begin."

Moving Again

At the fall election, candidates who had run on an economy platform gained the majority on the Richfield council. A few weeks after the new council took office, the new mayor came to my office to talk about the plans of the new group. They had been discussing where they could cut costs, he said, and had agreed that the $12,000 salary they were paying me was more than a city of their size should pay. He said they felt I had accomplished the job I was hired to do, to take the government through the change from the old mayor and board of trustees form to the council-manager plan, and they probably could hire a manager who would do an adequate job for $7,000 or $8,000. He said there was no hurry, but they would appreciate it if I would figure on making the change in the next three or four months.

I agreed and began applying around the country. To help the council find a suitable replacement, I prepared a notice of the vacancy and sent it off to the International City Managers Association to be carried in their semimonthly newsletter.

Late in March the chairman of the city-manager selection committee at Daytona Beach, Florida, telephoned to invite me there for an interview. In a letter of recommendation to the Daytona Beach committee, the mayor of Richfield wrote the following, published together with other recommendations in the Daytona Beach newspaper:

Here're Recommendations Concerning City Manager

Daytona Beach's new City Manager came well and highly recommended. Many letters of recommendation were received by Commissioner Long, chairman of the applicant committee.

Here are excerpts from three of them:

Fred C. Reller, Mayor of Richfield, where LeRoy F. Harlow is manager—"It is respectfully suggested his employment would solve the problems your municipality is experiencing.

"Mr. Harlow's integrity and forthrightness are his outstanding characteristics. He has the ability to guide and direct subordinate department heads, rather than supervise; plus the patience to hear both sides of an argument as in interdepartmental disputes and arrive at a logical conclusion without offending either party.

"In your letter you state you are most axious to secure a man capable of doing his own reorganizational survey and managing at the same time. That is precisely what Mr. Harlow was employed to do in our municipality.

"During December of 1950 he was engaged by us to bring Richfield from a disorganized, slumbering village, run by a group of amateur, part time, patriarchial politicians, to a well organized city. His mission has been accomplished.

"In the interim Richfield (or Mr. Harlow) has established a financial department, engineering department, and a strong Manager-Council form of government. It is almost impossible to paint a word picture of how far back Richfield started and how far organizationalwise it has progressed during the intervening months."

William H. Toussaint, member of the City Commission, Fargo, N. D.

—"If you have had an inefficient government, I can think of no one who has greater capabilities of analysis and correction than Harlow. He is also a man of integrity and moves swiftly to correct corruption of any kind. He is a man of deep religious convictions, and is very fearless in the steps it takes to secure efficiency and honesty in City Govt."

C. C. Ludwig, executive secretary of the League of Minnesota Municipalities—"Mr. Harlow is a man of unquestioned character and integrity. As a manager he is highly principled. His work habits and efficiency are unexcelled. He is one of the few managers in the country who can do an exceptional job of the survey type. His experience with Public Administration Service, with the Minnesota Hoover Commission, and with village of Richfield indicates this.

"Mr. Harlow is diplomatic and has a good public relations personality. This is not just a public relations veneer but a real understanding of the points of view of both the citizens to be served and the employes who make up the municipal bureaucracy. I would expect that he would not be comfortable in any situation where he is expected by the Council to make political concessions or to compromise with principles."

Daytona Beach, Florida

What precipitates reform movements
Citizen involvement in local government
Politics vs. public service
Racial integration
Weaknesses of the flesh
Favors for officials
Every vote counts

A Chance for Reform

Probably the contrast between snow- and ice-covered Minnesota and Florida's semitropical climate made Daytona Beach especially attractive. I was thrilled by the beauty of "the world's most famous beach," the Intracoastal Waterway, the colorful oceanside homes and motels, and the stately royal palm trees, brilliant flowers, and lush greenery.

But the political climate was totally different, and anything but beautiful. My interview with the mayor-commissioner and the other two commissioners of the selection committee ran late into the first night and all the next day. Listening to them relate Daytona Beach's long history of political corruption, chicanery, and turmoil was a sobering experience.

Since before 1937, when the governor of Florida sent in the National Guard to remove city officials for malfeasance, misfeasance, neglect of duty, and incompetence, the history had been one long story of wide-open gambling, strong-arm government, fraudulent elections, vice-connected killings, intimidated citizens, and governmental waste.

In 1948 aroused citizens had formed a civic affairs committee, gotten themselves deputized by a state court, raided the gambling casinos, drafted a fraud-proof election law which the legislature passed, purged the election rolls of dead and absent voters, and in 1950 won a 3-2 majority on the city commission by a write-in campaign. But the reform mayor switched sides, fired the new city manager, and appointed a $260-a-month clerk to the $10,000 a year post, precipitating a recall move that forced the mayor to resign. His resignation resulted in the election of another reform candidate.

Again the reform group had a 3-2 majority: on one side thirty-two-year-old mayor Jack Tamm, a lawyer and restaurateur who flew the India-Burma "hump" in World War II; thirty-three-year-old Dr. Hart Long, a dentist and active churchman; and thirty-year-old Hugo Quillian, a civil engineer-contractor. On the other side were LeRoy Hall and Combs Young, holdovers from the former administration. Commissioner Tamm's and Commissioner Quillian's election zones were on the Atlantic Ocean "beach" side of the city; Commissioner Long's zone, which straddled the Intracoastal Waterway, was partly on the beach side and partly on the "mainland" side; Commissioner Hall's and Commissioner Young's zones were on the mainland side, including the Negro section of the city.

The new majority had just seven months before the next election to demonstrate that professional city management would be good for Daytona Beach. Their appointee would be the city's fifth city manager in sixteen months. If they lost one seat on the commission, the manager would be out.

Following the day and a half of interviews, the selection committee called a conference where all the commissioners and I could meet, but commissioners Hall and Young did not attend. After waiting a few minutes for the absent members to arrive, the three-member majority informally offered me the position at a salary of $15,000 a year.

According to a later newspaper report, at a meeting of the full commission after I returned to Minnesota, Commissioner Hall stated, "I hate to go outside the city to bring in a city manager; I believe there're people here that are capable." Commissioner Young protested that he "didn't even know the man." I was appointed by a 3-2 vote and notified by letter.

Back in Richfield, I received a different kind of offer—to become the first director of the newly formed Citizens League of Greater Minneapolis. This was a promising opportunity, but for several reasons I leaned toward the Daytona Beach situation: the Florida climate was enticing, the job paid about two thousand dollars more a year, and I preferred being an administrator on the firing line to being a researcher removed from the action. Mostly, though, it was the exciting challenge to see what could be done in so short a time, working with that kind of a commission majority and in a city with that political history. I thanked the Minneapolis people with sincere appreciation, and we cast our lot with Daytona Beach.

I had no way of knowing that Agda and the children and I were headed into three dramatic years that would include a vicious city employee strike, death threats that would force us to take the family into hiding, implementation of one of the nation's first federal court racial integration orders, and several disappointing instances of official misconduct on which I would have to act.

My period of public service in Daytona Beach demonstrated clearly how much the quality of local government that we have in any community depends on what the people want, whether they know how to get what they want, and whether they act on what they know.

Honest, Impartial, and Courteous

On the return flight to Minnesota I had jotted down some ideas about what I thought needed doing and when, based on what the city attorney, a few other city employees, and the commissioners had told me. I sent the list to the mayor. He approved all of them; so I had some plans made before I went to work.

One idea was to try to get all five city commissioners publicly committed to the kind of city government I assumed they wanted. I drafted for their approval a "Declaration of Purposes," dated May 1952. It read as follows:

"It is hereby declared to be the purpose of the undersigned members of the Daytona Beach City Commission:

1. To return the government of Daytona Beach to the people of Daytona Beach;
2. To build a structure of City government which conforms to tested and proved principles of good government;
3. To provide *all* citizens of Daytona Beach with the maximum of efficient governmental services consistent with economical and sound governmental policies;
4. Above all else, to serve the citizens of this City, and our guests, with courtesy, impartiality and absolute honesty."

We had many copies of the Declaration of Purposes printed, on 20" x 30" poster board. All five commissioners signed them, and the statements were posted in city buildings and other facilities throughout the city.

Another plan was to keep Hewitt Edmondson, the acting city manager, on as the assistant city manager. During my first three days on the job, he and I visited all the city departments and facilities. Between stops, he brought me up to date on his activities. At night I studied the departmental payrolls, budget, charter, and financial audits to get a picture of the city's organizational setup and financial position. The payroll did more than show me salary levels and position relationships; it helped me familiarize myself with the employees' names so that when I heard them, they would not be completely new.

Because several invitations for speaking engagements were waiting for me, I was soon spending evenings, lunch hours, and even some breakfast times addressing local organizations and representing the city to visiting groups. The local people pressed for answers to numerous questions of both policy and administration. I remained as noncommittal as I could on both, partly

City Commissioners sign Declaration of Purposes, Daytona Beach, Florida, 1952. Left to right: Mayor-Commissioner John R. Tamm and Commissioners Hugo Quillian, Dr. J. Hart Long, Jr., W. Combs Young, LeRoy J. Hall. (Courtesy Daytona Beach *News-Journal* Corp.)

because I simply didn't know the answers to many of the questions and partly because I wanted to get a feel of the community before making any moves.

But these occasions and dozens of conversations with individual citizens brought me quickly to these conclusions:

- This really was a crusade for honesty in local government.
- The people had to be brought to feel there was something they *could* do about the political situation, that this was *their* government.
- The full light of publicity should be thrown on every action we contemplated or took.
- We could not afford to appear to be only slightly different from the previous administrations; rather, we had to both express a philosophy and present a program of honest, impartial, courteous government so distinctive that the voters would know what we stood for.
- The present administrative setup violated most of the basic principles of sound organization and procedure, and changes

had to be made soon—but only after I had all the essential facts well in hand.

- There was need to show the employees that the city commission and I understood their problems of low salaries and job insecurity and intended to do something about them; furthermore, I had to ignore the fact that most of the employees cooperated as little as possible—just enough to avoid being fired. They were well aware of the approaching election and took no chances of appearing to be loyal to the current administration.

- And, finally, this was the city commission's battle as well as mine; therefore, I must keep the commission fully informed, in advance, of every major step I intended to take regarding administrative policies and programs.

For me this meant working for and with three different groups—the skeptical and worried city employees, the divided city commission, and the many-sided public—some of whom were optimistic, some pessimistic; some knowledgeable, some confused; some trusting, some cynical; some supportive, some antagonistic. The demands, the needs, and the problems of all three were not in neat, separate packages but came thoroughly mixed and tumbling over one another.

By the end of the first week I had prepared and distributed a request for information about all city departments and agencies.

The next week I arranged meetings with the presidents of the several civic groups to propose they join in sponsoring a civic survey of community needs and participate in a tour of city problem areas and facilities.

Then followed my first meeting with the heads of all the city departments, boards, and commissions, thirty of us in all. After outlining some changes they might expect but assuring them there would be no shake-ups just for the sake of change, I concluded with a plea for faith in one another's good intentions—the employees', the city manager's, and the city commission's. I said, "I know you've taken a terrific beating in recent months. From now on, so far as humanly possible, the practice of making decisions wholly by political considerations will be stopped.

"It is a privilege to be a public servant in a free nation—to be 'the servant of all.' With this privilege goes the responsibility of performing our work honestly, impartially, and courteously. I know as well as anyone else that the casualty rate for city managers is high in this city. But so long as I am city manager, the people of this city are going to get absolutely honest government, absolutely impartial government, and as courteous government as we can provide. This means, for one thing, no more use of city employees, city materials, and city equipment to do work on private property. As for courtesy, we can borrow a saying from Voltaire: 'I can't always say yes but I can say no obligingly.'

"Every one of you is a vital part of this important team. No department is more important than another. Please remember we are not a group of individual, temperamental stars but are all part of the same team. The city manager is surplus baggage without you. His is just one of the jobs. Yours is just as important as his; in fact, in many respects more so. I don't know all the answers, but together we can find most of the answers."

Citizens Speak through Surveys

The presidents of the several civic clubs went right to work on the suggestion for a community-wide survey of civic needs. At city expense we printed thirty thousand colorful survey blanks, which read in part as follows:

WHAT DO YOU THINK DAYTONA BEACH NEEDS?

"What do YOU think would improve Daytona Beach ... her beauty, facilities, government, business, economy, reputation? ...

This Daytona Beach civic survey is being conducted jointly by: Daytona Beach Business and Professional Women's Club; Lions Club; Exchange Club; Kiwanis Club; Pilot Club; Rotary Club.

"I SUGGEST that to make Daytona Beach a better place in which to live, work and play, WE SHOULD HAVE ... OR DO ... OR STOP the following:

Blanks were distributed at service clubs, on city buses, in theatres, and in hotels and motels; they were stuffed into shopping bags and handed out to pedestrians on the street and at several tourist recreation centers. Three hundred collection boxes, identified with a civic survey committee banner listing the sponsoring clubs, were placed in banks, drug stores, dress shops, grocery and department stores, and wherever else people congregated. Completed blanks could be mailed also to the committee in care of the City Hall.

Out of all the suggestions, between twenty-five and fifty of the most frequently mentioned would be selected. These would be printed in ballot form and mailed to a scientifically selected sample of residents to establish the community's priorities among the most popular ideas. As far as practicable we would base city programs on these findings.

I hoped that in addition to bringing the people and the city government closer together in a practical way we could tap what I called our reservoir of ideas. Daytona Beach residents came from all over the United States. Many of them were retired executives and professional people. They had lived in many places where they could see how things were done better than we were doing them.

When early returns offered no suggestions other than that the city repair its sidewalks, provide free wrecker service for cars stuck on the beach, build a huge parking lot in the main business district, build a new ball park, and bring in horse racing (also an opposite suggestion: get rid of the dog track), I thought I had better make an effort to get the people in our "reservoir" to respond with ways to save, not spend. The newspaper did run a small, low-key story. It said I had "expressed gratification at early responses to the civic survey but noted that of the first twenty suggestions not one person told how the city might save money. Most were ways of spending it." The story quoted me as saying, "We hope sincerely that suggestions in large numbers will be forthcoming that will point the way to more efficient operations and a substantial savings."

I arranged with a much larger group of organizations—community associations, veterans organizations, the chamber of commerce, educational institutions, and others—to designate representatives to participate in a conducted tour of the entire city. We filled a city bus and followed a route that took us into every area of the city, over paved and dirt streets, past the best homes and the poorest, and through the major city-operated facilities. This included a foot tour of city yards, with a description of what we hoped to do there; a stop at one of the water reservoirs so that they could personally view the rusted and hazardous condition; and a firsthand look at our fire equipment.

Representatives of local organizations tour City Yards, Daytona Beach, Florida, to see planned changes in city operations. (Courtesy Daytona Beach *News-Journal* Corp.)

The group included men and women, blacks and whites. They agreed to take back to their organizations a report of what they saw and what their reactions were. Although I had no way of knowing what their reports would include and assumed that different persons would emphasize different things, I hoped the overall effect would be to help them all see the community as a whole, not as a collection of unrelated pieces.

A Company Town That Wasn't

The largest single group of city employees were those who worked at or out of the city yards: truck drivers, garbage handlers, street repair crews, tree trimmers, truck and bus mechanics, and time clerks. Half or more were blacks ("colored," "Negroes," or "nigras" were the terms used then).

The city yards were generally considered the political dumping ground, the patronage center, for the city. Few jobs were under the civil service. Men lined up every weekday morning to be picked for that day's work, and there was continuous payroll turnover.

One morning a grocer came to my office to complain he was having trouble getting a check from the city. I asked him what we had bought from him. "Oh, nothing," he said. "It's what one of your employees bought."

On investigation I learned the city had a longtime practice of giving employee paychecks, especially checks for city yards workers, directly to the employees' creditors instead of to the employees. It worked like this: An employee would run up a bill at a store. When payday arrived, the storekeeper came in, got the check, cashed it, took his share, and gave the rest to the employee. (Since the creditor had possession of the check, the employee had no choice but to endorse it.) In some instances the payroll office made out the check directly to the creditor (presumably with appropriate internal adjustments of the books). In most instances, the creditor got the check without the employee's formal consent by merely presenting evidence that the employee was indebted to him.

Although I neither had nor looked for evidence that creditors had cheated any employee, the opportunity and temptation were there. Moreover, the practice seemed arbitrary and repugnant to free men.

On completing my inquiry and verifying that the practice was currently followed, I issued the following memorandum to all department heads:

"I find that it has been the practice in the past that creditors of city employees have come to the payroll section to ask to pick up the checks of employees to cover bills owed by city employees.

"As of now, we will discontinue the practice."

Why Use One When Two Will Do?

Fewer than half the city employees had competitive civil service standing, but they had a full-fledged organization and a program to serve them. There was a five-member civil service board to adopt and enforce civil service rules, authorize and approve examinations, certify eligibility lists, hear employee grievances and appeals, and conduct all the other activities normal for a municipal civil service system. The board had a full-time secretary who maintained civil service employee records, recruited personnel, gave examinations, and administered the board's program.

In addition, the city had a personnel officer who maintained records on all employees. He recruited candidates for non-civil service jobs and performed functions that paralleled and sometimes repeated the functions of the civil service board's secretary. The personnel officer reported to the city manager. Both the civil service board's secretary and the personnel officer frankly acknowledged they were duplicating each other's work and recommended consolidation of the two offices.

But the holdover members of the five-member civil service board, who had been appointed by the previous administration, objected strenuously when I met with the board to propose the consolidation. The opponents contended the positions were not parallel and that one man could not hold down both positions. When another board member pointed out that Miami and other cities had consolidated the positions, one objector claimed that the two cities operated under different laws, and besides "you certainly can't compare Daytona Beach with Miami." He claimed that consolidation would mean the city manager would be running civil service in the city, and the civil service board would "go to pot." He charged that my purpose was to bring politics into the office and appoint somebody from out of town.

I responded that I understood that the civil service board and the city commission, as well as I, wanted to bring most city employees under civil service and accord them equal treatment.

I said I had no desire to appoint the person to fill the combined position, now or later, and would be happy to accept the board's appointee, including the present secretary, to serve as personnel officer. I suggested the two positions be combined, with the understanding that if either the civil service board or the city manager was dissatisfied, the arrangement could be terminated within two weeks after written notice by either party.

At their next meeting, the civil service board approved the merger under the arrangement I had suggested. The secretary to the board continued in office and assumed the additional duties of personnel officer. I appointed the former personnel officer, Al Bornmann, to head the new purchasing division.

Even Cities Need Water to Grow

Water is literally the lifeblood of every city. Consequently, one of my major concerns was the interrelated physical/financial condition of our municipal water system.

On my first day's round of city facilities I noted the precarious condition of the thirty-year-old Seabreeze water tank, one of the city's two elevated reservoirs. Even from ground level I could see how badly rusted and eaten away the supports and stringers were, and I could imagine the condition of the tank. (A subsequent inspection by engineers revealed that in some places rust had reduced the tank walls and bottom to less than half their original thickness.) I called for the latest engineering report on the water system and found that it was six years old. Fortunately, that report had been prepared by Dr. A. F. Black of the University of Florida, a nationally known authority on water and former president of the American Water Works Association, who was available and willing to bring the report up to date.

My concern was deepened just a month later when daily consumption of water exceeded the system's rated capacity for twenty-seven out of thirty days, and motel operators reported their patrons were unable to flush second-floor toilets. I had to appeal to the public to curtail water use until we had rain.

Even without Dr. Black's updated report our own capacity and consumption figures showed the need for expanding the plant. Daytona Beach faced a choice: expand the plant or stop growing.

Although a few citizens would have liked to see the growth stop, most of them felt otherwise. Furthermore, we had no legal or other means to stop people and businesses from moving into our community. But how to finance the expansion? The city's debt was already triple what it had been five years before, a circumstance virtually ruling out more bond financing. Fortunately, the $4.2 million worth of water and sewer revenue bonds still outstanding were callable. That is, the bonds issued for the last expansion of the water system were being paid off from the revenue of the system, and the city had the right to require the investors who held those bonds to sell them back to the city.

We checked the municipal bond market and found interest rates lower than the rate negotiated at the time the bonds were sold. It looked as though the city could call in its bonds and issue new bonds—"refund" its water system debt—and save enough in interest over a period of time to pay most or all the cost of needed improvements.

At this point we needed professional help. I told the commission my opinion that refunding municipal bonds was such a highly specialized field we could not afford to rely on our own limited knowledge and experience but should use the services of others of proven ability and experience in this field. We could engage an experienced bond dealer to set up the refunding and act as a consultant and adviser to the city, or we could engage an experienced financial consultant who neither buys nor sells bonds.

Four firms offered to do the work for us—three national brokerage houses and one independent financial consulting firm. The proposals of all three securities houses were below the cost of the independent consultant's offer. The possible savings were tempting, but I concluded that the city's interests might be better protected by engaging the independent consultants. In my written recommendation to the city commission I said, "The principal loyalty of investment houses is to their clientele. The investment houses must buy bonds at one price and sell at a profit. The higher the interest rate, the more buyers they will have. If an investment house were to serve as financial consultant, it might be inclined to set the sale at a date when the market is glutted, to the disadvantage of the city and the advantage of its own clients."

The commission engaged the independent financial consulting firm and authorized us to proceed with comprehensive plans for improving the system. The financial consultant and the engineers gave our urgent needs their immediate attention and soon had their work completed. But a local attorney opposed both the long-range plans for solving the water problem and the refunding and took us into court. Eighteen months later, the court upheld the refunding, with the judge's added comment, "The ten-year plan for extension, improvement, and modernization of water facilities indicates wise planning and long-range thinking. I wish that other cities would follow your example. It's high time for governmental agencies to wake up to the fact that they have got to plan twenty to thirty years in advance."

During the eighteen months the case was in court, interest rates on municipal bonds advanced. Consequently, we did not realize the full amount of saving originally anticipated. Such savings as there were went back into the system.

There's No Substitute for Planning

For months before my appointment the city planning board and the city commission had been at odds over rezoning matters, especially "spot" zoning—the rezoning of small tracts to permit more liberal use of that tract than permitted in the general area of which it is a part. The procedure on rezoning requests was to first refer each request to the planning board. The planning board then held a hearing and made its recommendations to the city commission. Upon petition from a prescribed percentage of property owners in the vicinity of the property proposed for rezoning, the city commission was required by law to hold a second hearing, then render a final decision on whether or not to permit the rezoning asked for.

Occasionally the commission made decisions contrary to the planning board's recommendation. When this happened, the planning board members felt they were being "bypassed," "overridden," or "sabotaged" by the city commission.

The two bodies asked me to study the situation and recommend an improved procedure. I met informally with the planning board to exchange ideas and sense their version of the problem. I also sought the views of the zoning board of appeals because that agency had the responsibility and authority to act in cases where the zoning ordinance imposed a hardship on a citizen and spot zoning might be justified. Then I prepared a report to the city commission, the planning board, and the zoning board of appeals. I attempted to lay the groundwork for agreement among the three public bodies, followed by a concrete proposal for a workable procedural change. Briefly, I recommended the following three-part procedure:

1. that the planning board stop handling any spot zoning matters and spend its time on long-range planning;

2. that the city commission send to the board of appeals all requests for rezoning that the commission was not required by law to hear; and that the commission declare a moratorium on spot zoning until we had a comprehensive city plan and zoning ordinance to follow;

3. that the zoning board of appeals hear and pass on requests for rezoning and hear all hardship cases.

The three agencies adopted the recommendations in principle and generally followed them thereafter, and before long we embarked on a comprehensive planning program.

Budgets: the Reins of Government

Three months after my appointment the *Evening News* hit the nail on the head in their editorial concerning the task of putting together our first city budget. Here is part of what they wrote:

"One of the ironies is that wasteful government usually is spectacular, and in that way impressive. The other is that efficiency often is just the opposite, sometimes even on the humdrum side in its painstaking methods, and seldom startling. . . .

"It is human nature to expect a miracle from every city hall housecleaning. It is human nature also to hope the miracle will be spectacular, somewhat in the pattern of extravagance which made the housecleaning necessary."

It *was* a painstaking job, and it *did* require a miracle to prepare a budget that would satisfy everyone.

One painstaking part was designing and installing a new budget and accounting system, including a budget calendar to keep budget preparation on schedule, estimate forms that would show anticipated revenues and proposed departmental expenditures in detail, cost accounting to show the quantities of work being done for the money spent, and allotment and encumbrance systems to avoid overspending the budget.

But we needed a miracle to produce a balanced budget that could pay for both the traditional services—fire, police, health, streets—and the unusual list of special semigovernmental projects, in the face of the following facts: Departmental expenditure requests exceeded revenue estimates by $800,000 or nearly 40 percent; a just-completed property reassessment program had raised the amount of homestead-exempt property from 23 percent to 32 percent of the total valuation of the city; under a new law consolidating tax collections, the city's total assessed valuation was down 27 percent; by an error that the assessor called "an act of God," the city lost $150,000 in revenue over two years, and a month after adopting the budget, the commission majority broke ranks for the first time and capitulated to demands that a major recreational facility be "free" rather than be put on a self-supporting basis.

The budget is the key instrument, and almost the only one, by which the people and their elected representatives can control the government. Yet if they do not understand the budget or know what it contains, this instrument is useless to them. I was determined to give our people access to the city's budget and do all we could to help them understand it. When the League of Women Voters asked if they could have any part in the budget-making process, I invited them to name a representative to sit with the assistant city manager, the research assistant, and me through the entire process. They did so, as observers, for five twelve-hour days. The league also sponsored and advertised a public meeting on the budget. They invited a member of their national board of directors from nearby Orlando to moderate the meeting. An estimated four hundred citizens attended.

I also initiated a move to get the budget before business and civic leaders. Knowing that the civic and service clubs schedule their weekly programs as far ahead as they can, I called the presidents of all the clubs several weeks ahead of the budget season to ask if they would be willing to hold one at their usual noon luncheon meetings jointly with other clubs—perhaps at an evening meeting—and let us put on a program about the city budget. Fortunately the Rotary, Kiwanis, Lions, and Exchange Clubs were able to adjust their schedules, and all were agreeable to the suggested program. To help the citizens better understand what we would be talking about, the evening of the meeting I arranged to have most of the city's garbage trucks, pickups, fire engines, and street equipment lined up facing the sidewalk on two sides of the Palmetto Club, where the joint dinner meeting was held. In this way no one could reach the meeting without passing within three or four feet of trucks with broken headlights, wired-on fenders, missing doors, and skewed dump bodies. They could see also, firsthand, the thirty-year-old fire equipment. From the remarks I overheard as the men entered the club, it was obvious that most of them had no idea how badly we needed new equipment.

Cut *and* Spend?

Now and then I've been asked what I found to be the hardest part of the job of being a local government administrator. My answer: having to deal with inconsistency. Here's an example of what I mean.

Shortly after the announcement that we were starting work on the annual budget, a chamber of commerce committee came in with a written request that we budget for construction of a waterway terminal, to handle incoming and outgoing waterborne freight. They explained that it was widely rumored the federal government was going to widen and deepen the Atlantic Inland Waterway located between the mainland and beach side of the city. The chamber thought it would be good for Daytona Beach to be ready with terminal facilities if and when that happened.

I asked for details that would justify the project—classes of freight, annual tonnage, revenue to the city—but the committee had not yet done that kind of research. I asked if they had estimated what the project would cost. They had—about $2 million. We talked briefly about the many worthy projects the city commission had to consider. They left, after handing me a one-page letter containing the formal request.

I had a feeling this would not be my last visit from the chamber about the budget. They were housed in a city building, and the recreation director had recommended a new or enlarged building for them. Also, the convention bureau wanted money. And the city had traditionally financed a variety of chamber-sponsored events. I laid the request for the waterway terminal in my center desk drawer, where I could easily reach it.

Sometime later, after release of the first preliminary budget figures, the chairman of the chamber's city budget subcommittee called for an appointment. Accompanied by other members of his committee, he announced they were there to talk about reducing the city tax load, that undoubtedly there were many places in the budget where we could make cuts without hurting city operations.

I handed each of them a copy of the budget document, and we started through it. Did they want to cut the police?

Oh, no; if anything, we need more policemen.

What about the fire department? Where should we cut there?

Well, we really hadn't better cut any there; that is, not more than you've already cut.

Special events?

No, you've already cut out the fishing tournament and reduced the Fourth of July and other celebrations to half of what's needed.

Maybe we ought to close some of the playgrounds.

What? You can't do that!

"Well, gentlemen," I said, "you're here to tell me we should reduce the budget. And I'm not arguing with that. But you have the budget right in front of you. If you think it should be cut, you tell me where."

"Roy, we just think it's too high. The community can't stand it," the chairman said.

"I know that's what you think. And that's exactly why I am asking you where you think it should be cut further."

After a moment's pause the chairman said, "Actually, Roy, that's your job. It's up to you to make the cuts."

"I don't think it is, George," I said. "I've made every reduction I think I can. If you think it should be cut any further, you're going to have to tell me where."

They got up and started for the door. As they did so, I moved toward my desk. "Men," I said, "just a minute before you go. I have something here I need your advice on." I reached in the drawer, took out the request for the $2,000,000 waterway terminal and handed it to the chairman.

He read it. He turned red-faced, then handed the letter to another committee member. When they had all read it, someone handed it back to me. As they went out the door, the chairman let out a string of cuss words, ending with "Someone's sure going to hear about this!" I don't know what he told the board of governors, but I didn't get any advice from the chamber on how to reconcile the inconsistency.

Looks Like It's Gonna Rain

Because of the location of the city garbage dump, most of the garbage trucks passed my office on their way to and from the dump. Consequently, one of the first city services that appeared to me to offer some opportunity for improvement and cost reduction was the garbage service.

Most of the trucks lumbering past city hall had five men aboard—a white driver and four Negro loaders on the seat, the running boards, the fenders, or wherever they could find a place to ride. At the rate and distance the trucks traveled to and from the dump and between work site and city yards, I estimated they had time for about two loads a day and averaged about an hour of deadheading travel time for each load. That is, we were paying for thirty-two man-hours a day of loading service and getting twenty-four man-hours of work per truck.

On my first conference with Cliff Gittens, superintendent of city yards, I asked him about the garbage and trash collection operation. "Have you given any thought to rotating the trucks," I asked, "so one driver can take the loads to and from the dump and the loading crews can move from one truck to another and not have to deadhead to and from the dump?"

"No," he replied, "we haven't tried anything like that. You don't know the South, Mr. Harlow. You can't work these men down here like you can up North. They get sick—get TB."

I asked if each truck crew had a route they followed.

"No, we just assign them a section of town. It's up to them to clean up that section."

"What about the schedule of pickups?" I asked.

"Oh, the people pretty well know when we'll be around. We try to make it about the same time, but it's pretty hard to keep to any schedule. The amount of garbage and trash and the amount of labor change all the time."

Before we finished our conference, I asked him if he would make up a map for me showing the sections assigned to the crews, what days they were picking up in those sections, the routes followed by any of the crews that usually followed the same route, and the number of men working each day over a period of about a month. He assured me he would get me that information when he could get around to it.

During the next few weeks, when I happened to run into the city yards superintendent I asked him how he was coming with the information I had asked for and when I could expect it. Each time he said he was working on it, but he'd been real busy. He'd get it to me as soon as he could.

As we moved into the summer season (in Daytona Beach an even bigger tourist season because the cool ocean attracts people from the Deep South) complaints about garbage and trash collection increased. Gittens responded there was nothing he could do. He had only so many men and so much equipment, and they were hauling all they could haul. He said he was losing men to easier jobs that paid more.

I asked the assistant city manager to meet with the superintendent and try to work out a plan for "dawn to dusk" pickup, using forenoon and afternoon crews so that we could double-shift the trucks. We could also pay a bonus to men who worked a full five-day week instead of quitting after two or three days' work. Gittens objected to such a plan, saying the people didn't want the Negro loaders around their houses in the early mornings and late evenings.

For several days after the Fourth of July holiday, backyards, driveways, and parkways were littered with overflowing cans of watermelon rinds and other garbage and trash. After a tour of this disgusting sight, I decided to have a firsthand look at how our crews operated. Although I had not yet received the maps or other information I had requested weeks before, I picked out a section of town during the forenoon and drove around until I found a truck. The first truck I came upon was stopped next to the curb in the middle of a block. As I approached it from the front, I could see there was no driver at the wheel nor any loaders about. I drove around the blocks on both sides of where the truck was parked but saw no city employees. I drove into some driveways, thinking the men might be working behind the buildings but found no one. Finally I decided to return to the truck and wait until somebody showed up.

This time I approached the truck from the rear. It was a beautiful, cloudless day, and the bright sun cast a shadow under the truck. But when I drew up to park a distance behind the truck, I could see figures of men under the truck. I got out and walked up to the truck.

"What are you fellows doing under there?" I asked.

They looked at each other and grinned. Then one of them said, "It looks like it's gonna rain, Mr. City Manager."

At the time the remark about rain meant nothing to me. I thought it was just their way of saying they were taking a break out of the sun. In a few months, I was to find it meant much more than that.

I walked back to the car, drove to the office, and called Superintendent Gittens to let him know what I had happened upon. He made no response.

Feet of Clay

At the end of World War II the federal government turned over to the city of Daytona Beach a large Women's Army Corps (WAC) training center known as the Welch area. Attracting tourists and recreation seekers were two Olympic-size pools, for several years the location of the women's national AAU swimming and diving championships. The pools were under the direction of James D. "Doc" Young, the very popular city acquatics director, who had probably taught most of the community's youngsters to swim, had officiated in national swimming circles, and was credited with being the man who made famous the lady lifeguards. These were seven young women between eighteen and twenty-two, any one of whom could have won a bathing beauty contest.

It was Sunday, the weekend of July 4. With house guests, we had just sat down to dinner when the telephone rang. It was Hewitt Edmondson calling from the Welch Pools. Could I come out to the pools right away?

"What's wrong? An accident?"

"No, but I think you'd better get out here right away."

I excused myself and headed across town for the pools.

Hewitt and recreation director Sam Galloway met me at the gate. Betty Ann Flippo, the head lifeguard, was standing in the doorway to Doc's outer office.

Welch Area round pool, Daytona Beach, Florida, site of national AAU women's diving competition. (Courtesy Daytona Beach *News-Journal* Corp.)

"I guess we'd better let Betty give you the story," Hewitt said.

"What's up?"

"Mr. Harlow, have you ever been in Doc's private office?" Betty asked.

"Yes."

"Do you know that closet he has back there?"

"Yes."

"Well, today a woman came to ask about a mirror in the women's small dressing room. She said when she was fixing her hair she noticed the mirror looked funny. The top half was darker than the bottom half. I told her it was all right, probably just some of the silver on the back had come off.

"But when she left, I closed the door to the small dressing room and went into Doc's office to look behind the mirror. The mirror is on the wall between the dressing room and Doc's closet. The closet was closed and had a lock on it as it always has, so I had Dick come in and take the door off at the hinges.

This is what I found."

She handed me a 6" x 8" orange Kodak box. It was full of photographs. The one on top showed Betty stepping out of her bathing suit. The next one was of a young woman looking straight into the camera, scratching her waist. She was completely undressed. Among the more than one hundred pictures were teenaged girls, young women, and older ladies, all in stages of undress but most of them totally nude. Among the photos were some professionally posed ones, outdoors and in a bedroom. Someone had color tinted a few of the photos at selected points. There were also a few slide transparencies.

"Betty, where did you say you found these?" I asked.

"Let me show you," she said.

We went back into Doc's private office. The closet door was still off its hinges.

"This box of pictures was lying on that little stool," Betty said, pointing to a low wooden stool on the closet floor.

I examined the closet. It was ceiling height and about three by five feet. On the wall that separated the closet from the women's small dressing room was a window frame. A cardboard covered the bottom half of the small window. The cardboard had an improvised handle of masking tape attached to the back of it. When I took hold of the handle and lifted the cardboard out, I had a clear view through the bottom half of the window into the dressing room. The top half was silvered. The little stool was directly below the window.

"Evidently Doc stood on the stool when he took the pictures," Sam remarked, "because that way he could hold the camera about waist high and it came up to the opening."

"The mirror the woman complained about is the other side of this window thing," Betty said.

"Look how Doc had this place sealed off so that no light could penetrate," Hewitt noted.

I looked up and down the corners and at the ceiling. All the corners and every crack were covered with masking tape.

"And look here, Mr. Harlow," Betty said. "He even had peep holes into the main dressing room. He covered them with tape, too. He had two of them, and they're aimed so that he could see the whole dressing room."

"Betty," I said, "I'm awfully sorry this happened. Of course, word will get around. But I would appreciate it if you'll say as little as you can until we've had a chance to talk to Doc. He's up at Indianapolis at those Olympic tryouts, as you know, but

Daytona Beach's famed Lady Lifeguards, with the City's aquatics director, James D. (Doc) Young. (Courtesy Daytona Beach *News-Journal* Corp.)

he's due back sometime this week. In the meantime, we'll post a police guard here around the clock. The minute he gets back we will pick him up."

I had the mirror-window taken out of the wall and brought to my office, along with the photographs. I called the mayor to tell him what had happened, and called the chief of police and gave him instructions to pick up Doc Young the moment he arrived in town, day or night, and to call me as soon as he had him.

On Monday morning the first caller at my office was an ex-county commissioner I had not met before. "Harlow," he said, "my daughter is one of the lifeguards out at Welch. You'd better lock up Doc Young the minute he gets back to town, because if I see him before you do I'll kill the _____. I know the consequences, but I don't care. I'm a Southerner, and no _____ is going to get away with this with my daughter."

Obviously the word was already around town. This troubled me. How should we handle the public information? It was my practice to let the press know anything and everything about city affairs, with the understanding that they would not print items that might be harmful or costly to the public (like police efforts to apprehend a criminal, or the city's intent to buy a tract of land) or would damage the reputation of an innocent person. This situation involved a very popular man and his family, but it also involved a lot of innocent people.

To get counsel, I asked the editor of the newspaper to come to my office. He had not heard about the picture episode; so I told him what had happened and showed him the two-way mirror and an example of the pictures.

He studied the mirror and asked a few questions about the arrangement of Doc's offices.

"This thing's dynamite," he said. "When word gets out, every woman and girl in town who has been at Welch Pools will wonder if her picture is in that box. What are you going to do about Doc?"

"I don't know yet," I said. "It depends on what he has to say when he gets back."

"If you fire Doc, I think you're going to have to say more than simply there were irregularities at the pools. You're going to have to give the public enough information to let them know that only pictures are involved, nothing else. Unless you are at least that specific, people will have a thousand ideas about what's been going on out there."

I thanked him, and he left.

At eight o'clock on Tuesday night the police chief called. They had Doc at the station. I asked the chief to call the mayor, the city attorney, and the recreation director, and to arrange for all of us to meet in my office in thirty minutes. He was to bring Doc with him.

As soon as they all arrived, I told Doc the purpose of the meeting—to get the facts about what had been found on Sunday.

Doc was sullen. "All I can blame is my own stupidity. I should have burned those pictures when I burned the negatives."

"Doc," I said, "what we need to know is, did you take those pictures?"

"Of course I didn't take them. What do you think I am, a queer?" Doc replied.

"Then who took them?"

"I'm not going to tell you who took them. I'm already in trouble, and I'm not going to get somebody else in trouble. It's all because of my own stupidity."

"Doc, we want to help you. But we certainly can't do so if you won't tell us who took the pictures. Naturally, it looks pretty suspicious when the pictures are found in your closet, behind a secret two-way mirror," I said.

"That mirror was installed to stop the stealing going on. As for the pictures, if you want to know, they were taken by a woman photographer," Doc said.

"When?"

"During the last AAU meet."

"Who was she, and where is she now?" I asked.

"I'm not going to tell you," Doc answered.

"Look, Doc," I said. "We don't want to hurt your wife and children, and we don't want to hurt you. But word of this situation is all over town, and we simply cannot ignore it. If you didn't take the pictures, and you know who did, all you have to do is tell us who took them. We'll get the facts and clear you."

"Nope, I'm not going to get anybody else in trouble."

I asked Doc about the slides and the tinted pictures. He said a salesman had given him the slides. About the color tinting, he said that a few times on rainy days when there was nothing else to do, he tinted them.

Mayor Tamm, City Attorney Judge, and I tried repeatedly to get Doc to say who took the pictures and under what circumstances. Although he consistently refused to reveal any names, his explanations varied. At one point he said he gave the photographer permission to try out a new lens, and he and she thought it was kind of a cute joke. Later he denied she had permission and said he didn't know at the time that she was taking the pictures.

At about 2:30 a.m., after pleading with Doc for five hours to help us help him out of the jam he was in, I typed out a dismissal letter dictated by the city attorney, who recommended we send a copy to the state's attorney.

The next morning the mayor and I went to a local bank and placed the pictures in a safe deposit box, under a double-signature arrangement so that neither could remove them unless the other was present.

The news story broke the same morning. The wire services picked it up, and for the next few days I had calls from coast to coast. The husbands of AAU swimmers were particularly irate and threatening.

I received word that Doc left town the day he was dismissed. A few days later Mrs. Young brought to my office a camera and some other equipment she thought belonged to the city. She was still in a state of great distress. Ten days later the state's attorney and the county prosecutor held a hearing. Doc Young was subpoenaed but did not appear. The city pressed no charges against Doc Young, and the city attorney reported that state statutes did not deal with cases of possession of photographs like these but only with their publication, distribution, or sale.

The following spring when Ed Aspinall, national chairman of the AAU Women's Swimming Committee, came to Daytona Beach to discuss details of the upcoming senior women's swimming and diving championships, the mayor and I asked him to look at the pictures to see if he could identify any AAU and Olympic swimmers and divers allegedly photographed. He was reluctant to be involved in any way. Finally he consented.

"Not one of the women in these pictures was ever in an AAU meet," was Ed's verdict.

Together the three of us walked to the power plant of the local electric company, climbed to the top of the furnace room, lifted a trap door in the floor, and dropped the box of pictures into the white-hot flames.

New Ideas and New Directions

By midsummer both the civic survey and the city government reorganization were nearing completion.

The civic survey committee read and grouped the more than three thousand returns, many of which offered half a dozen suggestions. This proved a demanding task for the volunteers. Finally they decided on seventeen topics that were referred to every tenth voter in a mail ballot. Thirty-seven percent of the people polled responded, and the commission and I were guided by these views.

Service club representatives tabulating returns from civic survey, Daytona Beach, Florida. (Courtesy Daytona Beach *News-Journal* Corp.)

The city commission was now holding its public meetings in the social hall, adjacent to the main concert hall of the auditorium. I presented the reorganization plan before an audience of about 150 intensely interested citizens, using large organization charts to describe and explain the proposed changes. Most of the reorganization of city departments consisted of new groupings of responsibilities, with reassignments of present employees. For instance, Cliff Gittens, former boss of the city yards, was appointed superintendent of the refuse division within the new public works department headed by the public works director/city engineer. Gittens could now give his full attention to the critically important garbage and trash collection and municipal dump operation. The full commission unanimously approved the new plan.

A New Police Chief

In many cities operating under the council-manager plan the police chief is appointed by the city manager, but in Daytona Beach the city commission appointed the police chief.

Although technically the position of chief was under the commission, the commissioners asked me to recruit a new chief and to have him serve under the city manager the same as other department heads. I placed a blind ad for police chief with the International Association of Chiefs of Police, including a brief description of our aims in "a medium-size Florida city." We received over forty applications, most of them of unusual quality—including assistant chiefs of several large departments and many chiefs of smaller departments.

Of all the applications, one stood out above the rest, although it violated much of the advice some placement experts give on preparing job applications and resumes. Instead of being on either an impressive letterhead or heavy bond paper, professionally typed, with lots of white space, it obviously was typed by an amateur typist and was on inexpensive yellow typewriter second sheets. It had narrow margins, was single-spaced, and ran nearly two pages; but it was written in flawless English and was crammed with concrete facts about the applicant's experience.

The applicant had a law degree and had risen through the ranks of the New York State Police from private to chief inspector, the highest career position.

I felt obliged to follow up on the top three or four candidates and did so, but the New York man was the most attractive. At the same time I was puzzled that a man of his experience would be interested in working in a city our size. After talking with him by telephone to let him know what city we were and to assure myself that his interest was genuine, I telephoned Bruce Smith in New York, then one of the nation's leading authorities on police administration. Smith knew the applicant, Albert B. Moore, and assured me that if Moore had applied for the job, he knew what he was doing.

Moore was invited for an interview. After showing him our city and giving him the political background, we met with the city commission. They offered him the position, and he accepted.

In his unhurried way, Chief Moore brought about a remarkable transformation in the department—physically and procedurally, and morale in the department began to climb.

He found department headquarters so crowded it was virtually impossible for the men to pass one another. He rearranged the use of space, allowing for a waiting room for the public, a tight but usable radio room, a small office for himself, and other facilities. He got the rusty, smelly, dirty jail repainted and brightened. And before long he had written a whole new manual of police operating procedures. The particularly gratifying thing was that he did it all without once complaining about what the department lacked. His standard response to every difficult situation was, "We'll make do." And he did.

The men in the department were enthusiastic. The chief was immediately accepted throughout the community and was frequently asked to address groups and to participate in community activities. And neither the other departments nor my office could have asked for more in the way of thoughtful, helpful, and wholehearted cooperation. Consequently, the circumstances under which Chief Moore left Daytona Beach two years later constituted the biggest disappointment of my time there.

A Blueprint for Good Government

With the crucial primary election for all five city-commissioner seats barely ten weeks away, there were rumblings of dissatisfaction with our philosophy and our type of administration. Therefore, when I was invited to write a guest editorial for one of the papers, I could think of nothing better than to restate our principles—the blueprint for good government we had followed the first five months and for which, I said, "we find no sound reason for discarding now."

Here is what I wrote on September 17, 1952:

"Our citizens have recognized that all the people of Daytona Beach have a stake in good government. They have been almost unanimous in their determination that we should build steadily, firmly, openly toward our announced objectives.

"Our objectives have been few and simple, but absolutely fundamental. Fitted together they compose our concept of good government.

1. We believe technical competence and efficient methods are essential to good government, but we believe they must be built on a foundation of integrity, impartiality, and consistency.

2. We believe that proven principles of sound administrative organization and methods should be introduced as rapidly as possible.

3. We believe our citizens are entitled to be served by the best available people, whose selection is based on *what* they know, not *whom* they know.

4. We believe we should leave no stone unturned to increase the quality of service rendered and to eliminate leaks that contribute to waste.

5. We believe that every act of the city government and all its records should be open to the public's watchdog, the American free press.

6. We believe the citizens should not only be asked, but they should be assisted so far as time and energy permit, to be fully informed about all phases of city business and that steps should be taken to learn the desires of the citizens."

Under most of the above items, I gave specific examples, hoping to remind the citizens of the changes actually made in keeping with those declarations.

A few days after my guest editorial appeared, I received a telephone call from Orlando, Florida. The man said he was a candidate for mayor and was running on a platform to get a council-manager form of government for Orlando, and would I be willing to fly over there to address a public meeting, make a radio talk, and cut a recording he could use in his campaign. I said I would be glad to.

While I was with the mayor-candidate's group, one of his supporters told me why his business was located in Orlando instead of Daytona Beach. When he decided to move his operations to Florida from up North, he first stopped in Daytona Beach. He went to the city hall to inquire if they could suggest any sites where he might locate the plant he intended to build. Someone there gave him several locations, and he started out to inspect them.

He had not been gone from city hall fifteen minutes when a man from the mayor's office caught up with him. After introducing himself, the man said, "It's election time here, and the mayor's up for reelection. It's going to be a tough campaign, and the mayor needs money to run it. Since you're thinking of locating your plant here in Daytona Beach, you might want to make a contribution to the mayor's campaign fund. He could use $1,000."

The Orlando man said, "I told him, 'Look, I haven't been in your town an hour and you're hitting me for a $1,000 campaign contribution. What if I had a quarter-million-dollar plant here and couldn't leave, then what would you be asking me? No thank you! I'm leaving, and I can tell you I'm going to build my plant someplace else.' "

First, Honesty

State Representative Thomas T. Cobb was the young legislator who got through the state legislature the new election law that brought a stop to votes being cast for people who had moved from Daytona Beach or were dead. He must have sensed the growing dissatisfaction that I had been hearing rumblings about. Three weeks after my guest editorial he wrote the following letter to the *Evening News*:

"Some of our citizens say that the honeymoon is definitely over, as far as the majority members of the City Commission are concerned. I can't help but feel that if the facts of municipal finance in Daytona Beach are known and understood, the achievements of this Administration will be appreciated. I hope no vote will be cast until these facts are thoroughly understood.

"Two years ago it was impossible to persuade mature businessmen of recognized integrity to seek a seat on the City Commission in opposition to the Titus-Padgett regime, which had brought us then to the brink of bankruptcy. Younger men stepped forward, knowing that their Administration would be one of receivership and retrenchment. Such an Administration, by its very nature, is never popular. Because of the Lancaster fiasco, the present majority has had less than a year in which to repair the damage of five years of political freebootery. They have faced up to the problems without fear of political consequences, and their courage is to be admired. Some of our citizens now say that it takes more than honesty, and imply that sound judgment has not always been present. As for myself, I will still list honesty as the No. 1

virtue to be sought, above all else, in a public official.

"This Administration, coming in as it did to pick up the pieces of a four year 'binge,' found the chaos almost unbelievable. The City, heavily in debt not only for current expenditures, but for so called 'improvements' such as a sewer system and a street paving program that clearly show the ravages of inefficiency and corruption, was met head on by yet another condition about which there is general misunderstanding. Tax consolidation forced the City to surrender its power to assess real estate within the City to the County Tax Assessor. His yardstick of valuation has produced a total assessed valuation of only about half of what it should be. Consequently, the millage instead of coming down, has had to climb, and even then it will not bring in as much money as before. So with higher millage the tax 'take' is actually less! The solution to that problem lies with our new Tax Assessor, to be elected in November, and if he puts property valuations where they are by law directed to be put, we will see the necessary relief for this and other Cities of Volusia County.

"If men who hold the political philosophy that is held by these members of our City Commission—that is, that a public office is a public trust and that political expediency must yield to public necessity—can't be elected to public office in Daytona Beach, then we will never see our government placed on the sound basis toward which we are now making some strides. I do not agree with every action taken by these men, but one thing is certain, and that is that they are doing their level best in an extremely difficult situation and a situation that can lead to eventual solvency if professional management coupled with Commission integrity is given a fair chance."

Genesis of Desegregation

I was taken by surprise one afternoon when the city attorney called to say the city commission would be meeting in my office in about an hour. Until the meeting got underway, I did not know the city had been defendant in a suit demanding admission of Negroes to the auditorium and that a federal district court had held recently in favor of the black citizens. Although the court ordered the city to admit the Negroes, it specifically authorized admission on a segregated basis. At the same time, it ordered the city to provide equal washroom and lobby facilities.

This was two years before the landmark U.S. Supreme Court decision in *Brown vs. Board of Education* that declared segregated schools unconstitutional and long before the civil rights confrontations in Little Rock, Birmingham, and Memphis. The department stores in Daytona Beach still had two drinking fountains, one marked "For White" and the other "For Colored," and black patrons on city buses still seated from the rear.

The city commission faced the question of whether to appeal the decision of the federal district court to a higher court. At the meeting in which action was scheduled to be taken, commissioners Hall and Young, the minority members, whose zones encompassed the Negro area of the city, were absent. The three majority members postponed the decision to an adjourned meeting. Again the two were absent. The newspaper quoted Commissioner Long as saying the question of whether to appeal the lower court decision had been postponed as long as possible to get the other two commissioners "on record." Now the three-member majority would have to decide. They voted to accept the district court decision without appeal.

The commissioners directed Henry DeVerner, the auditorium manager, and me to comply with the court order, but they gave us specific orders not to go one step further than was necessary to meet the court's requirements. Specifically, the races were to be segregated. We were to prepare equal washroom and lobby facilities. The commission left the details to us—physical arrangements of separate seating, lounges, smoking rooms, toilets, separate ticket offices, and other facilities.

DeVerner arranged a meeting with leaders and representative citizens of the Negro community for about a month prior to the fall season's opening performance. We met in the social hall of the auditorium. About twenty Negro citizens were there, led by Dr. Mary McLeod Bethune, a daughter of ex-slaves and founder and president emeritus of Bethune-Cookman College. Also present were a leading Negro medical doctor, the president and some teachers from Bethune-Cookman, the NAACP attorney, and various well-known members of the Negro community. The auditorium manager, the city attorney, the assistant city manager, and I represented the city.

To get the meeting started, I asked the city attorney to bring us all up-to-date as to what had happened so far and to tell us the nature of the matter we were dealing with. Step by step he recited the legal actions leading to the district court decision. He read and explained the decision. Then he moved into an outline of the racial history of the South, frequently referring to "the traditions of the South." He closed with a strong plea for understanding of the city's need to heed those traditions.

The Negroes heard the city attorney out with great deference and courtesy. After a moment's wait for comments, Dr. Bethune rose from her chair and walked to the front of the group. She was dressed simply but elegantly. She must have spoken to us for thirty minutes, starting with a word of appreciation for the meeting and the pride she felt in Daytona Beach, her native "city by the Halifax." She told something of her own background and experience; then she began asking disturbing questions.

Holding her right arm out in front of her, palm down, with her left hand she slid the loose-hanging right sleeve up to her elbow.

"What is wrong with this black skin and these black hands?" she asked. "They wash your clothes, feed your families, nurse your children—even put money into your cash register tills. But they aren't good enough to sit beside you to see and hear great artists—like Marian Anderson. Why?"

She noted that more than one white man had asked for those same black hands in marriage, but she would not leave the people of her race.

As had the city attorney, she too referred to the traditions of the South. But she presented them in terms of human rights and dignity, in a way that gave them a different meaning.

She touched on the highlights of her thirty years of fighting the battles of her people. "Sometimes waiting," she said, "but never retreating."

She mentioned having been the guest of presidents, premiers, and prime ministers and receiving high honors from other nations. This had accented the great hurt she felt when she returned to her home, where neither she nor her people could attend concerts or watch their children and grandchildren play in the sand of "the world's most famous beach."

When she finished and sat down, it was clear we were not dealing with a simple problem of how to arrange for people to enter and be seated in a public building. We were at the point of vibrant impact where the concentrated yearnings of a people for acceptance were pressing against a high wall of tradition and habit.

The city attorney and Dr. Bethune had presented two sides of a problem. Each had placed the case on a plane of such height as to make it difficult to return to the earthy question of what to do next. Yet, like many another momentous human impasse, this one had to be resolved by mundane means. We had to find a practical way to implement the court's order, to comply with the city commission's directive, and to act in good faith toward the Negro members of the community.

Getting and installing facilities would be no great problem. But the arrangement of the facilities and the handling of the people was delicate. At first it seemed the physical location of the auditorium would aid our problem. The auditorium was located on the corner of a city block; its main entrance and foyer faced one street, and patrons could go in almost a straight line through the entrance, across the foyer, and down an aisle of the auditorium. The assembly hall—a rectangular meeting room that could accommodate 200 to 300 people—faced the other street. It was positioned between the street and the main auditorium and was connected to the auditorium foyer by a short hallway.

Having our instructions from the commission, and needing to get down to specifics, I suggested we could open an entrance from the street into the assembly hall and set up a ticket window there. This would provide the Negro patrons with an entrance around the corner from the main entrance and would enable them to go to their seats in the auditorium without having to mix with the whites.

After some discussion of the details, Mrs. Bethune spoke up.

"We are opposed to segregated seating," she said, "but the court has permitted the city to require it; therefore we will abide by the decision. We will go to our designated places.

"But, we want to enter the building through the main entrance. We want to purchase our tickets just like anyone else. We do not want to enter the building through a side door, like second-class citizens!"

I could understand her feeling. I wouldn't want to enter a building through a side door like a second-class citizen, either. So I agreed; we would not cut a separate entrance. The Negroes would enter the building the same as the other patrons.

We discussed other points and reached agreement, including the seating arrangement. DeVerner suggested that the front half of the main floor center section, which included the best seats in the house, be assigned to the Negroes. The white patrons would occupy the remainder of the main floor seating.

Although I was satisfied that the agreements we reached were reasonable and just, I could not be certain the city commission or the citizens generally would think so. This was a tremendous cultural change. If the commission rejected the agreements reached at the meeting, there was no telling what might happen. I had not forgotten the preceding year's bombing of a Negro home in a nearby town and the few white people who had recently reminded me—ominously, I thought—that there never had been Negroes on the beach side of town after dark.

I was turning over in my mind how the Negroes felt, how some whites felt, and how the commission might react, when a simple idea occurred to me. I hoped it might forestall possible open conflict. I proposed it.

"Ladies and gentlemen," I said, "we have agreed that we won't make a separate entrance to the building. Also, we have agreed on the seating arrangement, with the understanding that the seating as well as other facilities will be segregated. Will you be willing to agree to one more thing—that we will try this arrangement for six months, with no commitment beyond that date? Six months from today, we will meet here again to take inventory. If it has not worked out, we'll make changes."

Speaking for her people, Dr. Bethune said they would be pleased to accept this arrangement. We parted company amid expressions of mutual appreciation and confidence that our objectives would be achieved without mishap.

Reaching agreement in midsummer about how people would be seated in the auditorium to implement the Court's order was easier than working out the details as the winter season approached. For instance, there was the sticky question of how to handle ticket reservations. Many patrons customarily telephoned for reservations, then picked up their tickets when it was convenient.

DeVerner quickly discovered that he and his office people could not determine over the telephone who was black and who was white. To ask them might offend them. Yet he had to know in order to know in what section to reserve their seats. After a brief conference about it, we decided to require all reservations and ticket purchases to be made at the ticket window.

A much more serious problem was citizens' attitudes. The city commissioners accepted the plan, but the citizens of the community were far from unanimous about it. No sooner had the radio and newspapers announced the plan than more than one "Florida cracker" called me to say, "It won't work. The coloreds have never been allowed on the beach side after dark before. They know that. And they won't be now—except the dead ones! There's going to be trouble. There'll be bloodshed. You just watch; it won't work."

At a meeting in Dr. Bethune's home about another matter, she asked me to stay a moment after the others left. She said to me, "I hear they are saying there will be blood flowing on the beach. I just want you to know it won't all be Negro blood."

I was unable to determine the extent of feelings on both sides. I knew only that no one had come forward to openly support our arrangements for the six months' trial period.

I called in Chief Moore to analyze the situation and to work out plans for opening night, when the opera "Carmen" would play. Fortunately, he had dealt with interracial and related problems both inside and outside this country, and I had complete confidence in his ability to develop a plan that would cope with potential violence. I made only one stipulation: that no matter what happened—even at the risk of someone's being killed—our officers were *not* to move first. We would take all possible precautions, but at whatever cost we would not allow anyone the opportunity to claim and prove that the city police were the ones who precipitated a tragedy. He understood and agreed.

The chief developed a detailed plan for opening night. The number of firemen usually on duty for a public performance at the auditorium was doubled. They were inside the building. Extra patrol cars were assigned to the area, to watch for and report unusual congregations or actions. The chief told me how many officers he had assigned to the area, but as I drove to the auditorium I didn't see them. However, when I walked the two blocks from where I parked the car, officers in plain clothes greeted me quietly from inside parked autos, at street corners, and even from rocking chairs on front porches. I was satisfied that the police department had the area well covered.

I circulated among the first-nighters in the foyer, noting the absence of a few of the regular patrons who had told me they did not want to be a party to what might happen. Despite their prophecies that dozens would stay away, only a handful of people boycotted the performance. One could detect some uneasiness and tension in the subdued conversation, in contrast to the usual preshow chatter and gaiety, but there were no incidents. The Negro men were impeccably dressed, several in evening clothes. The ladies were beautifully groomed and gowned. After showing their tickets, they were ushered to their places in the center front section.

Ten minutes before curtain time I took a seat in the last row of the left section. From there I watched Dr. Bethune and President Moore of Bethune-Cookman College and others come in and take their seats, nodding and quietly greeting friends they passed. White patrons took their seats. Soon the front half of the main floor was well filled, as were most of the other seats.

It was probably three minutes to curtain time when suddenly there was activity in the fourth or fifth row up front in the left section. Like a squad of soldiers, six or eight white men rose in unison to their feet. They stood still a moment, then methodically moved in a side step toward the aisle at their right—all still facing the front.

When the first man reached the aisle, he made an about face, walked half way up the aisle, halted and turned to face the stage. Each man followed him, until they all had cleared the row, and were in single file facing the stage at the right side of the aisle. Each man was standing at the left end of a row of Negroes. Again as by command, they all faced right, each looking along the row of Negroes he was facing.

There was dead silence. Hundreds of eyes were on that line of white men. We all held our breaths. My heart pounded as I waited for the next move. Was this it?

Then it came. As if by command, the men standing in the aisle lunged forward into the rows of seats. Each took firm hold of a Negro's hand or arm. I thought they were going to drag the Negroes out of their seats. But, no! Instead, each white man began vigorously pumping a hand—in a handshake of welcome!

What relief! Simultaneously, the entire audience expelled its bated breath. Someone laughed. The place came alive with conversation. In a moment, the lights dimmed, the orchestra struck up the "Carmen" overture, and shortly all attention was on the performers.

There were no incidents that night. Six months later we had our meeting but found no need for major changes in the plan.

As time went on, other performers came to the community to entertain or enlighten all of our people. On one occasion, when the segregation lines were generally ignored, the white speaker drew good-natured laughter when he quipped, "From up heah you-all look like salt and peppa!"

Thereafter I occasionally received unpleasant anonymous letters and calls. But after that first night I felt we were over the worst of it, and apparently we were.

The Spoils-System Crisis

In the routine of assuming office I had asked the city commission for a financial audit of the city as of the day I went to work. The audit showed that the city had a current deficit of $138,000, along with $175,000 in unpaid bills. I had to weigh this fact each time we made an organizational or procedural change, several of which reduced our costs but some of which increased costs.

The current debt plus the difficulty we had balancing the new budget (because of general inflation and the tax shortage), along with the complaints I was hearing that we were adding "brass" at city hall while cutting the budgets for traditional city-financed activities, probably would have been enough to make me take a hard look at where we might reduce our overhead.

At the same time, I was being told by earnest supporters of the administration that holdovers from the former administration were cutting our throats. They said the garbage and trash crews were openly campaigning for Commissioner Combs Young. Several brought me unsolicited reports of seeing people from my office in deep discussion with leaders of the former administration. They asked if I knew that instead of requiring all businesses that were operating without a city license to comply with the city license ordinance, the purchasing agent, whom I had assigned to make a compliance survey, was going from business to business criticizing our efforts to enforce the law.

Whether the reports I got were true and how much influence they had on the citizens generally I didn't know. But they helped me decide to reduce the size of my office by vacating two positions until we had a clearer picture of our city finances. I prepared letters to the assistant city manager, Hewitt Edmondson, and the purchasing agent, Al Bornmann, asking for their resignations. Hoping that the change could be made with a minimum of injury to them, I offered in the letters to assist them in relocating.

As for the touchy and visible garbage and trash collection problem, no one needed to tell me that was not going well; moreover, Cliff Gittens had never found time over a five-month period to supply any of the information I had repeatedly asked him for.

In the meantime, a puzzling situation was cleared up. During my first weeks on the job, I had seen names of garbage and trash loaders and other laborers going on and off the city yards payrolls about every other week. I had asked Cliff Gittens about this, and he explained that the men could work only a few days at a time at that hard work—that they got sick. Also, he said, when they got "nigger rich" with a few days' pay they quit on him. (This was why I had suggested a plan that would pay the men a bonus if they worked a full five-day week.)

But some time later a grocer came to my office with a different explanation. He said he was there because he had not been able to get any business from city yards employees. He hoped that maybe now he could, since there was a different administration. When I asked why he had not had any business he said it was because he was not willing to be part of the system. The system, as he described it, was that when a worker got on at city yards, he was given a numbered brass disc about the size of a quarter. The workman showed this to a grocer as evidence that he was working for the city, and the grocer would let him buy on credit. When he went off the payroll, he turned in the disc at city yards, and the disc was then given to the worker who replaced him.

The significance of the brass disc system was that the employees were told which grocery to buy from, and the grocer rebated a percentage to the city yards bosses, a form of collusion this grocer had refused to comply with. I thought I now saw the real reason for the labor turnover. If the grocer's story was correct, it was logical that the larger the number of employees with credit at the store, the larger the total sales—both when they were working and when they were off a few days—and the larger the kickback to the yards boss and whoever else was involved.

The combination of factors satisfied me that I had to replace the refuse superintendent if we were going to achieve our stated objective of "a trash and garbage system as efficient as any in the state." And since dismissing people is an unpleasant task under the best of circumstances, I decided to do all three on the same day.

I first invited Hewitt Edmondson, the assistant city manager, to my office. After expressing my appreciation for his helpfulness to me from my first day on the job, I told him that since we had cut back in the operating departments (as he knew we had, having participated in all the budget sessions), it was only right that we cut back in the city manager's office as much as we could. Therefore, I had decided to ask for his resignation.

I had prepared a letter to him, which I handed him. I hoped that it expressed adequately my appreciation and also my desire to help him any way I could in making the change. Hewitt read the letter and took it with him as he left the office without a comment.

I met also with Al Bornmann, the purchasing agent. (His official title was assistant purchasing agent because by law the city manager was also purchasing agent.) Al's reaction was essentially the same as Hewitt's.

But the meeting with Cliff Gittens was different. I expressed my disappointment that all my efforts to work with him had failed.

He said, "Then you say you're firing me?"

"No, I'm inviting you to resign."

"To hell with you. I'm not resigning."

"That's up to you, Cliff. But if you decide not to resign, your services are terminated as of now."

He didn't take the letter I offered him. On his way to the door he said, "This will just be a two-months vacation for me. You and the rest of your crowd will be out after the next election."

Thus began a hellish week, including a strike of city employees, sabotage of city equipment, slowdown of essential services, death threats, goon squads, and fear. For the following chronology of events, I have used actual front-page banner headlines and have added my own details.

(Evening News)
Oct. 9, 1952
CITY YARDS WORKERS ON STRIKE

Having been warned on the Wednesday night of the dismissals that trouble was brewing at the city yards, I was there at 6:00 the next morning when the men began to gather. Instead of starting the trucks and going to their usual jobs, they stood around in little groups. The yard foreman, Ben Blackwelder, arrived half an hour after I did, and at about 7:00 o'clock Cliff Gittens came in. A woman reporter was there also. When she asked Gittens what was going on, he replied, "It's going to be a rainy day, can't you tell?"

At about 7:15 I began addressing the 177 men from the refuse, maintenance, streets, and beautification divisions who were not at their jobs. I said I was told last night to expect trouble, that I thought the men would want to know what happened, and that they were entitled to know.

I gave them my reasons for the dismissals—that although I had much respect and personal liking for Hewitt Edmondson and Al Bornmann, we had to cut down as much as possible on operating budgets, and I felt we were obliged to cut down on city hall, too.

My two principal reasons for dismissing Gittens were that (1) he simply did not supply me with the information I needed about the refuse division's operations, which he had had ample time to provide, and (2) his general attitude was one of disapproval of the reorganization program.

Foreman Blackwelder then stepped forward. He said he was speaking for the men. They were giving me "an ultimatum"—they would not return to work until Edmondson, Gittens, and Bornmann were put back on their jobs.

I expressed the hope that the men would go back to work and offered to meet with a representative employee committee of their choosing or the regular civil service employees committee. They rejected the offer.

I said, "We will assume, then, that anyone who is on the job at 12 noon is on the city payroll; anyone who is not on the job at noon is not on the city payroll."

I returned to my office at about 8:30 and prepared a memorandum to the employees. Just before noon I returned to the city yards, mounted a pickup truck, and read the memorandum to the men. In it I reviewed the situation and told them, "We want you to go back to work. Your work is vital to the community. . . . There is no thought of mass dismissals now or later.

"A strike against the government is a serious matter. It threatens the health and safety of the public. It should not be entered into lightly. For this reason we have chosen to postpone any decision on this matter in order that those employees might think through the situation and arrive at a decision of importance to them and their families, as well as the entire community. . . .

"Some of you, I know, prefer to return to your jobs. The decision and choice is yours. Those who conclude that they wish to continue in the employ of the city of Daytona Beach are invited to do so and are welcome. Any who so choose shall be given the full protection of law in the performance of their duties in serving the people of this city."

No one returned to work.

The evening paper's report of the strike included this meaningful incident: "Gittens himself went to the yards early this morning. Asked 'What's going on here, anyway?' Gittens smiled and said: 'It's going to be a rainy day, can't you tell?' 'We're not working,' a striking employee spoke up. 'We're not going back until they hire Cliff back.' 'Why don't you tell them to go back

Daytona Beach City Yards as 177 city service employees go on strike. (Courtesy Daytona Beach *News-Journal* Corp.)

to work?' a reporter asked Gittens. 'I'm fired,' Gittens replied with a broad grin. 'I can't tell them nothing.' City Commissioner Combs Young, part of the group that had been conversing with Gittens, left as a reporter and photographer approached."

Apparently, when the garbage crew I had found sitting under a truck on a sunny day had said, "It looks like it's gonna rain, Mr. City Manager," they were using a prearranged strike code of some kind.

Through the newspapers Mayor Tamm asked the cooperation of the citizens. He specifically invited any who could help collect refuse to be at the city yards at 6:30 the next day.

At 10:00 that night, I went on the radio for a twenty-five-minute address to the citizens and the striking employees. I described the events leading up to the strike, announced the deadline for employees to return to work or be automatically dismissed, and said, "Tomorrow volunteers will begin manning the garbage trucks."

By 6:30 a.m. Friday there were enough volunteers to man

Daytona Beach

the trucks and help pick up garbage. But not a truck moved. All the keys were missing. The wires were either pulled loose or crossed in those that had button starters. Some were said to have sugar in the gas tanks.

(*Morning Journal*)
Oct. 10, 1952
HARLOW SETS 1 P.M. DEADLINE

An hour later I posted a notice at city yards, addressed to all city employees. It stated that as of noon Thursday all employees not at work or excused had been placed on a leave-without-pay status but had not been dismissed. But it gave notice that 1:00 p.m., this date, was the dealine for returning to work.

At about 8:30 a.m. Mayor Tamm began circulating among the men, proposing a secret ballot on whether they wished to return to work without Gittens. He said, "The city needs you. The people whose garbage is lying around need you. I'm asking you whether you want, in the democratic way, to put on a piece of paper whether you'd like to go back to work—yes or no."

In the meantime, the Reverend Lee Nichols, pastor of the First Baptist Church, who claimed many of the striking workers as his parishioners and was a close friend and political supporter of Commissioner Combs Young, entered the scene as a self-announced "unofficial mediator." He proposed setting up an arbitration committee.

I responded that I had already proposed that, twice, and the men had rejected it. I said I favored the mayor's ballot proposal.

Reverend Nichols, going back and forth between the men and us, succeeded in working out a compromise agreement. The men would come to the city yards office window for their checks at 1:00 p.m. When they got their checks, they would mark a ballot: "Back to work without Cliff Gittens. Yes ———; No ———." If a majority voted "No," the arbitration committee would be set up. Neither side would be bound but would consider the committee's recommendations.

In addition to agreeing to serve on the proposed arbitration committee, the mayor and I made these concessions: If the men will put on a temporary crew to make the daily garbage and trash pickups, the city will extend the dismissal deadline from 1:00 p.m. until after the arbitration committee makes its re-

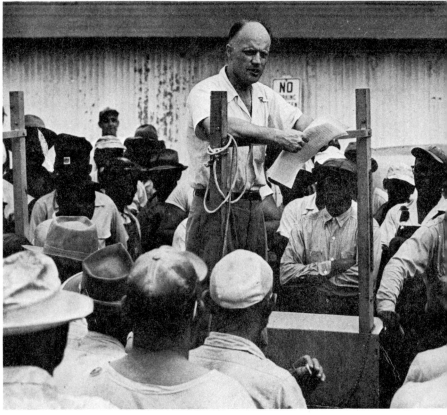

The author addressing striking city employees, Daytona Beach, Florida, October, 1952. (Courtesy Daytona Beach *News-Journal* Corp.)

port. Also, there will be no pay loss for the men if a full crew goes to work tomorrow.

(Evening News)
GITTENS STYMIES WORK VOTE

Reverend Nichols assembled the men at the far side of the yards and explained the plan to them. By show of hands, they approved it. He brought me the word, and we immediately began preparing the ballots. Our public works department supervisors started rounding up all the striking employees they could find, and I asked the radio stations to broadcast radio appeals to those at home to come promptly to city yards.

Minutes before the balloting was to start, Cliff Gittens came

into the yards office. He grabbed the microphone of the public address system and called out to the men not to vote "until two o'clock." His action cancelled the compromise agreement it had taken nearly seven hours to work out. Reverend Nichols pleaded with me to set the clock back thirty minutes to give him time to talk again to the men and to Gittens.

I agreed, but it was useless. Gittens's "until two o'clock" was not what he intended, and word went around that the men were not to vote at all. At 1:30 I walked to the microphone and said, "Please come to the window for your checks. Indicate on the ballot whether you wish to go back on the job. If you do, report at your regular place of duty. If you don't, you are automatically dismissed as city employees."

Because there was some confusion about the number of employees actually striking and the number who were staying away only to avoid violence or on instructions from their supervisors, we printed about two hundred ballots. The yards clerk handed out a ballot with each check.

From inside the office I watched the men pass the window. Gittens and another man stood outside, but so close to the window a man coming for his check had to squeeze between them and the window counter. After a dozen men had picked up their checks, I asked the clerk how many had voted. His answer: none. Just then a worker who had been outside came up to me.

"You know why the men aren't voting?" he asked.

"No, why?"

"Because that guy standing by Cliff has an open knife. When a man steps to the counter, there's a knife blade pressing against his back."

I went outside and told Cliff I wanted to talk to him over by the side of the building where we could be alone. He didn't want to leave the window, but I insisted it was important. Finally, he moved away from his companion and went with me. Until then I hadn't noticed, but now I could see he'd been drinking. It was heavy on his breath, he slurred his words, and he was coarser than usual. I stalled for time, talking about several extraneous things until all the men had passed the pay window. But it made no difference; there were no votes. Eighty-five men had picked up their checks. All of them either were following Gittens's orders not to vote or were afraid to vote. And all eighty-five of them no longer had jobs with the city.

By midafternoon Dr. Mary McLeod Bethune and the Reverend Nichols came to the city yards office. Dr. Bethune wanted arbitration negotiations reopened, and the two of them urged the city commission to hear the workers and to sit in continuous session until a solution was reached. But the commission majority declined. They said the city manager had acted within his authority, and they supported him in his action.

At the height of the tension someone suggested I meet with Dr. Bethune and seek her counsel. Although I had met her only once when we had made plans for racial integration of the auditorium, that had been opportunity for me to witness the objectivity, fairness, wisdom, and leadership ascribed to her by many Daytonans. I said I would be glad to meet with her—on a confidential basis, with no commitment of any kind. Someone made an appointment for me to go to her home on the campus that evening.

At home for dinner, I read this editorial in the *Evening News:*

"The men who went out on strike in the city yards yesterday were more to be pitied than condemned.

"That is why City Manager Harlow, handling the situation in a masterful manner kept his temper with them, dealt with their 'ultimatum' with firmness, but with patience nonetheless.

"He did not forget that behind the work stoppage—intended to force the retention of 'Cliff' Gittens as refuse superintendent after he had been fired for incompetence and noncooperation—lay long years of traditional operation of the spoils system.

"Under this system, men were not hired by efficient lieutenants of a professional city manager but by favor and as a political reward.

"These men were used to being 'put on' at a nod from a city commissioner. They thereby became victims of a confused loyalty.

"Their loyalty, according to the tradition of machine politics, was not to the city, not to the taxpayers, not to their jobs, but to their bosses.

"Harlow said nothing, be it noted, in his brief but eloquent appeal to these misguided men, about loyalty to him. He asked the men to consider that a strike against the Govt. was a threat to the health and safety of the public. He asked them to think. He asked them to decide freely of their own choice to return to work, without fear of reprisal.

"Can these men learn so quickly what it means not to have fear, not to have to think of their jobs in political terms, to be free from the old shackles of boss rule, to know that their jobs depend on how well they can do them and not on a nod from a Cliff Gittens or a Combs Young?

"The answer may be in by the time this editorial is printed. Meanwhile, the city vitally needs their services."

It was dark when I arrived at Dr. Bethune's home. A maid let me into the dimly lit house. Dr. Bethune met me in the dining room and asked if I would care to kneel with her in prayer. I was glad to. We knelt together beside the dining room table, and she led us in an earnest prayer to God for guidance in this time of trial in our community.

We went from there to the kitchen and sat facing each other in a breakfast nook. She graciously permitted me to tell her what was happening as I saw it: that if our policies and kind of administration were wrong and should be changed, they should be changed by lawful means available, not by threats, coercion, and force.

Citizens join city officials during city strike negotiations, Daytona Beach, Florida. Left to right, facing camera: Mr. T. G. Engram, Mayor John R. Tamm, the author, Pastor Lee Nichols, Dr. Mary McLeod Bethune. (Courtesy Daytona Beach *News-Journal* Corp.)

For the next hour we exchanged views. We discovered we fundamentally agreed that this country was founded on the principle of government by law and that what was done in Daytona Beach should be consistent with that principle. I went from her home to the radio station to report again to the people.

(*Morning Journal*)
Oct. 11, 1952
HARLOW STANDS FIRM ON GITTENS

Mayor Tamm and commissioners Long and Quillian joined me in the Friday night report to the people, each one declaring 100 percent support. I described the events of the day, then closed with this: "Through intimidation, threats, and generated fear of job loss, the men were deprived of their right of free choice.

"The 1:00 p.m. deadline was not changed. They have been dismissed. We are proceeding to make other arrangements for new employees.

"There is to be no compromise of principle. I do not propose to submit to coercion. So long as I am city manager, Mr. Gittens will not be employed by the city."

On Saturday forenoon, I met with department and division heads to work on plans to get the garbage and trash collection going, although we had no refuse division superintendent and no regular workers. Also, we needed to get employees of the other divisions who wanted to work back on their jobs.

At about noon Reverend Nichols had a letter hand-delivered to me, saying that Gittens and the workers' committee had agreed to recommend to the men to go back to work without Gittens. But at the meeting with the men, Gittens told them he had changed his mind. "I don't want to surrender the State of Florida to the State of Minnesota," he was reported to have said.

Without Gittens's approval, the second Nichols plan died. Reverend Nichols was quoted, "I think Cliff Gittens has made a mistake. I made a mistake, maybe, in pleading for you men. But I do know this. The loyalty you show for Mr. Gittens is the highest qualification a man can show for his job." Clearly, Reverend Nichols and I had different views as to where a public employee's loyalties belong.

By this time I had received enough threats, both veiled and direct, that I became concerned for the safety of Agda and our six children. I decided to follow the urging of some friends to take the family into hiding until the strike was over. That evening we moved in with friends, taking along the children's beds, bedding, and other necessities.

(*Evening News*)
Oct. 13, 1952
CITY HIRES GARBAGE CONTRACTOR

Over the weekend I negotiated a sixty- to ninety-day emergency contract with an experienced building contractor to take over the city's refuse collection. He was to pay the men slightly more than the city had paid, and he would use city trucks. Also, he was encouraged to hire former city refuse division employees if they applied.

When Cliff Gittens and the men learned this, Gittens sent me a letter via Reverend Nichols's secretary. He wrote, "The workers of the yards today have volunteered to collect the garbage in all places where the public health is endangered, without any cost to the city of Daytona Beach for labor."

I sent my reply back with Nichols's secretary, but I did not address it to Gittens. I addressed it to "The gentlemen who today volunteered to collect garbage where the public health is endangered." I thanked them for the offer, but said we had engaged a private contractor. I wrote, "If any of you men are interested in regular work of this kind, you may wish to let your interest be known to the contractor who will be glad, I know, to consider your past experience."

After consulting with Police Chief Moore, we had the twenty-one city refuse trucks moved from the city yards to a lot next to the police station and placed under lights and guards. The chief posted a police guard at the city dump because at least one individual who appeared at the dump with a load was threatened. The chief also assigned a police patrol and erected a sign at city yards prohibiting "unauthorized personnel" from entering.

During the day Gittens and discharged workers and their families milled around across the street from the city yards, and Gittens was quoted as saying, "It looks like another rainy day."

(Morning Journal)
Oct. 14, 1952
DEATH THREAT IN GARBAGE STRIKE

Late on Monday afternoon the garbage contractor came to me to report that Ben Blackwelder, the ex-foreman in the refuse division, had threatened him: "There won't be any trucks moved in the morning. If you attempt to move one of these trucks, we will kill you."

Again that night I went on the radio to report the death threat and the other events of the last three days. I said, "Citizens of Daytona Beach, I do not mean to appear theatrical. Until the present combination of intimidation, coercion, and threats was thrust upon us, I would not have believed it possible here.

"It is too much like Kansas City and Chicago of a few years ago. How can I convey to you the threat to human freedom that exists in this city tonight. Today I met in your city hall most of the day with city employees who wish to return to work—who say they and their families can't afford loss of pay—but who in the next breath say they can't run the risk of seeing the legs shot off their youngsters.

"Nearly forty employees, both black and white, described the terrorism of the last few days at city yards—of guns and knives flashed, of efforts to stop bus service, of orders to quit work coming from roving goon squads of men they have never seen before. Gittens himself called city hall today to urge that city hall employees go out on strike. . . .

"Today the mayors of Ormond Beach, Holly Hill, and South Daytona voluntarily called us to offer their services to help in any way they can if we need it. Dozens of our own citizens have done likewise. We hope we will not need outside help. If you can set your garbage where it can be found easily, we can get along without outside help.

"Ladies and gentlemen, I don't have words to describe it, but this situation is like a nightmare. It seems inconceivable that this famous city can be strangled by the terrorism of a few. This is not a dream—this is real, as real as if you were to feel a knife or a gun in your ribs, right where you sit.

"You can help. Be vigilant. Be calm. Think back through this situation in which we now find ourselves, and exercise the courage that only free men and women have."

(*Evening News*)
Oct. 14, 1952
10 QUIT AT WATER PLANT

When arrangements were completed for the private contractor to collect refuse, we asked employees in the maintenance, equipment, and streets divisions who had been on a leave-with-pay status (to avoid violence) to return to their jobs at the city yards. They promised, but only a handful showed up. Others said they wanted to work, they needed their paychecks, but they were afraid to go back on the job.

And despite police patrols assigned to protect the contractor's workers, several men he hired didn't show up, and others dropped out within an hour after the trucks pulled out past booing and threatening former workers.

To provide as much protection as possible, the chief put all three shifts of his men on alert; he roadblocked streets leading to the police station where city refuse trucks were stored; and he allowed only city officials and persons bearing passes into the area, stationing radio cars at three strategic locations.

For protection, city buses were lined up for the night on a downtown main street. Five days earlier the equipment superintendent had reported that the city buses had been tampered with. Oil lines were disconnected, and oil and water drained out of some of the buses to keep them from running. Gasoline tanks had been drained, and drivers had run out of gas. All of this had disrupted bus schedules. Since then, I had heard rumors that the bus drivers were going to strike.

Cliff Gittens's telephone appeal to city hall employees to strike had no direct effect there. But similar invitations presumably made to other employees were heeded in the place I dreaded most, the water division. If the city water system were incapacitated, we could be in extreme and immediate difficulty. So when the water superintendent reported that ten to a dozen water and sewer men had walked off the job, it looked as if we were headed for deep trouble.

(Evening News)
Oct. 15, 1952
'I'M OUT OF THE PICTURE'—GITTENS

Fortunately, after only a half-day "sympathy" strike, the water and sewer employees had second thoughts about their action and returned to their jobs.

And the bus drivers and bus mechanics, who had been the targets of numerous threats, never did go out. I sent a letter of appreciation and thanks to the drivers and other people in the transit department.

Later in the day when a newspaper reporter asked Gittens for a statement, he replied, "I'm out of the picture. I'm not the issue any more."

(Evening News)
Oct. 16, 1952
50 SERVICE WORKERS BACK ON JOB

One week to the day from the time the strike had begun, more than fifty painters, carpenters, plumbers, mechanics, mower operators, groundsmen, street repair, and sewer maintenance men returned to their jobs. During the strike, I had received dozens of telephone calls, letters, and telegrams of support, encouragement, and offers of help. I was grateful for them. But several letters were written to the editors of the newspapers, also. Not all of them supported our action.

With the tension relieved, Agda and I were able to return home, resettle the family, and reestablish our slightly less hectic routine.

You Don't Have to Run to Be a Candidate

Twenty candidates entered the November 25 primary election for the five city commission posts. Two were especially well-known locally: William H. G. (Bill) France, founder of the National Association of Stock Car Auto Racing (NASCAR) and later a key figure in establishing the famous Daytona International Speedway; and a justice of the peace, "Judge" J. C. Beard. "Judge" Beard was something of a local celebrity because of his odd decisions, such as the time, Solomon-like, he sawed in half a bicycle claimed by two parties and gave each a half. At another time he ruled the accused man innocent of stealing a watch but ordered him to return the watch to the owner.

The day before the primary election the *Morning Journal* ran an editorial titled, "There's a Man to Fit Your View." It read, in part:

"The basic issue is whether Daytona Beach will stick to the professional management form of government provided by its charter or will attempt to compromise and risk a return to politics as usual.

"It is contrary to the theory of professional management to treat the issue as a personality. But Harlow is here—brought in from the outside as the charter permits—and is not likely to be improved upon. Daytonans have found his ways to be winning as well as efficient.

"So the lines are sharply drawn and the voters should have no trouble picking the man they want in their zone, based on the kind of government they want."

I had never met "Judge" Beard or several of the other candidates. Nevertheless, in a local shopping news ad, beside his picture, the justice of the peace wrote under the title JUDGE BEARD SEZ:

"Harlow will be leaving town with his few months accumulations in a small handbag in early January. There's about 150 college graduates qualified to relieve Harlow at half the price."

In another ad, he wrote,

"JUDGE BEARD SEZ: If any of you taxpayers should want a good job, go see Harlow. Be sure to wear a white shirt and your very best clothes, tell him you just got in town, do not tell him you are a property owner or a citizen here—if you do — ?"

Tamm and Long won in the primary, getting more than a majority of the votes cast for all candidates in their zones. Coursen and Judge Beard led the five candidates in their zone, thereby eliminating the other three. The day after the primary Judge Beard withdrew, with this statement:

"If the results of the general election on December 2 should find me a minority on the commission, I would be unable to do the things for you taxpayers in my zone in the way of better streets, sidewalks, lighting, and other badly needed improvements." His withdrawal left Coursen unopposed except for possible write-in opposition. Coursen publicly thanked Judge Beard for what he called Beard's "considerate" act.

In the general election Coursen overwhelmed a write-in candidate nearly ten to one. A twenty-seven-year-old attorney defeated minority Commissioner Combs Young about three to two. The front page *Morning Journal* headline, December 3, read: COURSEN, McCARTHY, WARREN IN. The subtitle said: "Harlow Backers Take Five Seats on Commission."

Now They Can Talk

With the election over and the results conclusive, people who had lived in Daytona Beach a long time—both city employees and private citizens—seemed to feel freer to talk about past political happenings.

A few of the stories were almost beyond belief, yet they fitted the pattern. Some that I remember from persons who seemed credible were these:

Tom Pendergast, for years the political boss of Kansas City, Missouri, spent many winters in and near Daytona Beach. It was from Daytona Beach he learned some of his more successful political practices, such as casting ballots for "voters" whose names were taken from tombstones and getting monopoly control of an item the city had to have (in Pendergast's case, concrete) and seeing that the city used excessive amounts of the item and purchased all of it from the boss's firm.

Two lifetime residents, a man and a woman who were neither related nor acquainted with each other so far as I know, told me of unhappy occurrences during their depression-era childhoods. Jobs were scarce, and you didn't get a job in Daytona Beach if you didn't support the administration. The man said the family often went hungry because his father was an outspoken critic of the city officials and nobody dared hire him. Finally he got a job in a gas station. He had worked only a day when the station owner got a call from city hall. The person at city hall wanted to know if this man's father was working there. The station owner said yes, he was, why?

The spokesman from city hall said, "Well, he's not very friendly to the administration."

The station owner replied, "I don't know anything about his politics. He's a good man, and I needed a man so I hired him."

"We just wanted you to know," came the response from city hall. "And by the way, we've just been looking over the property assessment records here. We see there must be some mistake; your assessment is only about a third of what it ought to be. We may have to make an adjustment in those figures."

Fortunately, the station owner was about as independent as the man's father and kept him on. Nothing more came of it.

The woman's story was similar, with an added bit of interesting information. Apparently her father was not the outspoken kind, but he had made the mistake of voting against the administration. As a result, his employer's tax assessment was more than doubled; he lost his job; and as a child she sometimes thought they were going to starve. Luckily her father found a job out of town and was able to support his family.

"How did they know he voted against the administration?" I asked.

"The city officials controlled all the election records and polling places. That was before voting machines, when they used paper ballots.

"If they were in doubt about anybody, when that voter came to the voting place, he was handed a ballot that, unknown to him, was marked by pinholes. After the polls closed, when the election officials counted the ballots, they held them up to the light. Pinholes that were not observable to the voter showed clearly against the light. By using different arrangements of the pinholes, they could tell who cast what ballot and, therefore, how he voted."

A final example of the hard-to-believe stories was this one told me by an individual who claimed to have been personally involved: A bitter fight was going on within the city commission over a petition to rezone a parcel of land from residential use to commercial use. Two commissioners willing to vote for the change stood to pocket a considerable sum (property zoned for commercial use will often bring a much greater sale price than if zoned for residential use, and owners may be willing to share the difference with officials who vote the change), but they needed another vote. They tried various inducements to get one more commissioner to vote with them. He steadfastly refused, but they did not give up.

Finding they could not win him over directly, they tried an indirect means. A local police officer was married to an unusually attractive redhead. Arrangements were made to have the officer's wife begin to play up to the commissioner. The affair progressed to the point that the commissioner, although married and with children of his own, decided to spend a night with the officer's good-looking wife at a convenient hostelry. They had retired, and he had just reached a compromising position when the door came open, a camera flashed, and there was the officer and other witnesses to the scene.

The individual who related the story to me was a close friend of the commissioner, at least close enough that the commissioner contacted him, told him of the frameup, stated that his entire life was ruined, and said he was going to take his own life. The man's story was that he managed to get the commissioner into his car with him, drove him around town all the rest of that night and into the next day, finally convincing him he should not commit suicide, that he should make a full confession to his wife, plead for her forgiveness, and go on living. The former commissioner had taken the counsel and was still a respected member of the Daytona Beach community.

Happy First Anniversary

April 21, 1953, was one of the most rewarding days of my city-managing career. The employees arranged a surprise "birthday" party to recognize our being together one year and presented me with a plaque designed and made by members of the trades at city yards.

When I entered the large recreation hall where we had first met, the town's most popular pianist was playing "Happy Birthday," and one candle burned on a cake with the words "First Anniversary." I guess most of the city employees were there; at least, there were a lot of them.

Three employee spokesmen stated that "employees no longer need feel that our jobs are dependent upon some political connection." They said, "Employees feel free to express views

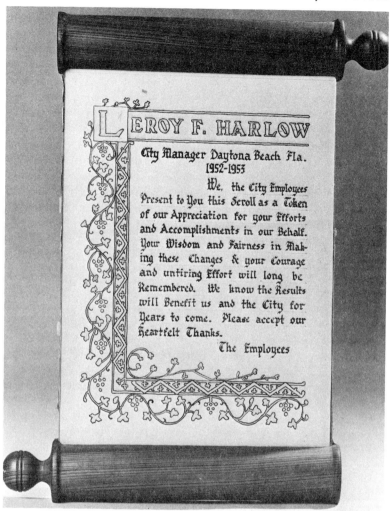

Plaque presented to the author by Daytona Beach municipal employees.

without prejudice or fear of reprisals; there're no longer kick-backs at city yards; you don't have to go to a certain grocery store to do your buying."

I suppose that looking back on happy occasions like this, we all wish we could have thought of something more appropriate to say. In my case, since tears come easily when I am deeply moved, I noted that "it looks like the hay fever season has arrived a little early," then went on to say, "As I told you here at our meeting about a year ago, you could take any one business out of this city and after some adjustment there would still be a Daytona Beach. But if the city government were taken away, with the kinds of services you provide for all the people, it would not be long until there would be no civilized community here." I thanked them.

With that, we all went back to work.

Continued Vigilance: the Cost of Good Government

As we approached the time to present our second annual budget, it was apparent that public interest was waning. Our new budget format showing much more detail than in previous years (Commissioner Combs Young had criticized the first new budget because it weighed nearly four pounds), the extent of citizen involvement, ample time for public inspection of the budget, and opportunity to be heard at a public meeting—these were no longer exciting to very many citizens.

In addition, despite much effort on our part to prepare factual materials, have department heads describe on radio the services of their units, and accept every opportunity to present our programs and answer questions about them, people were hearing and repeating rumors that we were hiding things at city hall.

Again we arranged for a presentation before a joint meeting of the civic clubs. The League of Women Voters advertised widely a general public meeting on the budget. A few days before the league-sponsored meeting, I wrote a letter to the editor of the *News-Journal*. After commenting that rumors were circulating, I wrote, "There are no secrets at city hall. If our taxpayers are asking for information from any of our departments and are not getting it, I want to know. Our citizens do not have to go one step further than the city hall to find out what they want—about city expenditures, where we buy things, how much we pay, what salaries we pay, expense allowances, condition of the budget, what our employees' duties are, why we are doing what we are, why we have the policies we have, and anything else that is public business." I closed by stating the place, day, and time of two public hearings and invited all our people to attend.

The public turnout at the League of Women Voters meeting was less than 20 percent of what it had been the first year; the other meetings were reasonably well attended, but the newness had worn off.

The Check That Was Never Cashed

I'm looking at a check I wrote twenty years ago that was never cashed. The reason it wasn't cashed relates to favors for public officials. I want to talk about that problem, but first let me tell you why I wrote the check.

The owner-operator of an automobile wrecker and towing service came to me to ask if he could get special permission to park his tow trucks on the street across from his place of business. He said the police department was hounding him because some of the neighbors were complaining.

In the course of our conversation we got on the subject of merchants and others doing favors for city officials. I don't remember how we began the topic, but I recall I made an offhand, probably cynical, remark that I doubted very many businessmen did favors for officials without expecting something in return—if not immediately, at some time in the future.

He thought differently. He said he thought lots of people appreciated what the mayor and the commissioners and other officials did for the community and just liked to show their appreciation, with no strings attached and no ulterior motives.

As to his parking problem, I said I would personally visit the location after I talked to the police and would be back in touch with him.

The police said that complaints were coming from a group of residents, most of them elderly retired people. The towing firm was located on an arterial street. When the trucks were parked across the street from the tow company garage they blocked the view of the arterial street traffic from motorists trying to enter the arterial street from residential side streets. This was a hazard and a worry to the elderly motorists.

I drove out to look at the intersection. The trucks were parked on the street. When I attempted to enter the arterial street from the residential area, I could see that the residents had a problem. Also, I noted that the towing firm had a vacant lot next to their building with ample room to park all their trucks. When I pointed this out to the owner, he acknowledged that he had room; but he felt that if the city would grant him a special parking zone at the curb, he could use his land for other purposes, and the city permit would stop the residents' complaints.

I told him I could see it would be more convenient to park on the street but that he was not suffering a hardship, and I could see no justification for a parking zone. Further, giving him what he asked against the wishes of the residents and posting official city signs wouldn't quiet the neighbors. I turned down his request.

A few weeks later my wife and I were on a Saturday afternoon drive. We went out to look at an abandoned gravel pit that I had heard might make a suitable new city dump when the present one reached capacity. We finally located it—actually a series of old pits. The old truck road that circled the pits was full of potholes but looked passable.

We got halfway around when I ran into loose sand; we were stuck tight. I walked a mile or so to the nearest house, telephoned the only wrecker service I knew by name—the one owned by the man who had requested the special parking permit. I described my predicament and asked them to send someone to pull me out.

Shortly a driver arrived with a big, crane-equipped wrecker. Our car was in an awkward place on a one-lane road at the edge of a pit; so he had to maneuver to get us hooked up and out. He towed us to the nearest surfaced road.

When he got us unhooked and his gear back in place, I asked him the amount of the charge. He said he didn't know, but they would send me a bill. So I gave him my name and address.

Several days went by, but no bill came. I waited until the end of the month, thinking maybe they billed only monthly. Still no bill. Finally I telephoned and asked for my bill. They said they had no record of the service.

I said, "Even if you don't have a record of it, I can tell you where I was and the distance from your place to there. Please tell me what a run of a man and a truck that distance, plus the tow out of the sand, would cost." The person on the telephone said that would probably be about ten dollars.

On August 22 I made out a check to the wrecker service for ten dollars. In the lower left corner I wrote "Gravel pit, west end 3rd St. in Holly Hill" to indicate the location. I mailed the check.

I received in return the following letter:

FRYER'S WRECKER SERVICE

ANYWHERE -:- ANYTIME

**BODY AND FENDER REPAIRING
PAINTING, WRECK REBUILDING**

580 BALLOUGH ROAD

DAYTONA BEACH, FLORIDA

August 26, 1953.

Mr. Le Roy Harlow
513 Silver Beach Ave
Daytona Beach Fla

Dear Sir:

    Check for ten (10) dollars enclosed.

    We do not have a record of this charge.

                Sincerely,

                Fryer's Wrecker Service

I telephoned the owner-manager, explained what had happened, and said I wanted to pay the tow charge.

He said, "Forget it. It wasn't anything. Glad to do you a little favor."

"Thanks," I said, "but I want to pay you for the service."

"I don't want any pay. If you send me the check again, I'll tear it up."

"Look," I said, "if LeRoy Harlow, private citizen, got stuck in the sand and called for towing service, as I did, you would charge me. But because I'm LeRoy Harlow, city manager, you insist on giving me the service, free, as a favor to me."

"That's right. You've been doing a good job for the city, and I want you to know I appreciate it. This is my way of showing my appreciation." He laughed good-naturedly.

"Now that's settled," he went on, "I want to ask you something. Do you think you could reconsider that request I made for a parking zone?"

I didn't say a word. There was silence for a long count.

Then, "Oh, oh, what *have* I said!! Forget that I said anything! Please! There's no connection between the free tow and my request. Forget it. Forget it!" He hung up. Because he sounded like it wouldn't do any good to send him the check a second time, I still have it. I never heard from him again.

Before going to Daytona Beach, I hadn't felt the need to pay much attention to incidents of this kind. The few times I was approached with suggestions of a little something for me on the side, I either ignored the hints, or in a couple of cases simply said, "If I understand you're trying to offer me something to influence my decision, you're talking to the wrong person. I don't do business that way."

In Albert Lea, a developer seemed to think that naming one of his subdivision streets for me would help me overlook his proposed violations of the zoning ordinance and subdivision regulations. When he showed me the subdivision plat with Harlow Street on it, I suggested a different name.

When vendors left small gifts—boxes of chocolates, pocket calendars, and similar offerings—I either distributed them around or used them at the office or at home. If the gift was too gaudy a piece of advertising focused on a particular firm, I threw it away.

When they brought to the house or left on the porch large and elaborate food baskets—hams, turkeys, fruit, or exotic packaged items, I took or sent the food to an old people's home or an orphanage in town, whose operators were always glad to get it.

The free trips offered to me usually had a clear city-business connection. For instance, in Fargo we were considering a large expansion of our water treatment plant capacity. The International Filter Company had patented a new high-speed mixing

machine that had the potential of saving the cost of constructing large mixing basins. When the firm's representative invited
our water superintendent and me to see some of their new
machines in operation and to visit their Chicago factory at their
expense, I accepted. And I didn't feel guilty when they included
a dinner and a good stage play. I knew they were trying to sell
us their product. But I also knew that if I didn't see some
installations at first hand and didn't talk to other people about
their experience with the new device, I could end up recommending to our city commission a costly machine that didn't
work.

But in Daytona Beach it was not that simple. There was a
history of kickbacks, payoffs, bribes, and embezzlement in city
government. That may have accounted for the general uncon-
cern about favors for officials—gifts, mostly at Christmas, but at
other times as well: clothing discount cards, expense-paid trips,
free meals, free passes, and season tickets. Perhaps it reflected a
resort community where gratuities are a major source of income
for many working people. Or it could have been just one facet
of southern hospitality. Whatever the reason for the greater
prevalence of favors for officials, it concerned me, and I decided
to try to think the problem through to a solution I could live
with, even though I felt from the start that I wasn't smart
enough to come up with a perfect answer.

I deliberately listed all the situations in which I received favors of any kind by virtue of my official position. Then I looked
for a pattern that might enable me to decide which favors I
would accept and which I would not accept.

When I did this, I noticed that most of the situations were
ones where I was part of the decorations for a particular occasion—for instance, when the host had to fill a head table or the
occasion was directly associated with city business. However,
there were a substantial number of situations in which the favor
could be used at any time, at my discretion. That is, while I
could not get that free meal any time I wanted, I could use a
clothing discount card or a baseball or theatre pass at my discretion. This discovery led me to the decision and practice I
followed thereafter: namely, to sometimes reject nondiscre-
tionary favors but to *always* reject gifts to be used at my convenience. The following letter is typical of several I sent after
making that decision:

Mr. F. L. Alig, Jr.,
Coastal Drive-Ins, Inc.,
1000 West Volusia Avenue
Daytona Beach, Florida

Dear Mr. Alig:

It was most thoughtful of you to send me a complimentary pass to the Volusia Drive-In for the year 1954.

Although I am returning the pass, I hope you will understand that it is not in any sense with lack of gratitude for your thoughtfulness in sending it to me. I have long made it a practice to not accept gratuities that have a continuing value which I may use at my own discretion and this, I think, falls in that category.

We appreciate your thoughtfulness.

Sincerely yours,

City Manager

All-America City

In 1952 a few people put together a presentation of the Daytona Beach story and entered the community in the All-America Cities competition sponsored by the National Municipal League and *Look* magazine. Daytona Beach was one of twenty-two finalists among fifty-seven entries, but the Daytona Beach representative who went to San Antonio for the finals was told that unless the new program survived the crucial election just ahead, the case was not strong enough.

In 1953 a more determined effort was made to win one of the coveted awards. A larger committee was formed, and a story-and-picture booklet was prepared. Mayor Tamm came into my office one day and found me toying with a design of a red, white, and blue shield.

"What are you doing?" he asked.

"Designing a shield to put on our equipment and on the police and fire uniforms when Daytona Beach is named one of the All-America cities."

"Aren't you a little premature and overconfident?" he asked, remarking that not even the next-to-last twenty-two cities had yet been chosen.

"I don't think so," I replied. "We were close last year, and now with the clean sweep in the election, I think Daytona Beach will be on the first team this year."

I had never seen an All-America seal used by other winning cities, but I had seen seals used by some companies and on patriotic occasions. So I completed the following design:

This time, out of 115 competitors, Daytona Beach was among the eleven named. The February 9, 1954, issue of *Look* carried the "salute" to the eleven. Shortly afterward the Daytona Beach story was dramatized over a nationwide broadcast; the city was provided a large blue and white flag carrying the words "DAYTONA BEACH — ALL AMERICA CITY"; and the award was formally presented to the people of Daytona Beach by the chairman of the board of the Chamber of Commerce of the United States at a citywide celebration.

Word of Daytona Beach's efforts to improve local government reached other places. During the summer following election of the five city commissioners pledged to continue the program, the *Ladies' Home Journal* sent a team of writers and photographers down from Philadelphia to do a story on our experience. The story came out in the magazine's November 1953 issue, with the title "Aroused Citizens Clean Up the Town."

In view of the negative publicity local governments sometimes get, one would have thought the community and the city government would have benefited from the favorable national publicity. Instead, it probably did more harm than good. Apparently desiring to make our experience even more dramatic than it was, the magazine and radio writers took liberties with the facts. Although the magazine had asked the managing editor of the newspaper to write the Daytona Beach story (going back several years), and he did, in their rewrite they left out some significant items, exaggerated others, added a few, and changed the sequence of some incidents. As a result, the published story was not only different from his draft; it was wrong about several specifics.

This did irreparable damage to our efforts. Opponents of the administration were able to take these stories to citizens who were on the fence politically and say, in effect, "Look at this story by our so-called honest administration. I know and you know that is not the way it happened. Yet that is what they are telling all over the country."

And even though information given the national media was correct, once the incorrect version came out in print and over the air there was nothing the administration could do to correct it.

Lies Fly Ahead of Truth

As we entered the second half of the administration's current two-year term, the community euphoria from the All-America City recognition was further dampened by stepped-up opposition to the administration. Opposing activities increased in tempo and directness.

The commissioners were feeling it, and some of it came my way. For example, in the Christmas mail I received a large fold-out card. On the outside it read "MERRY CHRISTMAS! As you unfold these wishes." When fully opened, it turned out to be a twenty-three-inch pair of long red paper underwear on which the sender had written, "To be use (*sic*) in Minnesota. '55 Committee."

Some other anonymous person mailed me the following clipping, stapled to a blank card: "*Today's Chuckle*. Don't strut. The fact that you have a certain title doesn't prove anything except maybe in selecting you somebody made a mistake that will be rectified later."

Still another anonymous person clipped and mailed me a news photo from a local paper, showing the head table at the kickoff dinner for the United Negro College Fund drive. There were thirteen people at the table—six Negroes, including Dr. Bethune, and seven whites, including Agda and me. The sender had typed at the top of the picture, "You might do this back

home but it is not done in Daytona Beach by people of refinement."

On another occasion, while standing on the curb watching a parade in which the sponsors had asked us to enter the new fire-fighting and public works equipment, a woman spectator standing in front of me grumbled aloud to her companion, "What kind of a parade is this? Nothing but showing off all the expensive equipment the city bought with *our* tax money!"

This stepped-up activity didn't pass the newspapers unnoticed. On March 20 the *Evening News* pointed out editorially what was happening in Daytona Beach. The writer drew a parallel with other reform movements, such as those reported by Lincoln Steffens, famed author of *The Shame of the Cities*, written fifty years before:

The Editorial Page

Daytona Beach Evening News

The Editorial...

Let's Not Follow The Rule

IT IS A SAD and baffling fact that reform administrations on the local level, are short lived.

There are several reasons for this:

— People expect too much of officials who have been elected to restore just and orderly processes after a period of abuse and bad management. That they should have confidence in these new officials is fine, indeed. But they indulge in fantasies of perfectionism which no human being could bring into line with reality. When this perfectionism is not realized, when in the natural course of events well intentioned mistakes are made, there is a tendency to resent such mistakes to a degree not felt toward equivalent errors by a machine group.

— In everybody's subconscious there is just a little touch of the anarchist. We are inclined to resent the restraint of laws, no matter how much we may accept them in principle. A reform administration, being made up of men essentially just, naturally tries to enforce laws equitably. There develops then on the part of some voters a feeling of irksomeness, a consciousness of government, a yearning for laxer days, perhaps for days when things could be "fixed," or at least when pleasing voters was purposefully placed ahead of order and justice.

— Not all people in business live by the splendid Rotary Club motto of "service above self." Years ago, Lincoln Steffens, the great exposer of municipal corruption, pointed out that reform governments tended to be swept out of office by an alliance, not always formal but nevertheless real, between selfish business interests and the racketeers. Business, he indicated, often would rather pay venality than submit to discipline.

— The day a reform administration goes into office, the professional politicians start their campaigns to get their noses back into the trough. Whispering campaigns get going. Advantage is taken of every mistake made by the administration. Geographic sectionalism is stimulated. Personalities are indulged in. Every little divisive flame is blown up into a fire.

— The very honesty of the reform officials militates against them. They are frank and open in expressing their opinions, even when they do not agree among themselves. Sometimes they give the appearance of "splitting up." They are not always politically minded and they neglect their fence building. Their minds are on the business of government; not on being reelected. All too often they are busy

men who are making personal sacrifices to serve one term and have no intention of preserving continuity by running for office again. Also, they are usually sensitive men, unused to the carping criticisms which they find go with the office.

— People are inclined to expect a reform administration to put a governmental house in order too rapidly. They do not realize that one term or so is often too little to set an inherited mess in order. Taxes brought about by past extravagances can't always be lowered overnight. Inefficiencies due to the spoils system can't be immediately rooted out. It couldn't be done in industry; it can't in government.

— Finally, the carping criticisms heretofore mentioned are multiplied by the simple fact that nobody has to be afraid to make them. Reform officials are sitting ducks. They have neither the inclination nor the lack of morals to make reprisals.

* * *

COMES ELECTION time and the reform officials are tired of it all. They step out. New candidates are hard to find: Other public spirited citizens do not want to face the music, either.

This is the kind of situation we face here in Daytona Beach if the great body of the citizenship which voted a year ago last December for first class government in the City Hall with a professional City Manager who has made a wonderful record here, do not stand firm in their determination to keep first things first in their appraisal of the government we have. Eternal vigilance is the price of liberty, they say. Eternal cool headed cooperation is the essential of retaining good government in a municipality.

* * *

LET US APPRAISE our administration as a whole—not on isolated issues—criticise when we believe it wrong without generalizations, avoid carping, watch out for undermining propaganda, and prove an exception to the rule that the "rascals" in American municipal government, always "get back in."—H. M. D.

The reference in the editorial to whispering campaigns proved prophetic. As we neared election time, hardly a week went by that someone did not bring me the latest story being circulated about me—that my salary had been doubled; that I had more than half a dozen personal assistants; that the city was paying my rent, utilities, and car expenses; that I was getting kickbacks from the private garbage contractor.

The secretary in my office was infuriated by one of the stories she overheard and brought me. She had gone across the street from the city hall to have lunch in the little cafe owned by County Commissioner Ralph Richards, the former city commissioner who had once been convicted of taking a $10,000 bribe for his vote for mayor.

She overheard the loud conversation at the next booth. One of the men was saying, "I've got *proof* that Harlow has just finished building a $200,000 motel in Ocala. I saw the building permit."

These lies came so thick and fast it would have been impossible to refute them. My friends joked about them and shrugged them off. "Forget it," they said. "Everybody knows it's just politics."

But I found them frustrating. As the author of the editorial wrote, I found myself a sitting duck. A liar can make a statement about another person without expending any more energy than it takes to get the words out. The person lied about can wear himself out getting proof of his innocence and trying to follow the trail of the liar and correct the wrong impression. But he will no sooner get close to undoing the damage caused by the first lie than the liar will make another wild, unsupported statement and send the innocent person on another exhausting effort to defend himself. And so it goes, the liar always in a position to keep the innocent person off balance and on the defensive. I can understand why the admonition against bearing false witness against others is among the most fundamental of commandments.

To Their Benefit

On the second anniversary of my appointment, the employees again surprised me. This time the employees' committee arranged a little ceremony in my office. "As official representatives, in behalf of and as a token of appreciation by the employees of the city of Daytona Beach," they presented me a framed resolution that listed accomplishments that had accrued to their benefit: "such as the establishment of better working conditions, a five-day work week, job training schools, expansion of civil service coverage, job classification and a graduated pay plan, better opportunities for promotion from within the ranks, the institution of Social Security benefits and the dissemination of the knowledge that any employee may be heard without prejudice at any time he may so desire." The fireman, policeman, and secretary from city hall who constituted the committee signed the document alongside the All-America City seal.

It's No Longer "Who You Know"

Commissioner Coursen, a semiretired photographer, lacked the energy and interest of the other commissioners; consequently, I was not so well acquainted with him and his views as I would have liked. So I was pleased when he came into the office one morning for a visit.

We talked about a few current items before he said he would have to be going. As he rose to leave, he took a small piece of paper from his pocket, laid it on my desk, and said, "Roy, will you take care of this for me?"

I picked up the paper. It was a ticket for overparking. I said, "This is a parking ticket. What did you want me to do with it?"

"Yes, I know," he said. "One of my old customers overparked while he was at the studio and got the ticket. I told him I'd take care of it for him; that's why I'm bringing it to you."

"Maybe I don't understand," I said. "Do you want me to pay the fine, or do you want to pay it, or what?"

"No, I don't want you to pay the fine, and I'm not going to pay any fine. I'm just asking you to take care of the ticket— write it off, cancel it, or whatever you do."

"Bill," I asked, "Are you kidding? You know we don't fix tickets. That's contrary to what this administration stands for."

"Do you mean to tell me that I'm a city commissioner and I can't even get a parking ticket taken care of for a friend of mine when I want to?"

"If by 'taking care of a ticket' you mean I should excuse this violation because the individual involved happens to be a friend of yours, or of mine, or some other city official, then I have to say yes, that's exactly what I mean."

There was a period of awkward silence. The commissioner took the ticket from my hand and walked out without a word.

Second Disappointment: A Deliberate Mistake

Like the incident involving the pictures taken at the Welch Pools, another unhappy instance of official misconduct by a key city official took place in the personnel division.

The city had a residence requirement for most civil service positions. That is, an ordinance provided that no nonresident could take a civil service examination or be appointed to a civil service position unless the civil service board specifically authorized an exception to the rule.

The civil service board announced examinations for clerk-typist and clerk-stenographer positions, open to residents only. The personnel officer (also the secretary to the civil service board) set up the examinations and notified a dozen or more applicants that they were approved to take the examinations.

At the time the examinations were given, the personnel officer was out of town, attending a personnel administrators' conference. His secretary administered the examinations.

After the examinations were held, the secretary reported that some nonresidents had taken the examination. This information aroused my suspicion that something was not right. For one thing, I knew that the personnel officer was fully aware of the residence requirement. Also, I knew there was no shortage of qualified resident candidates for these positions. And my casual observation of the personnel officer's conduct around young women suggested to me that he might have more than a professional interest in some of these candidates.

I asked to see the examination papers to satisfy myself that some of the applicants gave addresses outside the city. Then I had photostatic copies made of the examinations, showing the answers as written or left blank by the applicants. I locked the photostatic copies in my desk and had the original examinations returned to the personnel office for grading by the personnel officer when he returned.

After the examinations were graded and the lists of eligibles (including some nonresidents) were posted, I invited the personnel officer to my office. I asked if the residence requirement applied to the examinations from which the eligible lists just posted had been drawn. He said it did. I asked if everyone who had been admitted to the examinations was a resident of Day-

Joint Committee Says Berrien Altered Tests

ANSWER	ANSWER
.(.2.0.36.)	(..2.0.2.6)
.(...7.1.8...)	(.....9.98.) 798
.(..4.6..299)	(50.2830.) 46.299
.(....29/32	(..29/32.)

Published photograph of altered civil service examination answers, Daytona Beach, Florida. (Courtesy Daytona Beach *News-Journal* Corp.)

tona Beach. He said they all were. I asked him to bring me the file on each one of the applicants, with both their applications to take the examination and the examination results.

With all the files in hand, I opened those whose applications to take the examination showed an address outside the city and asked, "What about these?"

He looked at them carefully, then said, "I guess that's a mistake on my part. I must not have checked those addresses closely enough."

I excused him. When he left, I compared the copies of the nonresidents' examinations with the examination papers the personnel officer had marked and graded. Where previously the applicants had left answer spaces blank, now there were answers written in. Where the applicants had given wrong answers, the answers were erased and correct answers written in. All the additions and corrections were in handwriting so different from the applicants' that even as a layman it appeared clear to me the examinations had been altered by someone.

I asked for a meeting with the board and the personnel officer/board secretary, reported to both of them the evidence I had that someone had altered the examinations, and with the board's approval suspended the official as personnel officer pending action by the board on his employment as secretary to the board. Three days later he resigned, and the board accepted his resignation without terminal leave benefits.

Although the personnel officer/board secretary had resigned and his resignation had been accepted, he engaged a handwriting expert from Miami and hinted that someone else in his office had made the alterations. To establish the facts in the matter, the city commission and the civil service board formed a four-member joint investigating committee. At the committee's request, I contacted two handwriting experts: Charles Appel, Jr., of Washington, D.C., a former FBI agent who had worked on the Lindbergh kidnapping case, and Edward Kilner of Jacksonville, Florida, handwriting expert for the U.S. Post Office Department and the federal courts. The committee engaged these two experts.

Appel and Kilner positively identified the alterations as having been made by the personnel officer/board secretary. The expert engaged by the personnel officer/board secretary acknowledged changes had been made but declined to give an opinion on who had made the changes.

Two months after the personnel officer/board secretary resigned, the joint investigating committee announced their unanimous opinion that answers on the two examinations were altered by the personnel officer/board secretary.

Did You Get Yours?

After the incident involving the commissioner's request that I fix a parking ticket for his customer, there was a perceptible cooling in his relationship with me. The situation was further aggravated by an incident at one of the premeeting planning sessions.

Before the mayor started down the list of potential agenda items, the same commissioner put a simple conversational question to the group.

"Did you fellows get your season pass to the _____ Theatre?" (I don't remember which downtown theatre it was.)

Several nodded or said yes, but Commissioner Long, a man known to be outspoken, added, "Yes, and I returned mine."

This seemed to startle the first commissioner. He turned to me. "What about you?"

"Yes," I said, "I received one. I returned mine also."

The fact was that I had no knowledge of what the commissioners received in the way of official favors, and neither Commissioner Long nor any other member of the official family and I had discussed what we did about them. My policy of not accepting favors to be used at my discretion was one I had determined completely on my own.

But whatever the circumstance, my answer clearly offended the first commissioner. He turned red in the face, put the pass he had in his hand back in his pocket, and made a loud "Hrrmpf!"

The mayor turned our attention to the afternoon's business.

"Not I," Said the Man

As the election dates drew near, the rift between Commissioner Coursen and the other four commissioners widened. Commissioner Coursen announced he would not run again. Mayor Tamm and commissioners Long and McCarthy (an attorney/restaurant operator, a dentist, and a surgeon, respectively) wanted to find candidates who believed as they did and were willing to serve so that they could get back to spending more time on their private professional practices. This proved difficult.

I was not involved at all in these efforts, but I did read the newspapers and knew who had filed for office and generally where they stood. Moreover, the subject of the coming election and the search for candidates inevitably came up at the commission planning session where I was in attendance. (The only request the four commissioners made of me was that I prepare a fact sheet, which I did and which was available for anyone who wanted a copy.)

The first big disappointment came to the four commissioners when the chairman of the civic affairs committee, one of the leaders in the reform movement and the man who made Daytona Beach's first presentation to the All-America City jury in San Antonio, informed them that his business partner had threatened to dissolve their partnership if he ran for the commission. He could not afford this. After that, man after man declined, several of them saying their wives refused to let them run for fear of danger to the men and their families.

Faced with this problem, Dr. Long and Dr. McCarthy decided they would run again. Commissioner Warren also would make the race again, this time against long-established County Commissioner Ralph Richards, who was running on a platform of "closer cooperation" between city and county officials by his being both city commissioner and county commissioner.

Unable to find a qualified man to run in the predominantly Negro zone, the Tamm-Long-McCarthy group approached Dr. Ruth Rogers, president of the local chapter of the League of Women Voters. Dr. Rogers was an unmarried, white physician who lived in that zone and was known to have befriended and provided free medical service to hundreds of Negroes and was respected and appreciated by them.

Finally Dr. Rogers consented to run. She resigned as president of the league to make the race and was succeeded by the league's vice-president, Mrs. Marion Fields.

Now the reform group had four candidates; they needed one more. Again they tried to find a qualified person who would be willing to serve, but with no more success than before. Reluctantly, Marion Fields also resigned from the presidency of the League of Women Voters and became a candidate.

Another Disappointment

At about this time the mayor called to say he had heard a rumor he wished I would check on: that several business places in town had received a postal card from the police department suggesting that because the community was experiencing a large number of burglaries and the department was not sufficiently manned to deal with the problem, the department recommended that they contract with the Dixie Detective Agency to provide them additional security.

"Mayor," I said, "I can hardly believe that. It's bad enough to be telling the businessmen we can't protect their establishments without recommending only one private security service when there are several firms in the business. I'll check on it right away and get back to you."

I immediately called the chief and said I'd like to meet with him as soon as possible about something that had come up. I'd come to his office.

When I got to the chief's office, I told him what the mayor had said and asked him what he knew about it. There was nothing to it, the chief said. "It's true that the owner of that new detective service came over here and laid some cards right here on my desk and asked if he could mail them out, but I told him 'nothing doing,' and that was that."

I reported to the mayor what the chief had told me.

A few days later the mayor came to my office. This time he had one of the postal cards, signed by Chief Moore.

I met again with the chief and showed him the card. He was upset. In so many words, he said, "The damned guy mailed them out anyway, after I told him he couldn't." I asked the chief if he had any connection with the Dixie Detective Agency. He replied he had none whatsoever.

I reported this conversation to the mayor. Both of us were concerned about the effect of these cards going out over the chief's signature, whether or not he had authorized it. The opposition was not likely to overlook this opportunity to show how the police chief was favoring one detective agency over others that offered the same service.

We didn't have to wait long. I had another call from the mayor. The rumor this time was that the opposition had evidence that the chief was an officer in the Dixie Detective Agency.

Knowing the detective agency was incorporated, I sent to the office of the Florida Secretary of State for a copy of the articles of incorporation. I was shocked to see Chief Moore's name and his signature as a member of the board of directors of the recently formed corporation.

With the commissioners' opponents exploiting this information, it seemed to me this was a matter for the city commission. Although, in accordance with their wishes, the chief reported to me, he was appointed by the commission. And by this time all the commissioners knew from one source or another about the police chief and the Dixie Detective Agency.

The mayor called the commission together and invited the chief and me to attend. The commissioners told the chief what they had heard and knew and asked what he had to say. What he had to say was pretty brief: his private affairs were none of their business, and his being a stockholder and officer of the Dixie Detective Agency in Daytona Beach was no different from his owning shares of A. T. & T.

The commissioners and I tried to persuade him that there was a difference, that here was a matter about which he could have considerable influence by virtue of his position as chief of police. But he was adamant; it was nobody else's business. They assured him of their confidence in him and their appreciation for the excellent job he had done. They said they did not want to take any hasty action. They asked him to think it over, then to give them a written report on the situation. They gave him three or four days to prepare his report.

In the meantime, the commission released the story to the press. On November 2, 1954, the *Evening News* ran an editorial on the commissioner's action under the title A COMMISSION WITH CHARACTER. It read in part:

"The character of the men who sit on our city commission was exhibited once again by the decision to bring into the open the unpleasant disclosure that Police Chief Moore has an interest in a local private detective enterprise and has plumped to get it business.

"They have told the public about it, cleanly and frankly, and at the same time they have given Moore a chance to explain his position in a written report. . . .

"Old line politicians sitting in the places of Tamm, Long, McCarthy, Warren, and Coursen would have done the politically expedient thing, with a city election staring them in the face. They would have hushed the matter up as long as they could. Then, if the matter had been exposed by opposition forces, they would have met the attack with silence or shrugged it off.

"They would have thought primarily of the election and they would have disregarded their duty to keep the public informed of everything of which it is the public's right to know. This commission has been different. All through their administration they have taken any errors they have made in administrative decision or in the selection of personnel squarely on the chin. They have let the chips fall. . . ."

The time went by for receiving the report, but no word came from the chief. I waited a while longer, then checked with the deputy chief. He said he had not seen the chief for several days. I made discreet inquiry of a few other people who might know his whereabouts, but none of them had seen him lately.

A few more days had passed when I received a telephone call from the manager of one of the large beach hotels.

"Are you looking for your chief of police?" he asked in a sarcastic voice. Without giving me time to answer, he gave me a room number in his hotel "where you can find him."

I drove immediately to the hotel and went to the room the manager had given me. I knocked on the door two or three times before I got a growling response.

"Whad dya want?"

"Al, this is LeRoy. I want to talk to you. Let me in."

"I don't wanta talk to anybody."

"I know you don't. But I want to talk to you. Let me in."

I suppose I waited only five minutes—it seemed longer—when he opened the door. He looked in pretty bad shape—pants pulled over half-buttoned underwear; several days' growth of beard; eyes bloodshot; a croaky voice.

"What dya want?" he asked.

"You know what I want, Al. I want to know if you're going to get your report to the commission."

"To hell with that. To hell with this whole penny-ante town," he said, along with several less complimentary remarks.

He was sitting on the side of the bed staring at the floor when I closed the door and left. I never saw or heard from him again—Albert B. Moore, one of the ablest and most cooperative law enforcement officers I've known, and a man I admired and considered a friend.

Without Fear or Favor

The day before the *Evening News* editorialized on the city commission's disclosure of Chief Moore's interest in the private detective enterprise, the *Morning Journal* ran a lengthy editorial that put me in the center of the upcoming election, although at the same time it acknowledged I was not a candidate to be voted on by the people. The paper titled the editorial ABOUT LEROY HARLOW and opened with:

"There is lots of talk in Daytona Beach these days about LeRoy F. Harlow. It is natural that talk is going on, and it will increase; for Harlow is the man responsible for the competent and efficient manner in which the city's affairs are now being administered. The forthcoming city election will decide whether or not Harlow will be kept on his job."

The writer went on to say, "Harlow is a dedicated man and believes every citizen is entitled to equal treatment and service from their City employees. He performs his duties without fear and without favor. In doing this on an impartial basis the City Manager must say "no" more often than "yes." People who demand special personal favors, large or small from the City, are often displeased when Harlow refuses to grant them what can't be given to every other citizen of Daytona Beach. . . ."

The last sentence in the editorial read: "The candidates pledged to retain Harlow deserve to be elected on the basis of the effective performance of our city manager in the two and one-half years he has been here."

I felt uncomfortable being thus thrust into the political lime-light. After all, I could do nothing about who was elected to the city commission. My job was to administer the laws and ordinances of the city and the policies of the people's elected representatives, and that was what I was trying to do. After a new commission had been in office long enough to know firsthand what kind of an administrator I was, they were certainly entitled to make a change if they felt it was needed; or if their policies and conduct were ones I could not agree with, I could resign. But until then, it seemed to me it was in the public's interest to maintain continuity in the conduct of the people's business.

I was not so naive that I did not know that professional public administrators and career public servants are often identified with the "in" administration and become targets of the "out" group. But I was concerned by the wastefulness and cost to the taxpayers of this kind of switching back and forth. Most private companies would go broke if they changed general managers every couple of years and if they always fired their key people at about the time those people got well acquainted with and proficient on their jobs. If these practices would destroy a private business, they are not likely to be healthy for the people's business.

My discomfort was further increased by receipt of another anonymous note. This one read, "Don't be surprised if the News-Journal lets you down." I couldn't tell the source of the note, whether friend or foe. But I was satisfied that the management of the newspapers and I had the same vision of what government should be in America. Furthermore, their ideas about "good government" were not some vague abstractions they wanted applied to government in faraway Washington or the state capital. Rather, week after week they laid on the line their beliefs about government in their own community, as I was trying to do in my daily work.

On the other hand, I had noted as early as my first months on the job the resentment of a number of people about the attention the newspapers gave city affairs. This resentment may have accounted for the threat to kill me that was telephoned into the police department. Or, since the call came just a week before the primary election, it may have been evidence that strong-arm political methods were still alive in Daytona Beach politics.

Agda and I had driven to Tampa to attend a Florida League

303

of Municipalities meeting. On our return at about 9:30 in the evening, a police officer met us at the city limit. He told us a man had called on the direct line to the detective bureau at 7:55 p.m. In a disguised voice the man said, "You'd better get a guard on Harlow tonight."

This is the incident as reported on November 24 in the local paper:

LOCAL NEWS

Man Calls Cops, Says He'll Kill Harlow

By GEORGIA FRANKLYN

Police maintained an all night guard on City Manager LeRoy F. Harlow after an anonymous phone caller to the Detective Bureau threatened to kill him.

Detective Sgt. Jack Lynady received the call from an un- identified man who issued the death threat.

Lynady received the call at 7:55 last night from a man who, the detective said, "sounded like he was disguising his voice." Lynady said he answered his phone in the usual way and the caller said, "Who? Who's speaking?"

Lynady identified himself and the man on the phone said, "You'd better get a guard on Harlow to- night."

"What do you mean by that?" Lynady said.

"I've tried to get a hold of Harlow but I can't find him," the voice said, "I'm gonna kill him."

When Lynady asked who was calling and from where the man said, "Never mind who is speak- ing, you'd better do as I say."

The detective said he could not tell if the call was from a crank or if it was the real thing. He added that every precaution was being taken to guard Harlow.

Lynady said he thought it peculiar that the man had called on the direct line to the upstairs detectives' office, as most calls coming into the po- lice station are on the down- stairs police phone.

At the time of the call, Harlow was out of town. He returned to the City about 9:30.

Harlow had no comment to make about the threat.

Lynady remained with Harlow while the City Manager finished some last minute work at City Hall and then drove the Manager home.

Patrolman J. D. Wallace guarded the Harlow home un- til midnight when Patrolman Vic Folsom took over until 8 this morning.

Acting Police Chief H. L. Allen, when informed of the threat, said "We will have the place covered. If anyone tries anything, we'll know who it is." Allen also said he had no idea if the call was the work of a crank or a real threat.

I left it to the discretion of the acting chief whether or not to continue the watch the next day. He decided to provide a twenty-four-hour-a-day plainclothes bodyguard at least through the primary election.

Your Vote *Does* Count

A few days before the election the opponents of McCarthy and Rogers distributed a four-page tabloid newspaper. Except for the candidates' names, telephone numbers, photographs, and one short article, the tabloids were identical. One was titled CALDWELL'S NEWS and the other DURDEN'S DISPATCH.

The fictitious news stories in the two sheets were so cleverly and humorously written I found myself chuckling at them even though every one of them was either an outright lie or an insinuation intended to mislead. Here are a few examples:

Harlow Eats Heavy

Only a few people know that City Manager Harlow has made plenty of demands of the present City Commission; and they have been answered. He is living in a city owned house, drives a city car with city gasoline; and it is rumored that he has a very substantial city expense account, and even charges his lunch to the city when he is too tired to leave his office and has it sent in. While small in size, Harlow is a big eater. Is this all additional salary? You tax payers are paying for it.

Harlow's Happy Chart Makers

Harlow's Happy Chart Makers will convene in Daytona to study under the Master Chart Maker, LeRoy Harlow. Representatives from all over the United States will learn from Happy Harlow how to make increased taxes look like lower taxes, increased expenditures look like savings accounts, and his phenominally high salary look insufficient.

After the convention, it is rumored that all in attendance will be hired by City Hall and thus come under the fold of Master Chart Marker Harlow. The only assignment to be given these new Chart Makers will be to hide the increased City payroll under cleverly contrived, multi-colored charts.

A Bedtime Story

Snow White Harlow (and the Seven Assistants)

Once upon time there was a poor, poor city Manager, who lived in a beautiful ivory tower in the City Hall of a little City called Daytona Beach. He was a poor man, with many hungry mouths to feed, and his only income was the meager sum of $15,000 a year paid him by the city. That wasn't very much money in those days, because with expenses, and everything, it was pretty hard to save any more than about half his salary.

To pass the time away, this City Manager would si tin a rocking chair, reading his lovely story books, many of which talked about a land far away, a land called Utopia. This City Manager would dream as he read, that someday he might reach this promised land.

One day, as he sat in his office, reading and rocking, the telephone rang with a loud noise. This startled him so much, that he rose in anger, that his reading and rocking had be interrupted. "This will never do" he thought, "if they interrupt my reading like that, think what they might do when I start to draw all my lovely, lovely charts."

With that, he wearily rose from his chair and sought out the Mayor. He didn't go to the Mayor's office, but went to the front steps of the City Hall, where he knew he could find him. The Mayor, who's name was Little Smiling Jack wa sa jolly, round man, who always smiled when a photographer was near, and as usual, he was standing there smiling, surrounded by reporters and photographers who wanted to take his picture with his arms around a garbargc truck.

Seing that Snow-White was troubled, Little Smiling Jack allowed the photographers only ten pictures, whihc, for him was unusually rude, and, taking Snow-White aside, asked, "What seems to be the trouble, Whitey?"

In a voice coked with emotion, and with tears streaming down his cheeks, Snow White told the Mayor how his reading had been so rudely distrubed when someone had the nerve to ring his telephone. "This will never do," he said, "what will happen when it's time for me to make my Charts? I must have Assistants who will see to it that my phone never rings again, and I must have a raise in pay too, because it wouldn't look nice to have Assistants and pay them without paying me more too."

The Mayor thought this was a splendid idea, because after all, he was busy with photographers all the time, so he toudln't help snow whîte; and the other Commissioners were busy pulling teeth, cutting bladders and chasing race track promoters and bond buyers. He called their offices but they were all too busy to talk, but they told him to spend whatever he wanted to;

that they might sent messengers on pure white horses to all points of the Country, and each messenger bore a shield upon which was inscribed the All-American Emblem. This was indeed a Crusade, a pilgrimage in search of the Holy Grail, to free for all time the worries of Snow-White, the City Manager, for more important tasks, as reading books and drawing Charts.

Soon the messengers came, bearing good tidings for indeed they had found the right men, in many distant points. They came on and on, waving their brightly colored suitcases, and thus became known as the Suit-case Assistants. They were at once brought before the Mayor, requested to kneel, and were tapped upon the shoulder with his All-American Sceptor, and were given their Titles.

There was an Assistant City Manager, and an Assistant to the Assistant City-Manager, who was called the Research Assistant. Then, of course, there were various Clerks who assisted the Assistants. Then there was the Personnel Officer, and the Assistant Personnel Officer, and their Clerks to assist them. Then there was the Purchasing Agent, and the Assistant Purchasing Agent, and Clerks to assist them. Then came the Equipment Superintendent and his Assistants, making seven Assistants in all.

That is why we call this the story of Snow-White and the Seven Assistants. When they began to work, the City Manager was never disturbed again, but went back to his reading and rocking, and drawing charts, because there was now nothing to disturb him. All he had to do was go out for his salary twice a month, because he didn't need an Assistant for that. And they all think that they will live off the taxpayers forever after. *Do You?*

The morning and evening newspapers, the three incumbent commissioners, the two women candidates, and a committee of the central labor union countered with editorials, fact sheet mailouts, and advertisements.

None of these straightforward presentations had the eye-catching, entertaining, and suggestive appeal of the cartoons, the ridiculous articles, and the innuendos of the Caldwell and Durden tabloid. And when the votes were counted, County

Commissioner Richards and Caldwell had been swept into city office, and the other three races were so close they required a runoff. The administration had to win all three to keep control.

At this point, Commissioner Coursen stepped into the picture. In a signed, paid political ad that carried his photograph and was addressed "to the people of Daytona Beach," he gave his reasons why Dr. Long's opponent "would make a more competent and effective city commissioner than Dr. Long."

The *Evening News*'s editorial for December 4, 1954, the Saturday before Tuesday's final election, recalled what the people of Daytona Beach had achieved, yet it carried a warning. It read, in part:

"It isn't just because we have had clean, impartial government here for the past few years that we are able to fly that proud 'All America' banner.

"It was for the job we did, we the people of this city, in pulling our way out of a slough. It was for the long way we had come since the days when this town had the reputation—along with the rest of the county—for being the center of the worst political conditions in the state. Those days, indeed, when people smiled at you disconcertingly when they heard where you came from and said, 'Oh, yes—and are you still in a political mess over there?' And when people tried it out here and moved away because they wouldn't stand for political pressures and political tyranny.

"That's why we got the prize, because we won a long, hard fight. Because we had a bad situation and because we did something about it.

"And now we are in danger of dropping right back into the slough. We are in danger because a lot of nice people may not realize what they may be doing if, for one reason or another, they let their judgment be ruled by petty resentment concerning some detail of municipal management which in some way or other restricts them, instead of listening to the calm voice of reason. Because they can't see the forest of long pull progress against the trees of, let us say, the inconvenience of having to box their trash.

"Let us not sell our hard won birthright for a pot of favoritism. Let us stick to the path of fairness to everybody and of spending where spending will do the most good for the greatest number. Let us avoid the siren who talks of reduced taxes out of one side of its mouth and out of the other promises one costly moon after another—and, believe us, moons with a political ring around them!"

Voting was heavy in the runoff election. More than 72 percent of the registered voters went to the polls. Commissioners Long and McCarthy won handily in their zones, but Mrs. Fields lost by eight votes out of more than 1,500 ballots. Thus, fewer than a dozen votes decided the direction the city would move in the next two years, and maybe longer.

No Second Place in Politics

The new city commission took office on January 4. At about noon that day, newly elected Commissioner Francis Morrison, whom I had never met, telephoned to say the commission was going to terminate my services, that perhaps I would like to resign before they took that action.

There seems to be a popular notion that it looks better on a man's record to say he resigned than that he was fired. And maybe this is often so. But in this case there was more to be considered than one individual's job record. I didn't give Morrison an answer. Instead, I telephoned the editor of the paper. "Herb," I said, "Mr. Morrison has just called to tell me I am being fired. He has said I may want to resign before they take that action. In your judgment, will it make any difference to the cause we've been involved in whether I resign or am fired?"

He thought a moment. "Yes," he said, "I think it might help sometime in the future if the record showed they fired you."

I decided I would not resign.

That afternoon, our thirteen- and ten-year-old sons had rehearsal for a tap-dancing program they were to be in that evening. Their instructor was the son of one of the county commissioners.

At the end of the rehearsal, ten-year-old John went to the telephone to call for a ride home. He picked up the telephone just in time to overhear a conversation on another telephone in the house. Someone was saying, "Tonight we're going to get Harlow." So at dinner the whole family learned that something was going to happen to Daddy. But after having been taken into hiding once, knowing of the death threats, and having had a police guard twenty-four hours a day, it did not come with the same shock that four-year-old Christine had suffered when in Fargo she learned that someone was going to "burn up Daddy."

The city commission meeting place was packed. (This was the same large recreation building in which city employees had presented me the cherished plaque two years before.) The commission's first act was to elect Commissioner Morrison, the man who had defeated Mrs. Fields, to the mayor's post. Commissioner Long moved the election be unanimous.

Commissioner Long then took the microphone and introduced a resolution reappointing me city manager. Commissioner McCarthy seconded the motion. The vote was: Long—yes; McCarthy—yes; Richards—no; Caldwell—no. After reading a statement calling for a city manager who "has a better concept of the needs of a tourist city, who understands the place of recreation in the city, and who has some promotional ability," Mayor Morrison voted no. The audience responded with shrieking, whistling, stomping roars of approval.

In the middle of this commotion Agda came in from the boys' dance program. We drove to the office at city hall and began packing my personal belongings until we were stopped by a policeman who said he was carrying out orders from the mayor. Shortly thereafter the city clerk—now acting city manager—arrived to oversee what I was doing, also under orders from the mayor. Their orders were that nothing was to be removed from the office, not even the waste baskets, until examined by the new commission.

Agda was indignant. She defiantly took from the wall a caricature of a forlorn, emaciated old man with a lantern in his hand—Diogenes looking for an honest man. The publisher of the *News-Journal* newspapers had presented it to me some months before. As she walked past the officer, she said to him, "The new administration will have no possible use for this; besides, it's my husband's!"

Mrs. Mordt, the acting city manager and a fifteen-year veteran of city service, seemed embarrassed by the whole procedure. She authorized me to remove the boxes I had packed with the help of the new personnel officer, my secretary, and Agda.

Most of the next two days were filled with calls from friends and others we didn't know, calling to express their regrets. I deeply appreciated these sentiments. But most of them came too late. Some of the citizens had taken it easy, being sure "It can't happen here." Like good citizens in other cities before them and probably many who will come after them, they learned two things: in an election, you don't dare leave the action to somebody else; and the time for action is before, not after, the polls close.

Symbol of All-America City ordered removed by incoming city administration, Daytona Beach, Florida, January 1955. (Courtesy Daytona Beach *News-Journal* Corp.)

Several of the callers were incensed that the first order of business after the reorganization of the city commission was removal of all evidence that Daytona Beach was an All-America City. The large shield at the north entrance to the city was dumped on the city yards junk pile. Patches on police, fire, and bus-driver uniforms were ordered removed, as were the All-America City shields on sides of city equipment and attached to lamp posts. The All-America City banner which had flown nearly a year below the American flag at city hall was not raised.

People wrote letters to the editor, expressing their concern about where the city was now headed and urging a campaign to get me back. Organizations passed resolutions of appreciation. On January 6 the *Evening News* printed this editorial:

Daytona Beach Evening News

The Firing Of Harlow

LEROY HARLOW packed his belongings in the City Hall Tuesday night and got out—a victim of hate stirred up by demagogues and men who knew they couldn't control him, and manifested dramatically by the cheers of their camp followers at the City Commission meeting which voted three to two to fire him.

Not he, but Daytona Beach is the loser. He will find another job somewhere where he will be more generally appreciated. This City, with its record of rapid fire changes, will not easily find a professional manager of Harlow's character and ability, if, indeed, an effort is made to find one. He is the kind of man we need in a City Manager; and such men make enemies of the impatient and the undisciplined. So a majority of the Commission has said to him, in effect: We don't want a man like you. We want a man who won't annoy us by standing firmly on principle; who won't insist on treating everybody alike; who won't let himself be shoved around, even by Commissioners. And many people have applauded this point, as they showed by their votes in some zones. Some have wanted a man who will run things on the cheap. Some have wanted a man who will spend the taxpayers' money freely provided it is for things they happen to be interested in.

* * *

WE SAY Harlow will not be the loser, will not be long out of a job. This sort of thing seems to be a hazard of his profession, unfortunately. But we felt for him just the same, as he packed up under the All American City Award hanging above his desk. No man likes repudiation in the face of a job well done; no man likes to feel that three years of hard work for a community have culminated in discard.

We say Daytona Beach will be the loser, and we know it will. But in the long run we feel, being incurable optimists, that Harlow's work here, his example here, will not have been wasted. Sooner or later we will settle down in this community to the realization that integrity, ability and down the line consistency in principle and in operation is what we need, is what, in our heart of hearts, we really want.

Some day we will be searching for a man in the image of Harlow. Some day we may even try to recall Harlow here. The chances are he will not be available.

* * *

PERHAPS the firing of Harlow, the prototype of the expert, over the protest of far sighted Commissioners Long and McCarthy, is only symptomatic of something which has been going on too long in America.

It is symptomatic of the sort of thing which has broken the morale of the Civil Service, and which has discouraged scientists from working for the government, which has led to the shortage of teachers and the dissatisfaction of the faculties in our colleges, and which has led to attacks upon foundations which have financed impartial research and study of the moral diseases which afflict this World.

Down with the intellectuals, roar the demagogues, and too many people mimic them. Down with experts, they shout, we don't want thinking, we want slogans. These demagogues don't want analytical minds, they want men who are "practical" in that they do not think. Let us make an idol of mediocrity, they demand, a demigod of commonplaceness! Let's not listen to the teachers, they exhort, and the preachers and the schoolfolk and the "eggheads." They would have, instead, set up a leadership of men who are against cerebration and who speak in terms that are oversimplified and which appeal to our emotional desire to find a scapegoat for our ills.— H.M.D.

Two Dollars a Vote

Before the election I had accepted an invitation to address the student body assembly at Bethune-Cookman College in about the second week in January. While seated on the stage with the student officers, awaiting my turn to speak, I was handed a note. It read, "Dr. Bethune would like to see you at her home when you leave the assembly."

At her home I was escorted upstairs to Dr. Bethune's bedroom. She had been ill with asthma for some time and was having great difficulty breathing, so much so that I disliked taking her time and energy. But she wanted to talk to me.

She expressed her great regret at the way the election had gone. Then she said, "Do you know why Dr. Ruth lost in our zone?"

"No, Dr. Bethune, I don't," I said. "I understand it was a surprise to a great many people."

"It was a great disappointment to me, Mr. Harlow," she said. "For over thirty years I have urged our people to take advantage of their opportunities; that's why it was such a great disappointment to me. They turned their backs on their opportunity.

"I'll tell you what happened. Of course they bought votes in this zone like they always have, two dollars a vote. But more than that. The night before the election, word was passed throughout our part of the city that any Negro man who voted for a white woman would be lynched before daybreak. The men feared to vote; that's why Dr. Ruth lost."

I thanked Dr. Bethune for the invitation to see her, expressed my great concern about the condition of her health, and left.

"The Seeds Will Grow"

On January 26 the publisher of the *News-Journal* newspapers, Julius Davidson, hosted a Godspeed dinner for Frank L. McCabe, a department store executive who was moving to North Carolina, and me. Two days later I received the following letter from Dr. Mary McLeod Bethune. This letter and the plaque from the city employees are the two things I treasure most from my experience in Daytona Beach.

I wrote a thank-you letter to Dr. Bethune. In it I expressed my concern for her health and my admiration for her faith,

312

Mary McLeod Bethune Foundation
Incorporated

TELEPHONE 2-3519

631 Pearl Street
Daytona Beach, Florida

January 27, 1955

Mr. Leroy Harlow
City Hall
Daytona Beach, Florida

My dear Mr. Harlow:

As a citizen of Daytona Beach for the past 50 years, I have a great, great interest in the building up and the welfare of our beautiful city on the Halifax.

I have become deeply interested in good government, not only for our city but for our whole country and the world. I have come to appreciate men and women who have within them the making of good government and the sound building of a city and community for the welfare of all the people. I have come to deeply appreciate men and women who have the training and spirit and the background to make a real contribution to this end. Therefore, your coming to our city as Manager at a time when we so sadly needed real leadership in that field brought great joy and satisfaction to all of us who thought in terms of good management for the city that we have learned to love.

I have had some experience of administrative work in a very, very small way, possibly. I have had some contact also with great administrators and there has been awakened in me an appreciation for an administrator with vision and with courage and a spirit of unselfishness that stands firmly by the thing that is right, not who is right. Such an individual we have found in you and to have your departure at a time when we need you most is grievous to us all.

I regret exceedingly that illness prevented my attending the dinner in your honor at the Princess Issena Hotel last night. I now want to bring to you and your beloved wife our appreci-

Page 2
Mr. Harlow
January 27, 1955

ation for the services you have rendered. I commend you and hope for you great success wherever God may choose to use you.

Rest assured, Mr. Harlow, that the seeds that you have sown here will grow. Some of them have gone too firmly down to be uprooted. The platform that you have laid will eventually be built upon and Daytona Beach will become the sound, solid, growing, far-visioned city that we desire it to be.

Bless your wife and children. You carry with you the admiration and gratitude of us all.

Sincerely yours,

Mary McLeod Bethune

Mary McLeod Bethune

B/c

constancy, keen intellect, courage, wisdom, and love. I wrote also:

"I shall never forget the evening in your home during the trying period in October, 1952. I was grateful that I could lay before you the problem as I saw it and that you would take the time to counsel with me.

"And how fortunate I felt we all were when I discovered the breadth of vision, the reasonableness, and the strength of your guidance as we faced together the responsibility for initiating integration at Peabody Auditorium. Had you not been there to hold firm to your convictions, within a broader framework of giving as well as getting by all, the outcome would probably have been markedly different.

"Words are so inadequate to express admiration and appreciation to a friend. We sometimes need help beyond ourselves to convey our innermost thoughts. I hope it will be my privilege to work with you again. May God bless you always."

Four months later, Mary McLeod Bethune passed away.

A Man Must Work

Before the end of the month I was offered the position of secretary to the Florida state road board, a job the road board intended to convert to state director of highways. Agda and I discussed the possibility in detail. She counseled me to be sure this was what I wanted, not to feel I had to take the first opportunity that came along just to have a job. She reminded me how I'd felt about every job I'd had, that I'd often wondered out loud, "How can I be so lucky, to be paid to do something I enjoy so much!"

In the meantime I had been applying for jobs wherever I learned there was a vacancy—Joliet, Elgin, and Highland Park, Illinois; the National Safety Council in Chicago; San Antonio, Texas; Tucson, Arizona; Alameda County, California. We had reviewed our financial situation and concluded we could hold out for the job I wanted until May 31. I was most interested in the city-manager vacancy in San Antonio, where some two years earlier a new council majority had squeezed out one of the country's top city managers, C. A. Harrell, by the device of reducing his $30,000 a year salary to about $300 a month, but where the reform group was now back in control.

On May 31, our deadline, I received a formal offer from Booz, Allen, and Hamilton, international management consultants, to join a team being put together to design and install a performance budget system for the Republic of the Philippines. We would be based in Manila; I could take my family with me; transportation, housing, and servants would be provided; we could come home through Europe; and I would have a permanent job when we returned to the States. I accepted and informed the people with whom I had filed applications. A few days later I received a cordial letter from the mayor of San Antonio. He expressed regret that they had not been able to reach an earlier decision because the council had concluded that I "might be the man" they were looking for.

Connecticut to California; Atlanta to Seattle

The pattern of local government arrangements
Taxation
Management of governmental performance and costs
The power of bureaucracy in a democracy

I am writing this chapter almost exactly twenty years after our return from Manila. One might think that in twenty years the local government situations, problems, and forces at play I have been describing would have largely disappeared. Not so. New settings and new names have been given some of the old situations and problems, but their natures have not changed. Official misconduct, low productivity, financial crises, crime, and corruption are as prevalent as ever—if not more so. Indirect thefts due to inefficiency and waste go largely unnoticed or uncorrected in many local governments, although competent managers know that unsound organization, poor management, and inefficient operations can rob more than the criminal who breaks in and helps himself. Urban growth, industrial development, land use, blight, labor-management relations, and minority tensions are still among the top items on most local government agendas.

During these two decades I have been involved almost continuously in efforts to meet problems plaguing dozens of local governments, first with Booz, Allen, and Hamilton, then as director of the Greater Cleveland Tax Policy Study Commission, executive secretary and consultant to the Cuyahoga County (Cleveland) Mayors and City Managers Association, director of the Utah Local Government Modernization Study and the Utah Local Government Finance Study, and several individual consulting assignments. The governments I have surveyed are in urban areas from coast to coast and from border to border, including Vernon, Connecticut; Richmond, Virginia; Cleveland, Ohio; Flint, Michigan; Atlanta, Georgia; Fort Worth, Texas; Salt Lake City, Utah; Twin Falls, Idaho; Seattle, Washington; and Pasadena, California. Firsthand experiences in these varied localities and situations reaffirm that there still is great room for improvement in the management of the people's business at the local government level. This chapter presents a few of these situations and some observations that apply generally—no matter what the kind, size, or location of the local government. Because some of my assignments have included a professional commitment to confidentiality, I'll forego mention of places and times. But the events are real, and the descriptions are accurate.

Organizational Mazes

Let's start with the basic facts of organizational structure. The geographical areas of all or part of 48 states are divided into counties. (Two states have no counties.) Most of the counties are further divided into the other kinds of local governments: cities, towns, villages, school districts, and other special districts. Cook County, Illinois (Chicago), for example, has 475 local governments within its boundaries; Los Angeles County has 225; King County, Washington (Seattle) has 138; and Cuyahoga County, Ohio (Cleveland) has 97.

This may sound like a neatly solved jigsaw puzzle, with all the parts carefully arranged in an orderly manner to comprise the whole area of the country. Actually, the arrangements of local governments are anything but simple. Although some local governments are side by side in good order, in most places several governments of different sizes and shapes overlap one another.

For example, in one state where the governor's office, a county, and two cities joined in commissioning me to make a statewide study of local governments, there were forty-one local governments in the one county. Examination showed that in several locations in that county one piece of property was overlaid by seven, eight, and nine separate governments, each with its own taxing power, governing body, employees, buildings, and equipment. Consequently, property owners in any of these locations were paying real estate taxes to the county, the city, the school district, the library board, three different water districts, a sanitary district, and the mosquito abatement district. The number of officials making up the nine tax levying bodies totaled more than seventy—some elected by those property owners, some holding office by virtue of election to office in a different city, some appointed by a court, and others appointed by other elected officials.

Because ours is intended to be a governmental system "of the people, by the people, and for the people," it is essential that the people understand their government and that they be able to keep track of their officials. Therefore, as part of this and a related study, I attempted to ascertain how much the county residents knew about the governments they were supporting: how many governments there were; how many officials had a voice in levying taxes against their property; what were the officials' titles; how they were chosen for their offices; and what their names were. In a meeting of one of the most prestigious men's clubs in the county consisting of leading businessmen, educators, and officials, only one member ventured to answer the questions. He didn't get past a bad guess as to the number of governments that overlay his residence. Later, in a scientifically designed statewide survey that included only the question about number of governments, fewer than three-fourths of the respondents even tried to answer, and all of them were far wrong. Apparently eight or nine layers of local governments and several dozen local government officials are more government than these citizens could be knowledgable about—not to mention the additional burden of keeping up with what the federal and state governments are doing.

These organizational mazes of local governments make it virtually impossible for citizens to understand or to exercise any control over their governments. It is no wonder citizens become alienated and frustrated, lose interest, don't vote, and refuse to trust or support their local officials.

There are at least four major additional reasons why citizens should insist on simplification of organizational mazes, especially in large metropolitan areas. These reasons are (1) the inefficiencies of small units, (2) the destructive competition among them, (3) the revenue disparities that often exist among them, and (4) double taxation.

Small units lose the dollar savings possible with volume purchases. They often purchase expensive equipment needed for an occasional job, but they have such limited use for the equipment that it sits idle much of the time. They do not have enough employees to give them training or to provide service in emergencies or when one employee is absent.

Small governments also carry on running battles with one another to capture new plants and commercial buildings. Their purposes are to provide more jobs for their residents and to increase their tax bases. What often happens is that industries considering new plant locations will play one local government against another, wringing from the successful bidder concessions and investments that must be paid for long after the incumbent officials who get credit for bringing the jobs are out of office. Also, the locations finally decided upon may be economically and locationally undesirable: they are long distances from rail and highway access, when they could have been on them; they require large investments in new or expanded water and sewer services and paved streets, when these too were available elsewhere in the area; and they disrupt orderly development along sound planning lines that consider traffic flow, residential and recreational needs, and others, not just industrial growth.

Tax Load Disparities

Separate governments within the same area, even side by side, can have great disparities in their ability to finance local services. The principal difference is in assessed valuation, because property taxes are still the main support of local governments. For instance, in the famous 1971 California case of *Serrano vs. Priest* it was noted that within the state the difference in assessed valuation per unit of average daily attendance in school from one school district to another ranged from $952,156 down to $103, a difference of more than 9,000 to 1. Within Los Angeles County alone, differences between school districts were as much as thirteen to one. Fortunately, in most places school tax base disparities are reduced by application of school equalization funds. But similar equalization plans are not often provided for cities, towns, and villages or for special districts other than school districts.

Dr. James A. (Dolph) Norton, Chancellor, Ohio Board of Regents (then President, Greater Cleveland Associated Foundation), left, and author, right, receive progress report on financial study of City of Cleveland and 104 other Cuyahoga County local governments from Harold M. Peelle, Research Director, Governmental Research Institute of Cleveland. (Courtesy Greater Cleveland Associated Foundation)

Without Fear or Favor

Where I made a study of local government finances in a large eastern county, two cities adjoining each other within the same county faced quite different problems of financing services. One city had within its boundaries a large steel plant but relatively few homes. Its immediate neighbor city had virtually no industry but had thousands of homes, many of which housed the people who worked in the steel plant. In the industrial city, where service needs were minimal, the assessed valuation per capita was $140,000; in the residential or "bedroom" city, where service needs were great, the assessed valuation was $2,000 per capita. Thus the ability to pay for equal service in the two communities differed seventy to one.

Finally, there is the complaint of city residents against double taxation. As I explained earlier, in the discussion of the pros and cons of annexation (pp. 151-57), every resident of a city is also a resident of the county in which the city is located. Consequently, residents of cities must also pay taxes to the county in which they reside, but they do not always get from the county the services their taxes help pay for.

On Tap, Not on Top

I had been invited by a state association of counties to address their annual meeting of county commissioners on a topic of my own choosing. (In that state each county was governed by a commission of three county commissioners and eight other elected officials.) Not wanting to take their meeting time to talk about something of little or no help to them, I telephoned a representative sample of commissioners, fifteen of them, from large, medium-sized, and small counties, and asked each of them this question: "What is there about your job as county commissioner that eats up most of your energy, is most frustrating, and is least satisfying?"

As I compiled their replies, I was surprised to note how nearly unanimous they were that the following two conditions were their major problems. First, they were expected to make decisions on matters affecting thousands of people and setting the direction for the county for the next half-century or more without adequate information on which to base their decisions. This was because they had no one to collect, organize, analyze, and help them interpret the data they needed. Second, once they had made their decisions, they had no one to follow up for them to see that their decisions were carried out. Often they didn't even learn of a violation until it was so irrevocable that it was politically impractical to require the violator to go to great expense to reverse himself and comply with their decision.

When I reported at the association's meeting the results of my small survey, there was much nodding of heads in agreement that these were major problems for most of them. So I took the occasion to inform them that graduates of schools of public administration were being trained to fill that need and that they could be hired at modest salaries which might often be paid back and more in a few months by the service they could render the commissioners.

At this suggestion the response was quite different. Several indicated their reluctance to employ smart young university graduates who might "take over" the county government. Although the commissioners had identified their own problem, they feared loss of control to the "experts." I tried to ease their minds by explaining that a professional administrator's role is to carry out the policies of the people's elected representatives as efficiently and effectively as possible, not to make the policy.

I added that one of the most important tasks of a policy-making body was to select and use a qualified person to direct the administrative details of the organization in carrying out the governing body's policies and that any time the governing body determined that their appointed administrator was stepping beyond those bounds the governing body had both the authority and the obligation to discipline or to dismiss the administrator. In this way the governing body would provide their constituents with the most effective administration of their policies, while assuring that at all times the professional administrator would only be on tap, not on top.

As I now note the increasing number of appointed administrators serving boards of elected local officials, in that state and across the nation, it appears that this concept of democratic representation with professional administration to better serve the public is gaining some acceptance, although numerically it is still the exception rather than the rule.

When Right Is Not Might

In another state a city had long had a professional manager. Following a municipal election during which new members were elected to the city council, the council became divided over whether the manager should be replaced. Half the council had worked with the manager and maintained he was as able a manager as they could likely employ at the salary all the council members agreed the city should pay any manager. But the new half of the council wanted to carry out their campaign pledge to get rid of the manager. Their reason: the manager was "a dictator," for whom the council was merely "a rubber stamp." The council chairman (mayor) remained neutral throughout the controversy.

After weeks of wrangling, with neither side able to prevail, they reached agreement to bring in a consultant to make an impartial study and evaluation of the city's organization and administration, which they reasoned should be a measure of the manager's qualification and value to the city. Specifically, the assignment they gave our firm, which I was to carry out, was to make "an overall review of seven aspects of the city government, namely, (1) organization, (2) principal functions, (3) levels and adequacy of service, (4) general administrative practices, (5) staffing, (6) utilization and maintenance of equipment, and (7) space adequacy, arrangement, and utilization."

Now, I know of no human organization that can't be improved, and our local governments are no exception to this rule. But in this case, after several weeks of detailed examination, I had to conclude, and so stated in the final report that "when measured against accepted principles of sound organization and the operational practices followed in the better managed cities throughout the country, [this city] generally shows up well." Of course, there were opportunities for improvements and refinements, and I recommended them, but they were minor.

This city was one of only a handful of local governments I've been privileged to survey where the weaknesses were so minimal. Yet the pressure and wrangling did not end, and not long after the survey was completed and the report filed with the council, the manager resigned to accept a similar position in a larger city.

Cost Control and Reduction

Critics of government often remark that if any private business operated the way governments operate, the business would soon go broke. I saw an example of this when I was inspecting a truck and heavy equipment garage and repair shop run by a city of about 200,000 people.

The usual layout of a vehicle repair shop is to have a line of stalls arranged along one or both walls of a rectangular building. As a vehicle needing repairs is brought in at a central entrance, it is directed to one of the stalls. When the repair work is completed, the vehicle is backed out of the stall and driven away. In other words, the arrangement is as shown below under "Private Repair Shop."

But that was not the arrangement in this city-owned garage. Instead, the vehicles needing repairs were driven in and arranged as shown under "City Repair Shop."

Private Repair Shop   City Repair Shop

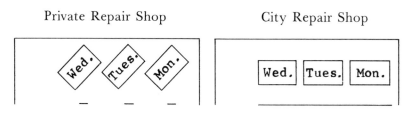

The result: Repairs might be completed on the vehicles brought in on Monday and Tuesday, but they could not be put back on the road until work was completed on the Wednesday vehicle, perhaps several days later. Expensive equipment in good running order was held in that shop many hours, sometimes days, unavailable for use because of the arrangement.

Every owner of heavy equipment knows that each hour or day his equipment sits idle means money out of his pocket. Therefore, he does all he can to see that idle time is kept to a minimum. In this case, the situation was described in detail in the survey report. It suggested opening up three drive-in entrances through the interior wall, which could have been done at small cost without damage to the building. But the city made no change.

Give Me Unit Costs

Elemental cost-accounting procedures call for combining costs of labor, materials, equipment, and overhead on a project and dividing the total of such costs by the number of work units completed to determine the average cost of each work unit.

Similarly, the unit cost of equipment use for any time period is calculated by combining a share of net purchase cost, oil and gas cost, and repair cost, and dividing that dollar total by the number of miles driven or hours operated, to get a per-mile or per-hour cost of operation. As part of the survey mentioned above, clerks kept meticulous records of oil and gas put into each vehicle and of the parts used in repairing the vehicles. But that's where the accounting stopped. There was no consolidation of the figures and no computation and analysis of unit costs of equipment operation for cost control, budgeting, or management purposes. When I asked both the clerk in charge of the records and the department head if they had ever considered determining their mileage or hourly costs of operations so that they could compare one piece of equipment with another or would know when it would pay to trade in a unit, they replied that that was not their responsibility. Their only purpose in recording the information was to try to make sure no one had taken any gas, oil, or parts for personal use—a laudable purpose, to be sure, but far short of the potential for reducing costs to the taxpayers.

It's Easier to Buy It Than Find It

I have visited and inspected county, municipal, and special district corporation yards from one end of the country to the other. With some notable exceptions, the pattern is the same, especially for the smaller governmental units. The yards contain a disorganized collection of concrete and cast-iron pipe, large and expensive valves, lumber, cement, street and road name and regulatory signs, steel members, corrugated sheet metal and culvert pipe, piles of sand and coarse aggregate, warning lanterns, barricades, and a miscellany of dozens of other items used by various departments and stored in the yards. Frequently, items are thrown one on top of the other, with no order, protection, or control. If there is a shop in the yard, it will have tires, oil drums, spark plugs, air and oil filters, vehicle parts, and other supplies lying around on the floor or thrown on shelves.

More than once I have walked into and through unattended and unsecured corporation yards containing hundreds of easily removed items. I have gone into stockroom areas and found bins covered with dust and cobwebs still containing brand-new, unused spark plugs, valves, fittings, nipples, and other items, with a scribbled inventory control card attached but no longer legible and obviously not used. Having previously been the purchasing agent responsible for approving bills in five cities, I have some idea of the cost of the items I have seen lying around these yards. Consequently, I have run quick tallies and have found

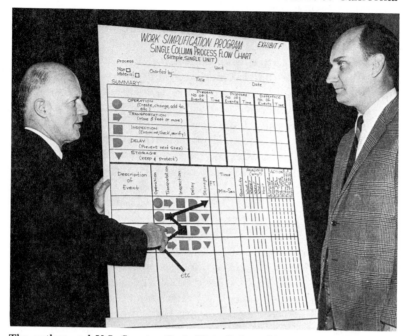

The author and U.S. Senator E. J. "Jake" Garn (then Mayor of Salt Lake City) discuss methods for simplifying local government work processes. (Courtesy *Deseret News* Publishing Co.)

that the corporation yard of even a small governmental jurisdiction can contain materials and supplies worth thousands of dollars.

When I've asked the people working in the yards and shops if they maintain any inventory control of these costly items, the usual answer is that it's too much trouble; if they need anything, they go to the nearest hardware or auto parts store and get what they need. That probably accounts for the number of unused items lying around in different places: it's easier to go uptown and buy an additional item than it is to locate what has already been paid for once by the government.

Merger Needed; No Takers

For most cities the costs of fire and police services constitute about half their operating budgets. With the accelerating crime rates, the ever-rising costs of both fire and police services, and growing taxpayer resistance to more taxes, it is only logical that management should look for ways to reduce the costs of these labor-intensive departments, at the same time strengthening the community's public safety protection.

Fire departments are special targets for such inquiries because it is often observed that firemen are paid for many hours when they are not actually engaged in fire fighting or related activities. Further, the objective of both services is protection of life and property, and they have similar requirements for employment in entry-level positions. Consequently, on two assignments I have made detailed studies of the potential for merging part of the manpower of the two departments into a single public safety patrol force.

The first study was for a large Pacific Coast city; the second, two years later, was for a smaller eastern city. In each case, the first factor to examine was the actual availability of manpower. For example, what were the facts about the amount of time firemen have that could be applied to police patrol service? If the amount were negligible, little would be gained by spending time examining other aspects of the subject such as organizational and command arrangements, personnel training, kinds and use of equipment, the attitude of the fire-insurance industry that rates cities for fire-insurance premium purposes, attitudes of the two departments, and whether one could expect any marked advantages to the citizens of the community if such a merger were effected.

In the two cities the leadership of both departments seemed to have an open mind on the question. In the larger city both the fire chief and assistant fire chief had stated more than once that they favored a merger if it appeared at all feasible. The chief had told his men the public would not much longer pay firemen to just sit around the stations. At the time, the fire chief was also national president of the Association of Fire Chiefs, a position that gave him both local and national status and would give impetus to the change if it were given serious consideration. In the smaller city the mayor and city council had defined the assignment as follows: (1) an evaluation of the efficiency of the present city operations; (2) development of concrete and practical measures for improving operations; and (3) identification of areas or opportunities for actual savings in administration and operating costs. Specifically, they requested concentration of attention on the three departments accounting for the largest outlays of city funds: the fire, police, and service departments.

In both cities, because of the increasing crime rates, the

police chiefs were anxious to get additional qualified manpower wherever they could. In the larger city, man-hour cost of public safety activities had increased 300 percent in the past decade. To cover this increasing personnel cost, the council had doubled its appropriation for these services during the same period.

Police statistics for the larger city showed that its crime rate was advancing much faster than the national average; the police patrol coverage was the thinnest it had been in years; and the number of department personnel per 1,000 population was below the same ratios for the other major cities on the Coast. The number of fire alarms had increased 30 percent in three years, and a recent insurance survey of fire protection strength had dropped the city one classification, threatening a 20 percent increase in fire-insurance rates.

In the smaller city, public safety expenditures had risen nearly 150 percent over the past decade. In the last seven years, major crimes had increased 130 percent. Fire losses had varied from year to year, although the city enjoyed a good classification for its size.

In both cities, manpower costs accounted for over 90 percent of the two departments' operations and maintenance budgets.

With the large city data on hand, I went to the fire department's operating records for the past several years. I tabulated the time spent by firemen on the three major department activities: fire combat, fire prevention, and training. For each activity I gave credit for anything related to the activity. For example, time spent by the men in post-fire cleanup at the fire site and in the station was credited as fire combat time.

When all the figures were put together, including the small 1.4 percent of paid duty time that was spent actually fighting fires, I found that the total time spent by fire officers and men on these activities was 32 percent of the duty time for which they were paid.

For the large city police department they had no past records that were usable for this examination. Therefore, I asked the department to conduct a two-week study of patrol officer activity. This was not to be a record of time spent on routine patrol but a record of time spent responding to specific radio-dispatched orders. Their survey showed that the patrol cars averaged fewer than ten calls per patrol district each twenty-four hours. Based on what the records showed for the time a car was out of service while on a call and on my request for time estimates from several individual patrol officers, I estimated that an average time per call was thirty minutes. Thus, out of each twenty-four hours of paid patrol duty, officers were engaged on emergency calls about five hours, or less than 25 percent of their time.

A similar analysis of fire- and police-department records in the smaller city two years later revealed an even larger amount of unassigned fire-department duty time. For the immediate past year the records showed that the department had made no runs on nearly one-third of the days of the year. Records for the past three years showed that the department spent about twice the percentage of time on fire runs as did the larger city, but department estimates of the other major activities brought the total amount of work time to only about 15 percent of total paid duty time. The larger amount of time shown as fire combat time was attributable to the great care with which the department cleaned up after a fire. For instance, I noted when I attended one residential fire that the department even vacuumed the drapes and carpets in homes where they had fought a blaze.

Police records in the smaller city were not as complete as fire-department records on use of manpower time. But by combining such information as was available with examination of the officers' activity reports and my personal observation, I estimated that the police officers spent about 60 percent of their time on specific duties. In both cities these data made clear that manpower time was available for additional assignments.

The amounts of time spent by firemen and policemen on their primary duties were not the only significant data that I gathered. Equally interesting were the percentages of fires being extinguished by hand extinguishers.

A fundamental principle in fire combat is to get to the scene in as short a time as possible in order to attack the fire while it is small. Even with the delay caused by firemen having to wait out the ringing of the fire alarm bell system to determine the box location, to slide down the pole, to find the precise fire location after reaching the box, and to travel to the scene on slow-moving rigs, in the large city 45 percent of the fires were extinguished by firemen with hand extinguishers carried on the fire trucks. In the smaller city the three-year average was 41 percent hand extinguishment. If fire fighters could reach the scene more quickly by traveling in faster-moving passenger-type cars that were already on the street and in motion, it appeared likely that the percentage of fires that could be extinguished with hand equipment while the fire was still small would be even greater.

No two cities are exactly alike; therefore, the surveys I have done have always been tailored to meet the particular city's needs. However, the situations and the recommended plans for partial merger of the two departments were sufficiently similar that I think this one summary description can suffice for both situations.

At this point let me interject an acknowledgment: the above findings about the percentages of time spent by firemen and policemen on specific assignments during their duty hours was no criticism of the officers and men. It is common knowledge that firemen are employed to be *available* for dealing with emergencies when they occur and that policemen are thought to deter crime by their presence, even when they are not engaged on a specific assignment. If the paid time of these men was not fully occupied, it was no fault of theirs. It was the consequence of a traditional pattern of organization and operations.

I acknowledged this in both reports. But the fact remained that both cities faced rising costs of manpower as well as increased service needs. At the same time they faced growing citizen resistance to higher taxes. Therefore, here are the essentials of the organizational and operational plans I recommended:

1. The plan would apply only in the predominantly residential areas of the city, not in the high-value commercial and industrial districts.

2. Present and future fire fighters and patrolmen would be employed and trained as public safety officers, with the training of each broadened to include the prevention and combat of both fires and crime.

3. Fire stations would be manned by fire commanders and fire truck drivers only.

4. Fire equipment would remain unchanged, but present police patrol cars of five-passenger design would be replaced with station-wagon-type public safety vehicles equipped with fire extinguishers and protective clothing.

5. Public safety officers would be assigned to public safety patrol cars by districts, to prevent both crimes and fires and to respond to both police and fire alarms. Except while functioning at a fire or a similar emergency, they would be under the command of the police commander.

6. The fire-company officers and drivers with their apparatus

and the public safety patrol cars would respond to fire alarms. Public safety patrol cars from neighboring districts would temporarily extend their coverage to the districts where cars had responded to fire duty. All this would be according to a preplanned response arrangement.

7. At no time would the public safety officers be under the command of more than one superior. They would be under the police district commander when on patrol or police call and under the district fire commander when dispatched to a fire or engaged in fire combat.

The survey reports concluded with estimates of cost savings that would result from the partial merger. For the larger city the amount was at least $1 million per year.

In both cities the reports received careful and generally favorable attention from the local officials and interested citizens. When I gave the fire chief of the larger city advance word that the report would recommend partial merger, he was enthusiastic. He said, "That has to come, and it would be great if we could be the first major city in the country to do it."

I remained in the city a short while longer, finishing up odds and ends of other parts of my assignment. Just before I left, the fire chief called me. "I'm sorry," he said, "but I won't be able to go along with the merger plan after all. I thought we could make it, but the resistance from the men in the department is too great for me to attempt it."

In the smaller city a couple of years later many of the survey recommendations were acted on, but not the one for partial merger of the police and fire departments. I never learned the reason there.

Not What to Spend but What to Provide

The first Hoover Commission, set up to improve federal government administration, recommended replacement of the long-used "line-item" budgets with "performance" budgets. The commission's criticism was that line-item budgets focus on how much money is to be spent by each bureau for various items, not on what programs and number of units of service are to be provided to the people. I understood and heartily agreed with their criticism because one example of the inadequacy of line-item budgets presented by the commission in its report was a navy budget item for which I had had staff responsibility while with the U.S. Bureau of the Budget. The budget showed only what the navy intended to spend, not what it intended to accomplish.

Both before and since the Hoover Commission reports were released, some local government officials recognized the inadequacies of line-item budgets and have led their units to adopt at least a semblance of performance budgeting. Many such performance budgets continue to show line-item information, such as expenditures by organizational unit, functions, and activities, and to break down the expenditure items by salaries and wages, materials and supplies, utility services, equipment, land, buildings, and other items. But in addition they show what the government is committed to do for the money spent. That is, they state the kinds, amounts, and quality of services to be provided; the cost per unit of service performed; the ways in which costs compare from one year to the next; and, where feasible, the ways in which costs compare among governments or departments.

Performance budgeting has become a controversial subject. There are sincere people who think performance is not an appropriate measure of government. I don't subscribe to that. Although I recognize that some governmental activities are difficult to measure and that it is not practical to try to measure some activities because of the cost of doing so or because of the several years that may have to elapse before results can be known (for example, measuring the results of a mental health program), the fact is that many local government activities are virtually identical to those in the private sector, where management has to measure performance and act accordingly or the business will go bankrupt. Just because we cannot easily measure every local government activity is no reason to not measure any. I have seen evidence that measuring performance produces tighter local government management and can result in greater citizen knowledge and control of local government activities.

Danger Ahead

Let me turn for a moment from opportunities to improve local government administration to the political side of local government.

I see two situations that portend danger ahead for the people's business. One danger is in the monopolistic nature of local government; the other is in the growing electoral influence of the local government bureaucracy.

In the private sector there are laws and legal machinery to prevent monopolies in order that consumers can be assured a choice of goods and services at fair prices. The major exception is in the utility field, where uninterrupted service to the public is so vital that monopolies are allowed. But even there they are allowed only under the control of regulatory agencies, established to protect the public.

By contrast, the purchasers of goods and services from local government have neither choice nor protection. With hardly an exception, if we want education, police or fire protection, garbage collection, water, sewer service, paved streets and street lights, or any other of the ninety or more services usually provided by local government, there is only one vendor from whom we can obtain them—the local government within whose boundaries we live or own property. In fact, we are required to pay for most of the local governments' goods and services whether or not we use or want them. Moreover, we have no counterpart of the regulatory agencies operating to assure us adequate quality at reasonable cost.

If we are dissatisfied with local government goods, services, or prices, three courses of action are open to us, none of which is very prompt or effective. We can file a protest, which can usually be ignored with impunity if the local official is so inclined. We can register our protest in the ballot box at the next election, a slow, imprecise, and undependable process. Or we can move out of the jurisdiction, a costly and time-consuming choice that carries no assurance that the situation in another local government will be better than the one we left.

In other words, local governments are under little pressure to seek and follow better ways of doing things. They are operating essentially in the same manner they did half a century ago, often with less courtesy and efficiency, yet with even higher costs, primarily because they are an unregulated monopoly.

As for the growing electoral power of the local government bureaucracy, I have sometimes wished that every citizen who could vote but didn't were with me in the city hall or county courthouse on election day—I mean not only the citizens who think they don't have time to learn something of the issues and the candidates or haven't time to go to the polls, but also the citizens who don't vote and complain afterward about what the local governing body and appointed officials are doing. They could see for themselves how the power over local government is slipping from their hands into the hands of their hired public employees.

On election day local government offices are abuzz with excitement. Informally, officials and employees encourage each other to cast their ballots. They make it a point to telephone relatives and friends to be sure to vote. They are given paid time off to go to the polls, ostensibly to set a good example for the general public but more directly to have an impact on the results. Elections are not only exciting at the centers of local government; they are serious business because public employees know how important each vote is in getting what they want.

The danger to continued citizen control of local government rests in the citizens' own attitudes toward voting, and in a paradoxical characteristic of any government that I will explain shortly.

In most communities there has been a steady decline in the percentage of eligible citizens who register and vote. On the other hand, voting by officials and employees of any government, and especially local government, is virtually a duty; and every convenience is provided to facilitate their voting.

The paradox I speak of is that in government the employees are the employers of their employers. Does that sound confusing? Let's follow it through. The people who vote are the ones who choose (employ) the persons who will head the government. The people who head the government are the ones who appoint (employ) the workers. The greater the influence of the workers in elections, the greater their influence over their own employers. As the proportion of the population who work for government increases (thirty years ago one out of twelve people in the labor force worked for government; today the ratio is one out of six) and the percentage of voting by private citizens decreases, the bureaucracy's votes will become a larger and larger percentage of the total.

Unless these two trends are reversed, eventually the bureaucrats, with all their relatives and friends, will totally control elections. Already we are seeing the effect of this paradox in the frequent failure of elected officials to act in the general public's best interest when to do so is contrary to the employees' wishes. Local government is especially susceptible because it is at this level that the number of governmental employees is growing fastest and where the voting strength of the bureaucracy is most beneficial to officials who want to stay in office and who depend on the bureaucracy to elect and reelect them.

Having spent the better part of this book describing situations and problems in our local governments, I want to make the point that there are practical things concerned citizens can do. These things are the subject of the brief final chapter that follows.

First Priorities
for Citizen Action

Elements of Citizen Control

A hundred years ago the French leader Clemenceau said, "War is much too serious a matter to be entrusted to the military." In our time we are learning that the governing of our communities is too essential to our social, economic, and personal well-being to be left entirely to elected officials and their appointed bureaucracy—no matter how great our confidence in their good intentions or how much we would rather spend our time on other things. To fulfill the dreams and the promise of America, citizens must be involved.

This does not mean we must return to town meetings, where all citizens assemble to decide every community matter. Nor does it mean total sacrifice of personal energy and time to achieve and retain "good government." What it does mean is the establishment of local-government situations in which citizens are not involved in name only but are *effectively* involved. As in one noted art of self-defense, where the weaker contender controls the stronger by the use of balance and pressure at critical points, so citizens must institute and operate a system of effective controls, few in number but strategically located.

The five-city experiences I shared with you in the early chapters of this book plus the twenty additional years of work with local governments I have described lead me to propose a minimum set of five controls I believe deserve first priority. These controls are not the traditional reorganization plans so often unproductive of improvement, nor are they by any means all that citizens should establish in their local-government systems. But they are the fundamental steps. Without them, the improvements in organization, management, and operations so badly needed in our local governments are not likely to happen. Here are the first-priority steps, followed by suggestions for implementing them:

Establish a system for alerting citizens to pending major policy decisions and actions of special concern to them. The greatest hindrance to citizen control of local government is the citizens' inability to know what is going on. Therefore, annually the local government should supply each registered voter with a blank two-part checklist showing (1) the districts comprising the local government's total jurisdictional area, by district number and geographical description; and (2) all the major services and functions of the local government. The local government should invite the voters to return to the government the completed checklists showing the districts in which they reside or have a special interest and the services and functions about which they wish to be notified when a major policy issue or action affects any of the checked services. Then, by computer programming or other means, citizens should be notified in advance of the time and place of meetings to consider these major policies or actions.

To avoid abuse of this citizen participation, the governing body should have sole discretion to determine, by majority vote of its full membership, what is a "major policy or action" requiring notification to citizens.

On the other hand, to avoid official excuses that the involvement of citizens to this extent is too time-consuming and expensive, the citizens should require that there be expressly authorized in each annual budget an amount adequate to finance the program.

Require employment and retention of trained professional administrators to impartially implement policies established by elected governing bodies and elected chief executives. When policies have been formulated by the people's elected representatives, including general guidelines as to their administrative implementation where appropriate, they should be referred for detailed implementation to trained professional administrators who have been appointed solely on the basis of demonstrated abilities, qualifications, integrity, and prior experience or training related to the duties of the office. For some small governments this may require sharing the services of a qualified administrator with other local governments.

To assure the people continuity in the management of their public business and to encourage candidates to campaign on policy issues rather than on minutiae, no action for removal of an administrator (except for malfeasance or misfeasance in office) should be permitted during the first nine months following an election in which there is a change of one or more members of the governing body or of the elected chief executive, and then only by vote of two-thirds of the full membership of the governing body.

Require all local governments to use performance budgets. Unless what a government does is measured, there is no proof that it has completed anything or made any progress. To assure that governing bodies, public managers, and interested citizens can ascertain what local governments have done, are doing, and intend to do with moneys provided, all local governments should use budgets that show goals, objects of expenditure, work units, unit costs, man-hours or man-years, progress-to-goals, and year-to-year and government-to-government comparisons of performance and productivity.

Require an impartial, outside professional management audit and public report at least every four years. Private business failure and public bankruptcies have demonstrated that traditional financial audits are not enough to let the people know whether their public business is being soundly managed—not only financially but operationally as well. Financial audits are after-the-fact, and they measure only what was spent, not what was accomplished.

Not less often than every four years the organization, management, and operations of every local government should be examined by an outside, recognized, and experienced management counseling organization. The management auditors should be required to publicly report their findings, based on the government's record and the auditors' professional judgments. Their reports should include at least the following:

- The results achieved by the government, as compared with its announced performance goals;
- Ways and places where the government's structure deviates from proven guidelines of sound organization;
- Violations of management practices and of operating policies, methods, and procedures regularly used by efficient and effective private and public organizations.

There should be expressly authorized in each annual budget an amount to be deposited in a cash reserve fund for the sole purpose of financing management audits and for publication in full of the management examination reports.

Require prompt follow-through and positive decisions on all management audits, examinations, surveys, and studies financed with the local government's funds or through its auspices, sponsorship, or initiative. After completion of any management audit, examination, survey, or study agreed to, assigned by, or contracted for by a local government, its governing officials should be required to publicly review the corresponding report within ninety days. Also, the governing officials should be required to formally adopt and publicly announce a plan of action within sixty days after reviewing the report, setting forth the recommendations to be implemented, a timetable for implementation, an assignment of each approved recommendation to an official for follow-through, and a schedule of quarterly and final public reports on progress and completion of implementation.

Concurrently with the announcement of the plan of action, any recommendation in the report not assigned and scheduled for implementation should be identified and the reason for rejection or deferral should be fully set forth and publicly announced.

How to Establish This System of Citizen Controls

The system of citizen controls just outlined probably will not come into being without citizen initiative and action. Here are alternative courses of action generally available to citizens who are serious about achieving results.

Start with local officials. Many local officials have a sincere desire to provide the best possible government for the community they are serving, but they do not know what the people want or where to begin. Therefore, the place for citizens to start is with an individual official who may be willing to take the lead in establishing the control system, or with the entire governing body in a formal session. At this time citizens can make clear their wishes, suggest alternative ways to achieve the desired results, and commit themselves to practical support of the officials in their efforts to comply with the citizens' request.

Examine the local government's charter. If the local officials are unwilling to take the lead, an examination of the local government's charter—whether a home rule charter or a state statute, either of which is probably available in the library or in an attorney's office—may reveal steps citizens can take to bring about the action they wish.

Take advantage of the right to petition. Citizens may have to go the initiative petition route. State constitutions, statutes, and local charters often grant the right of petition to the citizens. Any citizen can start a petition. By getting the required number of signatures, one citizen may be able to force a proposition onto the ballot. Once this is done, the citizens have taken the decision out of the hands of the officials. The voters will then decide whether or not the government will install the system proposed.

Work through your state legislator. If all efforts in the community fail, this does not mean the alternatives have been exhausted. In fact, the next alternative may be the fastest and most effective: work through the state legislators from the local government area.

In most states, local governments are partially or wholly creatures of the state. They are subject to state law, which tells them what they may and may not do, and what they must and must not do. If one or more citizens can get a legislator to introduce a bill in the state legislature to accomplish their plan, they may be on their way to achieving their goal.

A legislator may need citizens' help in getting joint sponsorship and support from legislators representing other parts of the state, because for his bill to become law it probably will have to apply to all the local governments of the same kind or same size in the state. Although this will add to the citizens' work, it may be helpful. It will broaden the support for the plan, give it wider publicity, and perhaps encourage the local officials to support what they see others supporting.

Stump for a constitutional amendment. If neither the local officials nor the state legislators will act, there is the constitutional amendment route. This is hard, but not impossible. The state constitution, available from the library or the office of the state secretary of state, will say what must be done to get an amendment. The easiest way may be to get the legislature to propose a constitutional amendment to the people of the state. But this may not be the only way. Amendments may sometimes be originated through a statewide petition or by a constitutional convention.

Resort to the federal government. Finally, if all local, legislative, and statewide efforts are ineffective, resort to the federal government. Because the federal government distributes billions of dollars to the local governments each year, federal laws and regulations have a great influence on the local governments. Write to the congressman from your district or one of your two United States senators in Washington, or talk with one of them when he comes back to the state and district during congressional recesses.

Managing: the People's Business

Now you have shared in the experiences of one local government administrator; you have observed the kinds of situations and conditions that sometimes surround or confront local governments; and you have been invited to consider some courses of action open to you and other citizens. Undoubtedly you know or will discover other challenges to sound management of the people's business and new and more effective ways to deal with them.

Perhaps, like my neighbor who loves America, you and your neighbors will want to "do something" to get better government in your community, in your state, or in the nation. If so, you may find encouragement in the words of Dwight D. Eisenhower, addressed to the American Bar Association on Labor Day, 1949. He said, "Every gathering of Americans—whether a few on the porch of a crossroads store or massed thousands in a great stadium—is the possessor of a potentially immeasurable influence on the future." How many gatherings will you be a part of in the days and weeks ahead—a civic club, a business meeting, a social occasion, or a family meal? Because of you, will any of these gatherings have an influence on the future?

Many of our local governments—on which millions of people must depend for their personal safety and much of their economic security—are on the brink of financial, organizational, operational, and ethical bankruptcy. Citizens need to act now. If you, your neighbors, and I don't act, what needs doing won't get done.

Selected Index